Skeletons Don't Sleep

Jeff & Kelly Halldorson

Pricky Hill Projects

Strafford, New Hampshire

By: Jeff & Kelly Halldorson

Skeletons Don't Sleep

Copyright (c) 2010 by Jeff & Kelly Halldorson

ISBN: 978-0-578-04997-7

All rights reserved. No part of this book may be reproduced without written permission from the publisher or authors.

Cover Design/Artwork & Formatting: Kelly Halldorson

www.kelly.halldorson.com/blog

Illustrations: Jeff Halldorson

About the Authors photo: Jessica Niles

www.capturedbyjess.wordpress.com

Editing: Catherine Johnston (http://bullyforme.wordpress.com/),

Ellen Fitzmaurice, Ann Grenier & Traci York

Transcription help … Kelly's lovely Mom, Ann Grenier

Skeletons Don't Sleep

By: Jeff & Kelly Halldorson

To Our Children:

No one knows the struggle or true consequences quite as defined as the three of you. You have been there by our sides unconditionally through the years, the smiles and the hard times. You all, forever willing, to provide the ever so necessary well-timed hug. We have seen you each grow into something to be proud of. As hard as these years have been, the three of you have proven just how strong the human spirit is.

Wolfgang you have worked so hard to become an individual and stay true to yourself. You have stepped up at the hardest time to take the reigns as man of the house and helped to lead us into brighter days.

Griffin you have brought fun and laughter into even the dark parts of our heart with your wit and humor. You have given us the strength to truly know that it will really be okay.

Zoë your determined love for others, us and life itself is an inspiration. You have the gift of a free spirit and it radiates to all those around you.

THANK-YOU! THANK-YOU! THANK-YOU! THANK-YOU! THANK-YOU!

Ellen Fitzmaurice, Eric & Julee Katzman, Margaret Wood, **Christophe & Malone Cloitre**, Robert J. Potenziani, Sara Shoedinger, Julia Kowalski, Alyssa Tuininga, Freedom Green, Laura Webb, Michelle Monroe Rowan, Chris Lawless, Tom Hudson, **Heather Cloitre**, Lee Sullivan, Fay Aucella, Toni Albrich, **Joe Simes**, Susan Mojica, Rae A Wilson, Wendy Carmichael, **Katie Condon and Tim Merry**, Roy David, Jim & Sue Forsythe, **Bl Pawelek**, John Hill, **Traci York,** Dena Hale, Joseph Overbey, Christine and Michael Hamrick, Kristi Hayes-Devlin, Matt Simon, Jamie Hupfer, Monique Vachon Cinfo, Anita Mathur & Steve Wourgiotis, Caitlin Carlsen, Stacey Lepage, Kasey Evans, Jennie Mosley, **Oyster River Alumni Association**, Hunt Howell, Ford Klaeson, Molly Capron, Amy Priestley-Roy, Shannon Wallace, Donna Proulx Holland, **Bob & Ann Grenier**, Sheryl Hebert, Amy Townsend DiCosmo, Stacey Noonan, Shirley Woodward, **Charlotte McPherson**, Jessie Forbes, Sara Gram, Ambre Proulx, Hilary McHone, Arlene Savory, Jackie Tarbox Valley, Marie-Andree Cleary, Donaldo Trejo, Keri-Lyn & Mike Hackney, Heather Driscoll, Elizabeth Burger-Shen, Robert Dworkin, **Catherine Johnston (aka Bully)**, Mara Kerns-Robertson, Paul Agakian, **David Castellano, Kelly Matthews**, Kim Hislop, Jennifer Marshall-Schuyler, Todd & Honey Puterbaugh, Tammy Alessandro, Catrina Lavoie, Ken Dunnington, Chad Talaiferro, **Jennifer Quinlivan**, Debra Hand, Matthew Smith, Gary & Tracey Leighton, Jennifer Layne-Eastman....and so many more

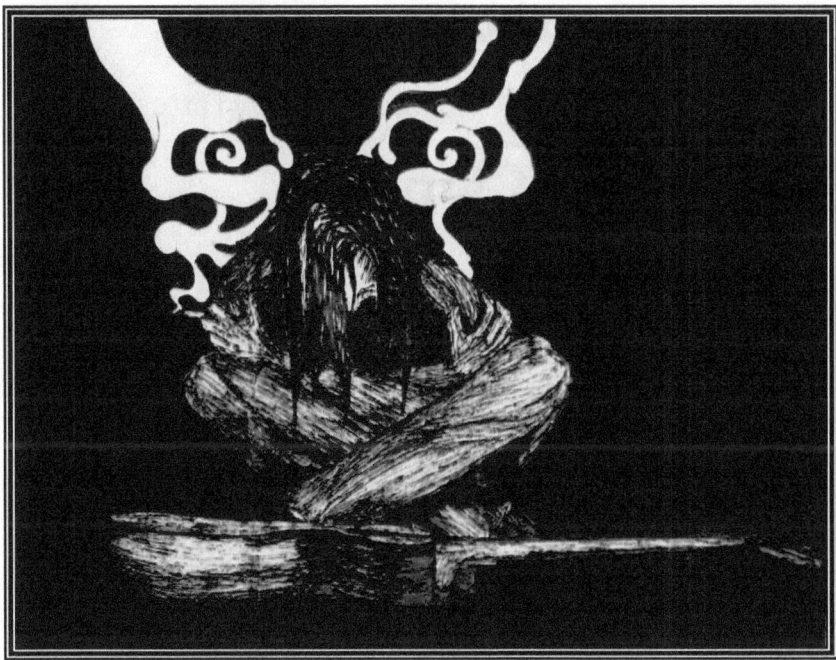

And thanks to those that didn't even know they were helping us...

NeedToBreathe:

Thank-you for your album, *The Heat* - you convinced us that..."just a few more months and we'll be fine"

Michele Weiner-Davis:

For your books *Divorce Busting and Divorce Remedy* you helped us stay together and reminded us why we fell in love in the first place.

Starbucks:

For making Kelly Green Tea Soy Lattes.

Chipotle:

For making yummy food and bringing the idea of compassionate eating to so many people.

Barnes & Noble:

For a place to regroup, get inspired and enjoy one of the above mentioned Green Tea Lattes.

Introduction

Jeff first asked me to write this book with him in February of 2009. The seven months prior had been the toughest ever in our marriage, which included a three month partial separation. He asked I write this book with him as a means to bring us closer. He had always wanted to write it on his own but something changed for him and he decided there was no way he could write it without me.

I was reluctant at first not understanding how I could really help. Then as the story took shape I saw how much I was already involved. My name came up again and again in the transcripts. I then realized, with Jeff's help, that he was right there was no way to write it without me being a part of it.

Throughout the writing of this book things continued to be tough. We have both struggled emotionally, physically and financially. We both have spent time in the hospital for physical and emotional concerns. We've moved into a broken down two bedroom trailer, from a beautiful Victorian house. We've had to give our vehicle back to the bank.

In September of this year, near the end of the writing of this book, Jeff had a breakdown. He spent a week in a psychiatric facility. While he was in the hospital our electricity was shut off. I mean, seriously...it couldn't get much worse. It's almost funny.

However, through the strength and support of each other, our amazing children and all those out there that have been, supportive to this project. We are going to do our best to right our wrongs, bring joy and learning to our children, and healing to ourselves and others affected by sexual assault. Peace, Love & Thank-you!!

☺ Kelly Halldorson

By: Jeff & Kelly Halldorson

New Beginnings

(Jeff)

It has taken seventeen years to get to this day.

I stand outside of the new residence of my father. My wife, Kelly, and I look upon the day after our drive. The scene is perfectly cast for a funeral in a movie. The dark clouds and cold rain combine to create a fitting day for a prison visit.

By: Jeff & Kelly Halldorson

We stand under the sheltered entrance to the Concord State Prison for Men waiting for the prison's Minister to walk us into the bowels of this hellhole to which my father's mail is now forwarded. I cannot shake the feeling I am standing in the beginning of a really crappy *Lifetime* original movie. Seventeen years. That is a long time to wait to get here.

I am what Detective Gabe Tarrants describes as a "late discloser." My father was a child molester. My older brother and I were his prey. There is quite a story to tell about how we got to stand here, freezing our asses off, in this cold brick front entrance. The problem is where to begin.

My name is Jeff Halldorson, a thirty-three year old married man with three children. I am six foot tall and well built. I have a strong stance from many years of physical labor. I am tattooed and rough around the edges. Some would say I am pleasing to look at, although their mothers might not approve. I have the battle scars of one who knows his way around a construction site. And I do, as that is where my work time is spent. I am well-educated in the ways of a hard-earned life.

My story begins in Wisconsin. It is the place of my birth, of which I had two. On the day of my arrival into this world, December 3, 1973, I was born as Jeffrey Dean Slattery. I know little of the time I spent passed around between my father, mother and other family members. I have been told tales from my adoptive mother, of abuse and troubling living conditions. I have little to no recollection of these first years; therefore tales are all they will remain.

The second birth is the one that matters the most for this story. At the age of three I was reborn as Jeffrey Watson Halldorson. I was adopted into the Halldorson family with my brother Erik who is thirteen months my senior. We are biological brothers. With the adoption, we were given the gift of a new family. We had a new mother, new grandparents, new aunts and uncles and, of course, a new father. It was magical. Erik and I had found peace at last. We were happy; we could be kids and live and laugh.

We were the picture perfect family for all to see. Susan, my new mother, was a stay-at-home mother by day and worked occasional nights in retail. James, or Jim, as friends called him, was my new father. What he did at that point for work I have no idea. They were both well educated college graduates. Jim held a Masters Degree in economics from an Ivy League school and Susan held an Associate Degree in retail management. The family looked and felt real. For the first time in our lives Erik and I had our own rooms complete with pictures on the walls and cozy beds. Love and affection was plentiful and the house was beautiful. It was large with more rooms than occupants. There was a yard with a garden and it was clean and warm. Instead of constant reprimand we were free to be children. Often in the morning I would set up pots and pans and drum on them with wooden spoons to my heart's content. Susan would simply close the doors and allow me to indulge in my fun. We were read books and tucked in at night. It was the family tradition to say every night before bed *Good night, sweet dreams, I love you. See you in the morning.* We all said it as a family every night.

Susan's appearance was frail and vulnerable. Her demeanor proved otherwise. She stood five foot eight inches, a tall, statue of a woman. Though lean and feminine, with long dark hair, she had no problem standing her ground. Susan enjoyed the spotlight, although she went about getting there covertly; making her presence known when it suited her needs.

Jim was exactly the opposite. A large man, six foot two and pushing two hundred and fifty pounds, he looked all man. When he spoke, out came a soft voice, just above a whisper. Not the loud boom you'd expect from such a big guy. Jim was reserved and would avoid conflict. His large broad chest and muscular frame were wasted on a passive, timid man.

The first Christmas present I ever remember receiving was my very own bicycle; fire engine red, large curving handlebars and cowboy images sprawled along a banana seat. Erik got one too. His was green with lots of chrome. To any boy they were the most beautiful things in the world. Erik and I passed our father tools and watched with eager eyes as this man of wonder assembled our dreams in our garage. He became our hero then and there. We had never ridden anything, much less our own bike. With patience and laughter my new parents spent endless hours picking us up and shoving us off again, our two wheels spinning with daddy running beside. Just like we had seen in the Wonderful World of Disney specials we watched together. Erik and I laughed, and when we cried Susan held us and comforted us with forehead kisses.

There was no doubt that we were loved children. Susan could not have been more of a mother. Having suffered a string of miscarriages she had an ever longing desire for children to love. She gave us her heart completely. Erik and I never longed for attention from her or our father. We were a close family. I started to learn, from them, what the meaning of love was. The family dog, Jake - a full-blooded Airedale- would stand guard as I played in the front yard. He did not play or sleep. If I was out playing he sat in the drive and wouldn't let so much as a paperboy within ten feet of the property line without intervention from our parents.

At the age of five my family moved to New Jersey. My father was climbing the corporate ladder. He was employed by The Woolworth Corporation in New York City. We moved from one big house to another. Erik and I were excited for the adventures to come. With the move to New Jersey came a lot of changes. It was a move back to the place my parents grew up. Our grandparents lived there as well as some of Susan's and Jim's old friends.

The biggest change, however, was in Jim. He was always a drinker but was becoming more of a drunk. He began as the average social drinker, drinking beer with friends on weekends. Now, he was consuming often and in excess in front of Erik and I during the week.

What was worse, he started to invade our nights. Something in him changed. In the comfort and security of our rooms adorned with loving toys and trinkets of happiness, our safety and security was shattered. My father allowed some sick suppressed demon within him to surface. Somewhere in this thirty year old man's head he looked at two young boys that cherished his love and adored him and saw sexual objects. Jim had become a male succubus with a preference for little boys.

It was the year before Kindergarten for me. In many ways I question my memories regarding the start of the invasions. Our move to New Jersey provides me with the first clear memories I have of the abuse and a marked change in Jim's drinking habits. I have some vague unsettling memories from the time before we moved but they are not precise. It is entirely likely that the lines had been crossed before we left Wisconsin but there is no real way to be sure.

Susan and Jim lived as loving parents by day. Jim lived out his sexual deviance at night. Slipping into our moonlit sanctuaries to fulfill some untamed desire, he left behind two confused, scared and hurt children. There was never any verbal exchange. He came in, did his thing and we didn't speak. When awakened we feigned sleep. I only lay there taking in the perfume of his alcohol. His deep, heavy breath filling my innocent ears, my tears stifled by fear; petrified I did not move.

One thing I always found interesting about the encounters is that Erik and I reacted in the same manner. We both laid there frozen in silence. It wasn't until he and I started to discuss it openly to each other did we realize this. We would ask each other if we got "visited" in quiet whispers over breakfast. It became a secret two brothers shared in quiet spaces where no one would hear. Erik became my savior, comforting me as a parent would comfort a frightened infant. He would wipe my tears and stand strong listening to my recounting of the previous night's visit. I was only six. He was seven.

Susan was always home. To us this became normal, as if this invasion was condoned and accepted in normal family life. Inwardly both Erik and I came to realize this was a dark secret that could end our family. Therefore we were willing to live as a happy family by day and on those nights of his choice, submit, reticent, to being his sexual play toys. We had been adopted into sexual servitude.

Erik and I both became increasingly difficult children. Erik started to lash out at our parents and had difficulty dealing with the separation from our biological parents. I would find myself standing outside the den as Susan and Jim tried to comfort him. Erik would shout words like, *leave me alone, you're not my parents* or *why did they do this to us*, never once mentioning the dominant source of pain he was feeling, Jim's betrayal as a father. Erik, being a year older than I, had stronger memories of our biological parents and it was far more difficult for him to let go. A year is a lifetime in the mind of a young child. He became withdrawn from the family at times and often didn't speak to Jim at all.

I had a cloudy vision of my years before being adopted. So, I lashed out in ways different from Erik. I became a constant problem at school. Academics were not my strongpoint, but stealing and lying came easily. It was convenient for my parents to attribute our actions to our first years on earth. To whoever asked or came looking for answers for our behavior, it was explained that Erik and I were abused as very small children and had attachment issues.

It wasn't long before I found myself sitting in a stuffy Doctor's office. Here came the therapy. I learned quickly and at a very young age whom to trust and whom not to. I would often go to these therapy sessions, walk in, answer a bunch of questions, walk out and sit in the waiting room while Susan talked with said therapist. During the drive home I would be either coached for the next appointment or reprimanded for what had happened in that session. I learned to shut up.

Meanwhile, Jim took us hiking, camping and generally, we had fun. The outdoors was our playground. He was teaching us the ways of the woods, which he had learned as an Eagle Scout in the Boy Scouts. Other than raping his children frequently and drinking, Jim was a good man. He worked hard, came home after work, supported a comfortable lifestyle for his family, paid his taxes and even went to church on Sunday. He was the everyday white collar stereotype. Anyone looking in from the outside would think of him as nothing other than the perfect family man.

The sexual invasions continued, as did Erik's and my silence. It all became an acceptable part of life. That's how the Halldorson family lived. There were times when Susan would come to me after Jim had left, comforting me as if it was all a bad dream. Lightly brushing my hair away from my tearing eyes she would whisper soft words of love in my ear. Susan would hold her crying son until his shaking stopped and he drifted off to sleep. Maybe to her that was all she thought it was, a bad dream. Erik told me of a time when he got up after an encounter with Jim to go to the bathroom only to find Susan watching television in the living room. The living room was directly outside his bedroom door. After returning from the bathroom she ushered him sweetly off to bed with the traditional, *Goodnight, sweet dreams, I love you. See you in the morning.*

Erik and I don't know what or how much that woman knew about the visits. The last time I spoke with her, many years ago, she would admit to no knowledge of any sexual assault by Jim or any suspicions for that matter. As you read on you may draw your own conclusions. I have and they are from the heart. Knowing Susan as intimately as a son knows his mother, I believe, without any doubt, that Susan knew there was something wrong within her family. She knew all too well that Jim was dealing with something deep inside that was cruel and destructive. She even mentioned many times throughout our lives that her own mother never wanted her to marry Jim. In her words, there was something *very wrong* with that man. I always loved my grandmother.

In New Jersey I had reached second grade and life in the Halldorson family continued down a sinister path. I finished out the school year then Susan and Jim told us that we would be moving to New Hampshire. Erik and I didn't experience the same feelings of adventure this time around. Woolworth had gone Chapter Eleven and my father had found a new job working for Congoleum in Portsmouth, New Hampshire. Another white collar job doing, God knows what. We moved to the outskirts of Durham - home to The University of New Hampshire (UNH). The house was the nicest yet. A Saltbox Colonial on a quiet, secluded dead end street. It was new and we were the first family to call it home. It sat on a good chunk of land surrounded by woods and farmland. Although we were close to all the amenities, to a young boy it was the middle of fucking nowhere. The other downfall being, there were few families around with children.

Life continued on as it had in New Jersey, except for me. My parents had decided to hold me back a year in school due to my lack of effort and the disciplinary issues. I was blessed with repeating the second grade. They also thought it best for me to be tested for learning disabilities. After my evaluation I was diagnosed with Attention Deficit Disorder. This diagnosis paved the way for my parents and teachers to begin treating me as though I was incompetent. It also gave them yet another excuse for my actions. I was by no means an easy child. I gave them all they could handle. I was removed from school for everything from kicking the teacher, to fighting and stealing. I was on fire and it wasn't long before they attempted to smolder it with medication. I was prescribed a daily regimen of Ritalin, issued to me by Susan with an oral inspection to ensure I was taking it every morning before school.

Erik, on the other hand, fit in well and found his place in sports. He made easy friends at school and was liked by most kids. He made average grades and stayed out of trouble. With the move came the start of us growing apart. He and I drifted in opposite directions and although we still spoke of our visits, conversations became brief and more infrequent.

In early 1986 Erik and I received the news Susan was pregnant. We were unclear what exactly it would mean to us. Erik and I had been constantly fighting and Jim was frequently gone on business now that the company he worked for went Chapter Eleven (funny trend). He was forced to take a job with Converse down in Massachusetts. *Whatever*, I thought, and just kept living. Life for me changed little.

As far as the sexual assaults went, Erik and I were still visited a few times a month and acted like it was normal with the exception that we never spoke of it even to each other, now. We were growing up and starting to become our own individuals. Erik and I could not have been more different. He was jock. I was leather. We came from the same yet we were nothing alike. Even in appearance, he was thin, unusually tall, short blond curls, had hazel eyes and a handsome face. I was an average height for my age, wiry but tried hard to act tough. I had long brown hair and dressed like trouble. Any resemblance between Erik and I could only be seen in our eyes. We may not have looked like brothers but we fought like them. Fights were loud and extremely physical. We no longer had each other to turn to. We had grown too far apart.

By seventh grade I was out of control. I was destructive to no end. I was completely withdrawn to the point of refusing to take part in family events. I was getting into lots of trouble at school and the therapy, though constant, was not helping. I found comfort only in my friends and they were every bit as destructive as I was. Most of them came from poor, broken or dysfunctional families; and although my family had money, this is where I fit in best.

Though my best friend Dave did not fit this mold, I often found his home to be a sanctuary from all the mess that was my life. His parents treated me well, though I think that they were afraid my rougher side would wear off on their son. Fortunately for them my exploits at the time did not prove contagious. If I went into a store to shoplift he would have nothing to do with it. If I skated down an unsafe hill he would walk down behind me. We accepted each other for what we were and didn't push one another to be anything different. He was a good kid with a good family and knew it.

In the summer of 1988, I was 14 and the visits had become less and less frequent. I was coming of age and confused and my body was changing. The visits were becoming harder to deal with as my body was now reacting to them differently. It was sending me on a whirlwind of emotions about the way we had spent our lives in the Halldorson family. I was becoming more protective of my body and wanted an end. I questioned Erik about his visits to which he responded they had stopped. The fact that it had stopped for Erik was hard for me. I had always known that I was the favored victim even though Erik's and my pain was equal. I felt alone to fend off the monster. What was even more confusing was Susan's pregnancy with her second child. The addition of our first younger brother meant less attention for Erik and me. This was no shock to either of us. We were constantly told that they were only adding more love to our family and not replacing us. Despite this reassurance it didn't feel that way. I didn't know who they were trying to convince more…themselves or us.

Their first biological son, Sam (for privacy concerns both the Halldorson biological sons names have been changed), was growing and I started to fear for him as I had feared for myself. What was to stop Jim from showing his dark side? I was falling apart and too old for my years. I knew what was wrong and I knew that there was no way out, unless I did something. So I did.

Our next door neighbor's boy, Grant, came to visit their father for summer vacation. Grant's parents were divorced so he would come and stay with his father during school breaks and all summer. We were the same age and naturally became friends over the years. We were very different. Grant was very reserved and into computers. He was exceptionally smart and knew it but was never patronizing. I was able to let my guard down and put aside the tough act when we were together.

In early August I confided to him my darkest of secrets. There was no reason for it to be that day. The sun was shining on us, sitting on our skateboards, just like any other day. We had spent most of the morning outside running around doing the things kid did. To this day I don't know what prompted me to tell him. But I did. I told him everything. It gushed out. I know it wasn't a conversation he expected to have when he woke up that morning. I could tell he was shocked and by the look on his face quite horrified. Grant did what any kid in his position should have done. He insisted that I go home with him immediately and recount all I had told him to his parents. I agreed. It was all I could do. I walked and talked like another being, it was all surreal. I had never discussed it with anyone other than Erik, until that day. He was the first person to know my secret and now I was off to tell someone else. I was beside myself, just going through the motions to get me to where I was headed. I was numb.

I sat in his parent's living room and told them everything. I told them what Jim had done to me and Erik with all the nastiest detail. It felt like I was telling the story of somebody else's life. It wasn't mine. I didn't want it to be mine. I answered all their questions with only one stipulation, that they not tell my mother until I left for overnight camp a week later. I wanted to be gone, anywhere but with my family when they found out that I had thrown stones at our little glass house. They agreed. Grant and I were sent outside while they pondered this new information. Grant's immediate discomfort around me was visible, almost tangible, not that I could blame him. I had just dropped my world upon his shoulders, and he was forced to deal with it.

Imagine my shock when later that afternoon, Grant's stepmother, Suzy, informed me that there was no possible way she could keep any of it a secret, even for a week and had already spoken to my mother. Looking back on it now the decision she made, of course, was the rational one but at the time I felt as if I was being sent into the wolf's den.

So, there I was at the age of fourteen staring down my very pregnant mother, sitting on her bed crying. She looked at me with red swollen eyes, filled with tears and only asked. *Is it true?* I was starting to feel extremely guilty, as if I had let my family down. I was ashamed of what I had just done.

I responded with a simple, *Yes it is.* Then I went off to my room to wait for the next page to unfold. I sat anxious, on my bed, consumed by the fear of not knowing what was to come as a result of the action I had taken. I grew numb with each passing minute. I began to blame myself for what had gone wrong.

If things went bad then it would be my fault.

Erik returned home from where I don't know. I heard him downstairs. I heard him climb the steps. I heard Susan call him and I heard her bedroom door close. I sat frozen in place. *Erik. I hadn't given much thought to him had I? What was he to do? We had never discussed telling anyone. How would he take it?* Time was now of no consequence to me. It was moving in every way. What seemed like hours were mere minutes and hours were irrelevant. *What have I done? What is going to happen now?* A knock at my door brought me to present. It was Erik. He asked if we could go for a walk and so we went.

What happened next was a defining moment in both our lives. I have forgiven him a thousand times over but I do not believe he has ever quite forgiven himself.

We crossed over Route 4, the main artery that fed UNH and ran behind our house. We walked in complete silence; he led with me in tow. The air was hot as we entered the field on the other side. We knew we would be lost to the outside world in the tall grass. Free from anyone or anything. We could speak of things as we had as children. Erik stopped walking and turned to me. To this point he had shown me no real emotion. He had remained blank. Now a heat rushed over his face and he could no longer hide his anger. I could see years of pain had weighed on him as they had on me. Conclusions were being drawn in his head. He was formulating some kind of a plan. It felt like an eternity before he spoke. With his silence and demeanor he had made the roles quite clear. There was not going to be a fight. He was going to talk and I was going to listen.

When he spoke he looked at me with pity in his eyes. *You are going to tell them that you lied. You will tell them that you made it all up. That you got confused and that none of it ever happened.*

He was stern and quite matter of fact though I could tell this was hurting him to say. He made it clear that that was the way it was going to be. It was final. I don't remember the rest of the conversation or even the walk back.

On my return to their world, for it was no longer mine, I did exactly what Erik told me. I told everyone that I lied. I told my neighbors and Grant. I told Susan. It was all a lie. It was the first time all day that I had had told a lie. The truth finally came out and it was already a lie.

Susan only asked me once after that. *Did it ever happen?*

To which I replied, *Well, you always take his side it doesn't matter what I say, forget it.*

It was all dropped and I never spoke of it to Jim or anyone else for some time to come. From that point on the entire family looked at me differently. Erik and I no longer spoke unless it was in anger and it generally escalated into a fight. I was cast out, emotionally, by my parents. We had very little interaction and they seemed all too eager to have me find any place else to be.

I was only visited once more and it left possibly the deepest emotional scar. Jim, in order to show how fatherly he was or maybe it was an attempt to reward me for my continued silence, had arranged an outing for just the two of us. I was to take a bus into Boston and meet him after work. He was taking me to my first ever Red Sox game at Fenway Park. After an hour-long ride, I arrived at the bus station I was told to get off at. I looked around for Jim but he was nowhere to be found. There I was, fourteen, standing in the middle of Boston Massachusetts holding my baseball glove, alone. I was scared.

About an hour passed and my fear was turned to complete elation as I saw Jim approaching. The joy did not last. The reason for his delay became quite apparent when he greeted me. I'd say he was drunk but shit-faced is a whole lot more accurate. He apologized that work had kept him late and we had to run to catch the game. Together we rushed off to the subway that would take us to Fenway Park. It was the first, and only, Sox game I have ever been to. Even Jim's visible state of intoxication couldn't suppress the thrill of the moment. Though sports were never really my thing I was drinking in the rush of the crowd and the excitement that flowed in the air. I was anticipating the fun I'd have bragging at school.

Jim and I ate hot dog after hot dog washed down with Coca Colas and beer. I felt so alive and truly happy. Jim taught me the mechanics of the game as the Sox played the A's. It wasn't until the bottom of the seventh inning that I came crashing down from my high. It was time to leave. *If we leave now we can beat the traffic and get home at a reasonable time.* I was visibly crushed so Jim reassured me we could listen to the rest of game in the car on the way home. He actually thought that I gave two shits about who won the game. I slept the whole ride home. It would be hard to brag at school not even knowing who won.

Once home I went to bed immediately, leaving my baseball glove in the car, never to be used again. With all the day's commotion it was no time before I drifted off to sleep. Then came that all too familiar sound of my door being opened from the outside. The house was not built with doorknobs instead it had cast iron door latches that had a very distinct sound. And there he was, my father coming to put the finishing touches on his "father son" day. This time was different. He left the door open. There was light flowing into the room from the hall. It illuminated the room for the first time. As he made his advances going through his checklist of pleasures, I stirred. I moved in resistance to him. I made my first noise. That was all it took and he was gone. He didn't even close the door on his way out. My head spun and my heart sank as I reached over from my bed and latched the door for him. The light was gone.

From that day on I became a terror with little to no fear of consequences. I started to take my destructive behavior where my friend Dave would not follow. He watched as I became something that he would not want to be around. Fighting with other boys from school got worse. I started to prey on the weak and didn't care. I became the playground bully. I was never without a concealed knife, easily obtained at the local flea market. I wore a full-length army trench coat with an AC/DC patch on the back. I got caught shoplifting at the local supermarket. School held nothing for me, other than, it was not home and I had friends there. I just plain didn't care about anything anymore.

Within nine months of my original disclosure I was fifteen years of age and my parents had me committed to one of the toughest drug rehabilitation centers in the country. The fuckers.

Rehabilitation

(Jeff)

On April 17, 1989 I was placed into Straight in Stoughton, Massachusetts, a last resort, highly intensive, drug rehabilitation center. I had never done drugs in my life. I had, at times, toyed with the idea because a few friends had bragged about drinking and smoking pot. It was certainly a road I was looking soon to travel down, but the day I walked into Straight it hadn't happened yet.

Straight was pure hell. It was, and to this day remains, the worst and most damaging place I have ever been. Straight was nothing more than long days of constant physical and mental abuse. I was tested for all the drugs that could be tested for. Every one of the tests came back clean. That's not what they told me though. The counselors told me they found, among other things, cocaine in my system. I had never even seen cocaine. I didn't know anyone who had. Yet, they still forced me to write to my parents and tell them how fucked up on drugs I was or I wasn't allowed to eat.

Straight was an inpatient facility. We didn't get to leave or go home for visits. We weren't allowed outside and we never saw the sun. I stood with boys and girls of all ages. Some, like me, were placed for accessory and stuck in their system while others were so messed up they were literally tearing skin off. We endured long days under florescent lights that turned the skin green with countless brutal hours of what they deemed therapy.

New arrivals were referred to as *Newcomers*. Our days would begin at our *Guest House* which was the home of a boy further along in the program, an *Oldcomer*. The rooms had caged windows, alarms on the door, and mattresses all over the floor. You would consider yourself lucky if you got blankets. Bathing was only permitted at night, usually only twice a week and always fully supervised by an Oldcomer. No privacy was permitted. Shower curtains were non-existent. God forbid you have even a speck of dignity.

After the morning at the Guest House you were shipped off to a bus pickup point at 5:00 AM. On the bus boys sat on one side, girls on the other. You would face stern reprimand and severe consequences if you even looked at the opposite sex. The bus ride would last up to two hours and sleep was not permitted.

At the Straight compound everyone gathered, upon arrival, in the Common Room, where we sat waiting for the remaining buses to arrive. Then all were ushered into the Assembly Room, a large gathering hall set up with two sections to segregate the sexes.

For the next sixteen to eighteen hours we were subjected to gruesome interrogations and mental abuse. Sitting in standard plastic school chairs with hands on our knees and our backs straight, we were questioned, screamed at and insulted. To prevent slouching, the Oldcomers would walk up and down the aisles running their knuckles down your spine. It wasn't long before your back was so bruised from this action you made damn sure you sat as directed. I watched, incredulous, as countless children were brought to tears from this unbearable pain. I was one of them.

No Newcomer was left alone, ever. Anytime you were standing, whether it be walking to the bus or taking a piss, an Oldcomer would place their thumb through your back belt loop and twist their hand to knot it in place. Often boys would get stage fright and would be forced to pee sitting down. These boys were then referred to as girls. If you needed to shit an Oldcomer would stand in front of you and watch. There were no doors on the stalls.

If anyone at any time had an outburst, got up, or moved the wrong way, they were immediately restrained. What this involved was being torn out of their seat, thrown on the floor by a group of Oldcomers and wrestled to the ground. You'd end up held down by five boys one on each appendage and a fifth sitting on your chest or back. I had this happen to me twice. It was humiliating and painful.

Everyone was expected to admit to being an addict. Unfortunately for me, I got caught up in the *denial* trap. I would not admit I was an addict. I was told I was "in denial." In denial I was subjected to a different form of therapy. I was refused food or received smaller rations. I was denied bathroom privileges and was not allowed to advance in the program. I was told that until I fully admitted I was an addict I wasn't going to see my family and would never get out. Inevitably I did what everyone eventually did. I played their game. It was only a matter of how weak my will was that would determine the length of my stay.

Then there was *Spit Therapy*. Brought into a small dark room followed by five or six Oldcomers, with maybe a counselor or two, I was thrown onto an infirmary style cot and the *therapy* began. What they did was all get as close to my face as possible and shout insults at me, covering my entire face, hair and neck in layers of spit. If I tried to wipe it away, my face or hand would be slapped.

They raged on about how I hurt my family and how shitty of a son I was. I was a druggie and a liar. They went off about how I lied to get Jim in trouble. On and on it went. This would continue for about forty-five minutes to an hour, or as long as their voices would hold out. If one got tired he would back up to make room for another. Then without warning they were gone. I was left, locked in that dark room for hours. I only had the shirt I wore to clean the spit of all those people off my face, my mouth full of other boy's spit. I cried for my mother. I banged on the door for help, to no avail, with only the light from under the door for comfort. One of the two times this happened to me, I remained locked in that room so long I pissed my pants for the first time since I was a toddler. When I was finally released from their spit chamber I was paraded in front of everyone so they could all get a good look at my soiled pants and a whiff of my stench. I was forced to sit like that for the remainder of the day.

Other times I would watch, in horror, as they would come and pick some poor soul from the crowd and drag them to that room. Everyone knew what was coming for that person; we also knew that if they resisted they would be restrained, dragged away, and locked in for the entire day.

Girls had it just as bad, if not worse. One girl was locked away for bleeding all over herself. Staff would not allow her a tampon or pad.

They reprimanded her in front of the entire group. This cruelty was so frequent we all became somewhat desensitized to it.

While in Straight I never once had any contact with my parents, nor did most of the kids around me. Ninety days exactly from the date of my arrival, I was forcefully ripped out of my chair and dragged out of the hall to a back entrance. The door was kicked open and I was literally thrown out as a drunk would be thrown out of a bar. The door was slammed behind me.

I found myself standing there bathed in sunlight for the first time in three months. Waiting for me in the back alley were my parents. I collapsed and Jim picked me up and carried me to the car. It could have been Satan himself for all I cared as long as I was getting out of that place. I knew I was one of the lucky ones that escaped Straight's hold.

Over the next several years all the Straight Rehabilitation Centers across America were shutdown. Many were sued for child abuse and neglect. Some cases were won. The children, they supposedly helped, often ended up broken or lost. Some committed suicide after they released themselves when they reached eighteen, while others have formed support groups to help them cope with the pain they suffered in the institution. The founders of Straight went on to open other rehabilitation centers under different names, using the same program model. Some of those centers are active today.

I was pale green and considerably underweight, but I was not yet to return home. This was made clear to me after Susan and Jim got me the first real meal I could remember having since entering Straight. It was Burger King. My parents explained that now I would be taken to Brookside Hospital in Nashua, New Hampshire because I wasn't ready to come home. After eating they took me to a K-mart to get me some clothes. I only had the ones I was wearing and I didn't even know if they were mine.

I thought the nightmare was over, and in many ways it was but I longed to go home. I told them. *I learned my lesson. I'll be good.* I begged and pleaded with them, but I had little fight left in me. In the end I accepted the disappointment and was thankful, for at least I wouldn't be returning to Straight.

Brookside was bright and clean. I was relieved. The people seemed nice enough. In the admission room I sat with my parents as they explained where I had been and why. They told the admission director exactly what they were expecting from my stay at their hospital. Susan took the opportunity to go into great detail of my actions the previous summer. Laying particularly hard into all the pain that I brought upon the family with the *lies* I had told. She went on about all the therapy it took Jim to deal with how my actions affected him. It was of great importance to them that I be placed in the drug rehabilitation ward. To them a drug addiction was able to explain away all of my actions and better yet if they could tell everyone I was on drugs, in some way, it freed them from any responsibility.

For the first time since my disclosure someone actually looked at me and asked what I thought. It was my turn to speak but I kept my mouth shut. I only told them that I knew that I needed help but wasn't on drugs and never had been. I was enrolled in Brookside's drug rehabilitation program anyway. The program, I was told, was to last four to six-weeks.

Coming from Straight, Brookside hospital was a resort. I slept for the first two days. I took my first shower alone in three months. I shared a room with another boy. The room had blankets and its own bathroom. The food was plentiful and good. The place was clean, comfortable, and coed, although it took some time for me to be able look a girl in the eye. If I behaved, I was allowed to go down to the cafeteria and eat as much as I wanted every meal. I began to get healthy and put back on a little weight.

Therapy at Brookside made more sense. To my relief no one yelled, or spit at me. We left the hospital to go to AA meetings and there we interacted with the outside world. Even though I was still caught in the denial trap I was not punished for it. Susan and Jim were expected to come every week for family therapy though Susan often showed up alone, explaining that Jim was traveling for work. I saw Erik in sibling therapy. Not much was accomplished in these sessions possibly due to my lack of trust in therapists or maybe because, well, I wasn't a drug addict.

In a private one on one session my therapist asked me about what happened that summer. She asked about the lies I told, about Jim's sexual assault. I looked her dead in the eyes and I told her the truth.

What happened last summer? Why did you tell your neighbor those lies?

Why do you think I'm here?

Why do you think you're here?

I'm being hidden. I'm the family secret. The black sheep.

So, what is it you're saying?

I told the truth last summer and my whole family knows it but it's easier to hide me in drug rehabs and tell everyone I'm a junkie.

So, what you are telling me is that what you said your father did is true, am I correct?

That's what I am saying.

It was never brought up again. Seventeen years later Jim confessed to police that Brookside asked him about my allegations. He told the Brookside therapist *no, the allegation are not true*. He explained that I was *definitely trying to manipulate the situation and was lying again* and explained that was why I was *in dire need of rehabilitation*.

Brookside was, at least, a pleasant place to spend my days compared with the hell that was Straight. After my six weeks were up I had seen a lot of kids coming in after me and leaving before me. I started to question when it would be my time to leave.

Back home Erik found himself in his first real bout with trouble. He and a friend got caught stealing a car stereo. As a result my parents decided to put him in a temporary foster home. They used the opportunity to take the two younger boys on a two-week *family* vacation. He returned home as soon as they did. This put me at eight weeks. Upon their return my state caseworker (who I had never met much less even knew existed) went on his two-week vacation. This put me into my tenth week in a four to six week program. Even the staff members began to wonder what was going on. It was never explained to me why but I ended up spending a full 90 days at Brookside.

After Brookside I was moved to a group home in Concord, New Hampshire for a two-month stay. That was a cakewalk.

From there I went to The Institute for Family and Life Learning, known to most as IFLL (pronounced if-full) in Danvers, Massachusetts. I should have gone there from the get go. It was not a drug rehabilitation center but a school for troubled teens. I was placed in the all boys house. I would remain there for the next ten months.

IFLL was set up much like a boarding school. There were two houses, one with all boys and a coed house. Under no circumstances were the two houses to interact. Each house was outfitted with a commercial kitchen, common room, living quarters and a main office for the staff. The facilities were equipped with a sports field and a basketball court. There was also a main building that was home to all the offices, infirmary and classrooms.

It was easy to get accustomed to life there. Two to six boys shared rooms. Everyone was responsible for keeping the rooms, bed and dressers in perfect condition. All the residents, as a group, cleaned the house every day. Days were regimented. Monday through Friday there was school, free time, mid-day group talks, and evening group therapy in the large common room. Meals fell in between.

Everyone started out as *Younger Peer* (YP) then would progress to *Older Peer* (OP) and would be responsible for looking after the new arrivals. Most kids only advanced to Older Peer. For those with the drive and ambition the next level was *Expeditor*. The job of Expeditor was to communicate all of the staff's wishes and commands to the lower levels. For the very ambitious there was *Overseer*. Overseers had all of staff's privileges without the paycheck. The position was rare and hard to obtain.

On weekends the YPs would stay at the house and the OPs and above would go home if they had one. For the students that stayed, weekends at IFLL were fun. The staff had a budget for things to do. They would take us bowling, to movies, into Boston, or anything else they could think of. Every Saturday morning they would gather us into the common room and put that weekend's possible activities to a vote. We also got a weekend allowance to spend when we went out.

Life there was hard at times, but if you watched your ass and did as instructed you could walk through the day just fine. For the most part, I did just that. In the beginning I pushed the envelope and found myself in some hot water but I came around real quick. At IFLL I was back in school for the first time in eight months and it wasn't hard to do well. The structure of classes and the personal involvement of the teachers was a good fit for me. Individual therapy was mandatory and I did what was asked of me. Family therapy was also required but for some time my parents refused to take part and once they did it was always only Susan.

That was the way life went for my first six month at IFLL. There was little change. I made friends easily. We were all from bad beginnings and could relate to one another. On rare accounts there would be physical confrontations among peers but they were dealt with quickly and sternly. No exceptions.

By the end of my first six months the staff thought I was progressing well. Although my family would have little to nothing to do with me and refused to take part in the family events on campus, I was promoted to an OP. I was the only OP that had a family yet still remained on campus during the weekends. I was also the only child there with a family that never once showed up for the Friday night family group the entire time I was there.

Eventually IFLL made it crystal clear to Susan and Jim that they had no choice but to go along with the layout of the program or be held accountable. If they didn't help me integrate back into society the staff at IFLL would have no choice but to notify the courts that my parents were noncompliant with the treatment. With this threat they began to sing along with the song. And I was to go home for my first weekend in well over a year.

I returned to a completely different home. I no longer had a room but was supplied a cot in Erik's room. Any possessions that I had before I left for Straight were either distributed between my two younger brothers or long since removed from the house. Erik told me two days after I was committed to Straight, that my remaining belongings were brought to Goodwill by my mother. There was no trace that I had ever lived there. All the pictures of me had been removed and replaced with baby pictures of *their* children. It was clear to me at this time they had no intention of ever letting me return home. I was not welcome there. They wanted me on the eighteen-year-old plan, locked up until I was old enough to legally sign myself out.

On that first weekend home my parents confined me to the house. All my excitement went out the window. I would have been happier back on campus. It was good to see Erik and my younger brothers but it was hard to see how Erik had moved on with his life. He was the star center on the school basketball team. He had his license and a car. He had a beautiful girlfriend and life had gone on without me.

I continued to return home for visits on the weekend and at IFLL I stuck to their program. My parents were getting good reports on me. The staff at IFLL always gave Susan and Jim the report in front of me. I believe this was intentional. They couldn't deny I was trying because the IFLL staff wouldn't let them. They started to let me out of the house on weekends.

It wasn't long until things were just as they had been before, as long as I told them what they wanted to hear I was free to do what I chose. My longtime friend Dave went to a boarding school in the White Mountains. He also only came home on weekends. I had mellowed out and was a lot less destructive and Dave lightened up a bit. We bonded, again and spent most of our weekends at his house. My parents were happy to be rid of me. I was fine with that. I even got a weekend job at a local sandwich shop.

Life was becoming quite normal considering where I had been, I thought. Then Susan and Jim threw their last Hail Mary. They told the Institute that they had suspicions of me sexually assaulting the older of my younger brothers. That put a quick stop to the home visits and the cot in the corner of Erik's room. Seeing as I had been very upfront with my employer about my living situation, they were accommodating and put my job on hold.

The interrogations at IFLL started. It was not done in private but out in the common room in front of all my peers. I was grilled for six long hours about my parent's allegations. They tried and tried but I never broke. I had learned the reasons not to in Straight. I didn't care what the consequences were. I was never going to admit to something that I didn't do, ever again. At midnight they brought me into private therapy and tried to get me to confess. Sleep deprivation was kicking in but I wouldn't let it break my resolve.

IFLL insisted that Susan bring in my younger brother to be evaluated in her presence. She had no choice but to oblige. It was their professional opinion that he had never been touched inappropriately. I was cleared to go home.

Two weeks later I was promoted to the rank of Expeditor. Only the third in the time I had been there. At IFLL I was doing great. At home I was better off not seen or heard. I was gone as much as possible. I had girlfriends. I followed the three IFLL rules of home visits: no sex, no drugs, no drinking. They were called the cardinal rules. Break them and you lose everything, bumped down to YP instantly. I followed them to the letter and gave my parents nothing to bitch about. I had my own money and asked for nothing but a ride back and forth from campus.

In my tenth month at the Institute I was requested to do the first ever house transfer. Due to the lack of OPs in the coed house it had gotten out of control. The boy's house was in good shape so the staff came up with a new plan. I was allowed to pick two of the OPs from the boy's house to come with me as Expeditors and was granted the rank of Overseer. It was the first time in IFLL history that they were going to allow interaction between the two houses.

With the move came added privileges. If I helped keep the coed house in shape I would be allowed to leave campus Thursday night and return Monday morning. I could interact with anyone on campus and go freely between houses. The three of us were allowed to leave campus during select free times to go to the store. I had worked my way up to King Shit. IFLL loved me and I worked hard to keep it that way.

My parents were happy to let life go on this way for as long as they could. There were no more interactions between them and the staff. They dropped me off and picked me up. They didn't even get out of the car, not even for my progress reports. The staff had to go out to see them. Eventually, they didn't bother and instead just mailed the reports.

It wasn't until I saw the two boys that I had brought over to the coed house leave, did I finally get fed up. I had been there longer, worked harder, and followed the program to the letter. I started to put the pressure on the staff. It was time for me to leave and they knew it. I had been at IFLL for fourteen months and seen both my sixteenth and seventeenth birthday in those walls. It was time.

As an Overseer I could go or see anyone on campus so I went straight to the head of the Institute with my request. I had done my job. He admitted to me that I had completed their program but they were having problems with my parents allowing me to return home. It wasn't until he contacted my state case manager and informed him that IFLL had nothing left to offer me, that my parents had no choice but to bring me home for good.

Of all the placements, I must give credit to IFLL for giving me the tools I would later use in life to help define myself. They provided a safe and secure place to teach and assist lost teens. I returned to IFLL many times over the years to tell my story to the kids there and catch up with the staff that remained. Unfortunately, the Institute was also forced to close its doors.

I spent two years institutionalized for something I never did. I was locked away with the family secret, in places that no one would believe me, even when I told them. In those years the world had gone on and forgotten about me. I felt as though I had served a sentence for a crime I not only didn't commit but was victim to. I would spend a long time trying to regain the foothold on the life that should have been mine. It was Jim and his crimes that had been kept safe; but that was only for the time being.

By: Jeff & Kelly Halldorson

Homecoming

(Jeff)

*"He said thank you mom for fixing
my clouded broken mind
but excuse me if I seem a little rude
while I was missing my childhood, my brother and my prime
you enjoyed the convenience of my solitude"*

-Edwin McCain *Solitude*

My return home did not unfold as I had imagined. I returned to school and I quickly picked up with my old crowd. They had all moved on with their lives without much thought of me. They had cars, girlfriends, jobs. They had shared time with each other laughing, swimming, talking and making mischief all the while I was locked away. The resentment I had toward my parents only deepened with this revelation. I became sinister and spiteful, determined to make up for lost time.

I sprinted down that road that I had contemplated two years prior. I knew deep inside I was failing myself with nobody to care enough to stop me. I was fueled and on a collision course to God knows where. I came home knowing that my family wouldn't be transformed into that magical beginning we had so many years ago, but somewhere in me there was a shred of hope that it may. The reality that I had been replaced by their new children left me lost. I was abandoned and depressed.

I longed for Susan and Jim's praise even though I knew there would be none. I had been cast aside like a broken toy just waiting for someone with the sense to toss it out. I was self-medicating. I was drinking, taking LSD, smoking cigarettes and pot. I got into a couple of fights but was able to keep a leash on the bullying. I had a bad reputation in school that I fed constantly and even ended up suspended for getting in a fist fight with the gym teacher.

The fear that kept me in my place for the two previous years had lost its grip on my conscience. With no goals to accomplish and no reward for positive actions I developed a fuck-the-world attitude.

My own family was willing to set me out to the curb on trash day. I had no one left to care about me or my actions. I no longer cared. The last two years were nothing but a way to dispose of the Halldorson's undesirable son. It allowed them to pretend, at least for a time, that I never existed.

I longed to be back at IFLL. At least there I didn't have to see my world for what it was. My parents didn't reintegrate me into society. They threw me in without any support or family to back me up. I was a hostile, angry kid that had been taught to trust no one. I hated and resented the world. I was destined to destroy both myself and just about anyone or anything that got in the way. My sophomore year of school was winding down. It looked as though I was going to squeak by. Teachers were easy prey for sympathy and I plucked them like guitar strings. I had learned how to work a system. All I had to do now was work it to my benefit. Manipulation became my passing grade.

Things were getting progressively worse at home. I made no effort to hide my disgust with my parents for what they had done. I allowed them no control over me. I gave them no respect. I came to realize they didn't deserve any. The disgust on Susan's face washed over me every time I entered *her* house. Family dinners were often eaten before my arrival. It was clear that my presence was a nuisance to their family life. Things were accelerating in the same direction for Erik. Their disdain for me was morphing into obvious regret for the day they signed the adoption papers.

Susan was resentful for the way we had turned out. She placed no blame on either herself or Jim and all the blame on our lives before the adoption. You can't un-rotten an egg. On the off chance I was home when she had company the comment echoed every time, *Oh, I didn't know you had an older son.*

Susan's response was always the same, performed flawlessly. *Oh yes, you know that. I have two older boys. Erik and this is Jeffrey. We adopted them when they were younger but I always thought of them as mine. We were blessed with four boys, what a handful.*

The sticky sweet love in her voice would drip from her mouth to my ears like an angry salivating pit bull. I didn't know which I hated more: Susan for faking love, yet casting her sons out or Jim for stealing our innocence. There was never going to be the affection I craved under their roof. If they were not going to love me then I was going to hate them with every fragment of my being.

Jim did his best to ignore me. I'd sit in the kitchen while he prepared himself something to eat without a single word uttered between us or any attempt at eye contact. I was an ant at his picnic. Reveling in his visible discomfort I would sit and watch him as he cut up slices of cheese, place them on little crackers then toast them. Other times he'd stand with the refrigerator door open just shoveling food directly into his mouth. He sickened me and I enjoyed watching him squirm.

When summer rolled around Erik and I were spending many of our days and some of our nights away from the Halldorson household. The time wasn't spent together. We each had our own groups. We both had girlfriends. It had become common practice for Susan and Jim to lock me and Erik out of the house when they were not home. They would provide neither one of us with a key. This often led to hours spent on the front porch waiting for one of them to come home and let us in.

One afternoon I wasn't up for waiting. I broke in. I entered through the first floor bathroom window, assisted by a friend. I grabbed a duffel bag full of my clothes and left. Susan had been waiting, ever so patiently, for an opportunity like this to present itself. She needed an excuse to get rid of me that she could blame entirely on me. She never wanted anything that may paint her in a bad light. By breaking into the house I had handed to her the key she was looking for.

Susan recounted, to anyone that would listen, the story of how she and Jim adopted us from a troubled background and worked tirelessly to provide us with the best life possible. *We took them in. We gave them a loving family but they just were trouble from the beginning. We could never repair the damage from their lives before us.* Hatched from un-cared for eggs we were destined to be rotten. To everyone else in the world, no matter how hard they tried there was little they could have done as parents to prevent us from becoming bad people. *All we could do was love them.*

Yeah, she had loved me alright especially when she called the cops and pressed charges on my ass for breaking and entering.

The Honorable William Shaheen was the Judge at my hearing. He was the very same Judge that had signed the paperwork for me to be placed into Straight and assigned me the invisible caseworker. He requested that Jim, Susan and I join him in his chambers. I walked behind my parents, into the chambers, trying my best to hide in their shadow.

What seems to be the problem here?

Well, Jeffrey broke in to our home.

Wasn't this also the place of Jeffrey's residence?

Yes.

Then please, tell me for I am having a hard time understanding, why is it that he was locked out of his home?

Well, Jim and I don't trust Jeffrey, or his older brother, in the house when we are not home.

What is it that he took exactly?

His clothes.

Wouldn't you say it is safe to assume that if Jeffrey was going to steal something from you, this would have been the ideal time to do just that?

I suppose.

The judge's next words will be eternally etched in my memory, for it was the first time I saw my mother put in her place.

This is the problem I am having here, Mrs. Halldorson. Jeffrey has been away for two years. He has come home to a locked door and you expect me to believe he is in the wrong for what he did. It is my opinion, that parents like you are the cause of these children not wanting to go home. Therefore they often find themselves in trouble with the things they do find to do. There is no justifiable reason for you to be locking your son out of the house. Essentially you are putting him on the streets. What if he was cold? What if he was hungry, tired or wet? You as a parent have the responsibility to provide safety for this child. You are not doing that. Maybe you should be the one standing up in my courtroom facing charges of child endangerment.

My mom had just gotten ripped a new asshole. All I wanted to do was giggle. Then he turned to me and the feeling was lost entirely.

Jeffrey, there is no doubt that you have caused your parents a lot of trouble and heartache. There comes a time when enough is enough. This is that time. Do you have any friends you can stay with?

Maybe, I don't really know.

Well you had better find one. In two weeks you will be legally responsible for yourself. With this your actions will also be treated as an adult. The court will contact the school to inform them of our decision.

He turned to my parents.

Mr. and Mrs. Halldorson it is your responsibility to provide a safe, and unlocked, home for Jeffrey, for the next two weeks. I hope to never see any of you in my courtroom again, especially you Jeffrey. I hope that someday your family will heal from all this. Good day.

With these words came the end of my childhood, washed away in the same unwanted water it had began with. It was bad enough that one set of parents had tossed me away. Now I was to be tossed out of yet another family banished once again from my clan. With me gone from their lives, they were free to raise their other children without the shadow of my tree to hinder their light. Erik was also asked to leave (by my parents) at the end of the school year. Susan and Jim wanted to purge their home of regret and begin anew. They had two new children now. This time they could get it right, couldn't they?

Erik was set to graduate high school and was heading off to boot camp, for the US Army Reserves, at the end of summer. Yet, they were so eager for us to be out of the house that they were willing to rent us an apartment in Durham for two months of the summer. Just enough time to keep Erik under a roof until he left for boot camp. I still had two years of high school to complete but was left to figure it out for myself.

I only returned to their house for help one time. I told Susan, as I stood on her front steps, that I was living on the streets and had no job or food. As cold as she could, she handed me ten dollars and told me to get off her property or she would call the police. She wasn't kidding. I was grateful for the money and her reaction was what I expected.

For the next year I bounced all over the place, helped by friends and their families. I found freedom from the weight in my heart with large amounts of LSD. It brought me farther from reality than anything else I could find. One time I tripped on acid for an entire week, hiding from the world. I spent a lot of my days high, hiding just the way I heard it told time and again in the AA meetings I was forced to attend in my placements. The trauma of my childhood was often hid only skin deep. Friends have recounted stories about me drunk or high ranting about the wrongs that were committed against me as a young child. I don't have any personal recollection of any of these outbursts but it would seem they happened, more than once.

I spent days not knowing where I would spend my nights. I slipped in and out of friend's houses hiding from their parents while they snuck food to me in the late hours. My home was a duffel bag with little clothes. I continued to go to school, often bathed in a deodorant shower wearing the same clothes as I had slept in, until I finally dropped out. I had only friends. I owned nothing. I couldn't get a job and I took to shoplifting to get what I needed.

My relationship with girls was unpredictable at best. I wanted to find security and I definitely didn't want to be alone. My two most serious relationships ended with their sexual betrayal. This compounded with having Susan as a mother and being given up by my birth mother left me with some serious women issues.

As soon as I hit the age of eighteen I left New Hampshire for another part of the country. I wanted to be free of the pain that surrounded me. I headed for L.A. but ended up in New Mexico. I worked dead end jobs that paid just enough to buy cigarettes, food, a roof over my head, and recreational drugs.

There were good times when I could hold myself together but I seemed destined to walk the tightrope that connected being destructive and being productive. I often found myself in bouts of deep depression. I would find a warped, artificial peace drowning myself in mind-altering substances. Alcohol had always been a last resort for me. It was Jim's curse and I wanted as far away from the memory of him as possible.

Unfortunately, sometimes it took the past to drown the past.

I had little to no contact with any of my family including Erik. If I was to be forgotten then I would make damn sure they would also be erased from my mind. I would get an occasional card on my birthday if Susan knew my address, but that was pretty much it. Erik was doing the Army thing and going to college full-time in New Hampshire. I wanted nothing to do with that part of the country ever again.

I was fighting a battle deep inside that made no sense to me. I was longing for my family. I felt the weight of their absence on my heart. I could subdue the feelings temporarily but try as I did, I could not extinguish the flame completely. I was both hurt and infuriated. *Why do I long for the love of those people? They hurt and betrayed me so blatantly?*

This would be a battle I was to fight for a long time.

New Love

(Jeff)

In 1993, I returned to New Hampshire for what was supposed to be a short visit. I wanted to catch up with some old friends and see Erik. I had absolutely no intention of staying. A good friend of mine, Malo, arranged with his parents for me to stay with him. After a month or so we were to return to New Mexico together.

While in New Hampshire I had brief encounters with Susan and Jim. I had dinner at their house and I even stayed a few nights. Surprisingly, they were kind and understanding of my life choices but Jim was concerned about my lack of education. I think it helped them to feel as though they were fulfilling the parental obligations.

My visit to New England was nearly over and the time for me to leave was fast approaching. Malo was coming up with excuse after excuse to delay our exit. Frustration set in and I became increasingly eager to leave. My short visit had turned into months. I ended up having to get a job to make money while I waited out my friend's indecisiveness. I wanted out of the state.

Then the unexpected happened. I fell in love, hard. *Leaving? What do you mean? I'm not going anywhere!*

Her name was Kelly Remick. She stood five foot three on a good day, weighed barely 100 pounds and had long brown hair with deep eyes to match. She had my full attention. She haunted my nights with longing; I had yet to feel this kind of desire for another human being. We had just met and the infatuation was instantaneous. We met and became fast friends. The bond between us grew quickly and all of a sudden New Hampshire was a fine place to be.

The connection with Kelly was clearly more than any of my past relationships. Kelly had seen inside the world of a hard life. We talked about our childhood and the dark places we visited in our lives. We shared not only our hearts and bodies but our minds. Kelly had felt the pain of growing up poor in the projects and seeing her violent, alcoholic father drift in and out of her days. She dealt with her pain by lashing out at the world then suffering the consequences of her actions for doing so. As beautiful as she was on the outside, she was equally scarred on the inside.

We spent all of our free time together. For the first time in my life I was completely comfortable spending all of my waking, and many sleeping, moments with a female. I wanted nothing more than to be with her. It was clear to both of us that we were growing close and a young love was unfolding. Kelly planned to leave for Los Angeles, California long before we met and she had no intentions of breaking those plans, even for me. As I had before, Kelly had her own reasons for leaving New Hampshire.

I was in a stalemate with Malo about New Mexico. So, Kelly and I, wrapped in the passion of the moment, decided we would go to California together. This was a daring move on her part. We had only been together for three months and Kelly had just gotten out of a three year relationship that had ended in betrayal. It was easy for me as I knew that I loved her and was willing to go anywhere to be where she was.

We left on October 4, 1993 - little did I know that I had just driven off with the girl that would become my wife and mother to my three children.

We arrived in Los Angeles set up with a place to live at Kelly's aunt's house. Between us we had four dollars, half a pack of cigarettes and enough gas to get to the next gas station. Ellen and Bob welcomed us into their home, gave us a room, food, and Kelly a job. Other than the two of them we had only each other for companionship.

In LA we spent all of our time either working or with each other. We had no friends out west and didn't have the time to make any. We loved, fought, and lived together. Often times were not easy but there we were side by side. She was all I had. I was all she had.

That was soon to change.

In January of 1994 we put a deposit on a studio apartment in Reseda, California. Exactly two days after we paid the deposit we witnessed the world crumble, literally, in the Northridge earthquake. We decided to get the hell out of there and at the end of the month. We packed up and moved to Phoenix, Arizona.

Shortly after our arrival in Phoenix we found out Kelly was pregnant. We were not married and hadn't any plans to marry. We were both only twenty years old. In those first few months in Phoenix we also discovered a technical school for motorcycle repair. I enrolled almost immediately. We both found jobs working at *The Waffle House*. Kelly waited tables and I cooked. It paid the rent. It wasn't an easy life for either one of us but we managed.

Kelly was beautiful pregnant. She was young and had a glow of life that would intoxicate me at times. A few months into the pregnancy we found out we were having a boy. I was proud but scared as hell. I was about to start my own little clan, one that couldn't kick me out. Little did I know this time it would be me that would fail.

October 21, 1994, Wolfgang Erik was born. I had become a father. As Kelly lay there a new mother, tired from labor, I knew that she and I were now undeniably bonded for life. The two of us occupying a small room in a hospital, far from any family, we only had each other but were no longer alone. I left Kelly alone in the hospital room that night, while I went out and celebrated with friends. I have never forgiven myself for that.

With the new addition came added pressure on both of us. We began fighting a lot. I wanted to go out with friends and naturally Kelly wanted me home with her and Wolf. Kelly decided she wasn't getting the support she needed in Phoenix so figured she'd move back home to be with her family while I finished school. She wanted to get some help for herself and give me a bit of space free from the pressures of parenthood. About a month after her move to New Hampshire I got a job working in a strip club. I started dating one of the bartenders and ended my relationship with Kelly during an angry telephone call. I left Kelly miles away with a baby, no money, and living in her parent's single wide trailer without the support she had been promised by me. I was twenty-one and was on the road to becoming a dead-beat father.

I had lost all faith in myself as a human being. I was a true failure of my own doing. I once again resorted to my destructive ways. I drank with new meaning, allowing alcohol to drown my pain. I became increasingly violent. I was involved in frequent full-on bar room brawls. I reveled in the negativity I surrounded myself with. I felt the fire in my heart extinguish. My heart froze. I no longer cared about myself or what I was becoming.

My puzzle piece was missing. I was no longer whole. It was becoming increasingly clear that without Kelly I was nothing but a shell walking through life in a haze of self-loathing. I began to hate what I had become. Kelly never gave up on her love for me. No matter how verbally abusive I was on the telephone she remained strong for us, for our son. Kelly carried the torch that was us in one arm and rested our child on her hip with the other, alone.

Through all the pain I had caused her, she still loved me. Even though I told her not to, she resolved to come back to Phoenix. I told her I wouldn't be there when she got there and it was a waste of time. She came anyway. Determined to work things out she took our infant son and drove 3,000 miles across country in her little blue Volkswagen Golf.

My heart fell the night she arrived. Looking upon her caused a pain that no man could ever inflict on me. She stood there holding our child and a piece of me died. I knew that my actions caused the pain in my soul. I had torn apart and hurt the only person in my life that had been truly mine to love and loved me unconditionally. I was the cause of her pain and the guilt was overwhelming. The only thing I wanted was the one thing that I had no right to. I wanted to run to her and take her in my arms and hold her tight. I wanted her to hold me, to comfort me and make the pain in my heart disappear.

Seeing Kelly I knew then and there that I would never amount to anything without her love. She was what kept me from becoming Jim. What Susan wasn't strong enough to do for Jim - keep his sexual demons at bay; Kelly's love was strong enough to do for me - keep my self-destruction demon locked up. With her help I would inevitably be forced to put that demon to rest once and for all.

On March 6, 1996 Kelly Remick became Kelly Halldorson. Wolfgang was the only family member present. He was also the best dressed. We returned to New Hampshire to live two days later. Our honeymoon was spent in a U-haul driving cross-country.

By: Jeff & Kelly Halldorson

Reunited

(Jeff)

Griffin Jeffrey was born on October 22, 1996 exactly two years and one day after Wolfgang. Kelly and I were working hard to carve out a quiet life for our little family. We were broke but blessed with each other. We were content to hold one another every evening, never spending a night apart.

I struggled emotionally. I experienced bouts of depression, anxiety and rage. The saying *you hurt the ones you love* rang in tune to our lives. Kelly found herself a victim to my instability. She became the scapegoat for all the pain the world had inflicted upon me. In my mind she vacillated between being my savoir and being my saboteur. For years she tried to help without really knowing how to help. At her insistence we did therapy both individually and together. Yet there were times therapy actually seemed to make matters worse. Antidepressant or anti-anxiety prescriptions would help but often I would abruptly stop medication and therapy citing various reasons ranging from feeling manipulated by Kelly (or the therapist/s) to financial concerns.

Kelly became increasingly concerned for her safety. I was refusing to seek help for my raging, this time for financial reasons. So, Kelly went to Jim for help. Which wasn't an easy thing to do; but she felt I had tied her hands. She felt if she went to her family or anyone else they would just tell her to leave me and she wasn't going to do that. So she called Jim and explained we had no health insurance and I was refusing to get treatment for financial reasons. She told him I was volatile and she was becoming fearful of me and she felt a good deal of it was because of what Jim had put me though as a child. She didn't go into specifics but she made it clear she knew exactly what had happened to me at the hands of that man. He offered to give her money, which she refused. She told him to just pay the therapist directly. As with the rest of my stints in therapy, it wasn't long before I bailed.

Despite my actions, Kelly held strong to her vows and was about to prove her love and strength once again. This time she would carry me through my past as it crept its way back into my life. This time it was our lives it would be affecting, for better or worse.

We had our own two boys now yet with some late nights, Kelly regained her pregnant glow. It would be our third. We were adults; there was no denying it now.

Erik and I rarely spoke, but when we did we reunited as true brothers. We played the hand we were dealt. Overcoming the odds, we both had become productive members of society. He was on his final year of school at Plymouth State College. I had become the motorcycle technician I went to school for in Phoenix.

I decided it was time to take a new approach with my parents. The relationship had evolved into a confusing one. I wanted to let go of my stained and gruesome past. I believed that Erik and I were the only true casualties of the war we were drafted into. I convinced myself that if I could let that be the end of it then the battle could be over. Maybe peace could be had for all of us.

I longed to be a big brother to my younger siblings. They were growing up fast and without me. I wanted them to know my wife and children and to be a part the family I had created. I felt they would be great, fun uncles. Yet, the sight of Jim repulsed me and it took an immense amount of strength to learn how to deal with that. I struggled hard to stifle thoughts which brought me back to my childhood bedroom, when he became the boogie man in my closet.

It was only when Jim saw my children did I question my decision to invite these people back into my life. Jim had been sober for a number of years now. He was exercising, eating better and professed to have found God. He was a changed man, or so he wanted us to believe. We didn't buy it but we made a half-assed attempt to pretend we did. There was no way we were going to take any chances with our boys so Kelly and I were in complete agreement that he was never to be alone with our children. We also vowed never to leave them alone with Susan if Jim was around.

With our strict rules in place it was easy to protect our children without ever having a mention of the abuse.

We got into the habit of visiting at times we knew Jim would not be there. I began to accept Susan for what she was and knew it was little more than an artificial smile on her face. She wanted all to look good for the outside world. It was how others perceived her that mattered most. She personified Approval Whore. I could get past that.

We were spending a good amount of time with my mother, Sam, and Will. We went to their hockey games and visited often. Sue watched our children on occasion, always when Jim was not there.

One day after a class Kelly was taking at a local college, she went to pick up our boys from Susan's house. Kelly was greeted at the door by a disheveled woman.

Sue, you look exhausted. Is everything okay? Did my boys wear you out?

Skeletons Don't Sleep

No, no. I haven't been sleeping much. Sam won't fall asleep unless I'm in the room. Sometimes I have to actually be physically touching him, rubbing his back or hair before he drifts off.

Do you know why? Is he having nightmares?

I'm not sure. I was thinking of moving the boys into the same room. That way I wouldn't have to stay in there until he falls asleep and then I could get some rest myself.

You should give Jeff a call. Maybe there is some way he can help.

Kelly did her best to retain her composure and got out of there as soon as possible. She wanted to share the conversation with me immediately. She walked in the door calling for me and she filled me in on the particulars of the conversation. Then she asked.

What do you think? Is there a chance? If there is we have to say something. We have no choice.

Everything crashed down on me, once again. I suffocated from the weight of my past. The pain bullied its way back to the forefront of my life and put me in a chokehold. I gasped for air. If I had any doubt that I needed to act it was put to rest with a phone call.

Hello?

Hello, Jeffrey

Hi Mom.

I was wondering if you could come by after work tomorrow to help me set up some bunk beds.

Sure, where are you putting bunk beds?

Will is moving into Sam's room.

I went rigid. In an instant I knew that I had failed in protecting those innocent, beautiful boys and it struck me like a fucking bulldozer. My heart shattered into a thousand pieces. And it was all happening in my kitchen nine years too late to save anyone.

Why?

He's been having a hard time getting to sleep. I think that it would be easier if they both slept in Sam's room for a while.

I will be over after work.

Thank-you.

I hung up the phone and fell into instant panic; the thoughts that invaded my head were pure torture. I had no idea what to do.

Kelly and I discussed the next move. My adorable little pregnant wife thought far more clearly than I was capable of. She was willing without complaint or hesitation, to carry whatever part of this burden was too heavy for me alone. We decided to go together. The plan was for Kelly to talk with Susan and try and get more information about what was happening while I set up the beds.

When Erik and I were younger, Jim often hid underwear, photographs, and letters, from other women around the house. His sexual deviance went beyond just what he did to Erik and me. He indulged in pornography and extramarital affairs. He had even brought me to a strip club once when I was 15 (we were promptly kicked out). So, the next night at the house while Kelly talked with Susan I decided to poke around some of my father's old hiding places we had found as kids. I needed evidence that he might still be that sick man I remembered as a child. Sadly, I found what I was looking for.

I walked upstairs and told my mother I needed Kelly's help bringing up some tools from the basement. When we got downstairs I handed Kelly the Ziploc bag full of photos and a pair of underwear. *He is the same man. I don't know what to do.* It was full of pornographic snapshots of different women of all ages, in various stages of undress some merely seductive and others explicit. We stood there shaking. Kelly was disgusted and confused. I had never told her Erik and I knew about these hiding spots or even that I had any intention of looking while we were there. Kelly stood holding my father's photo collection of filth and said *we have to do something I don't know what but we have to do something.*

Like Kelly the night before it was all I could do to hold it together. I assembled the bunk beds as my mother had requested. We left with little more discussion.

I was not willing to face this alone again. I had failed the first two times and this time the stakes were far higher. Erik was replaced now that my soft whispers fell on Kelly's ears. She became the one I turned to. To console me as Erik had done when I was a child. I found comfort in her soft embrace. Together we discussed the next move in the never-ending game of chess. Instead of resting my head on her pregnant belly talking of the future I rested my head on her shoulder and talked of the past. Jim had wormed his way back into my conscience and hung there like a taunting marionette.

With Kelly at my side, my next call was to Erik. Guilt crept in. I didn't want to awaken the feelings he had worked hard to suppress but I knew I had little choice

Hello Erik?

Hey Jeff.

I am so sorry to call you like this.

What's wrong?

You need to come down tomorrow.

Why? What the fuck is going on?

Mom just called and asked me to come and set up bunk beds in Sam's room because he's refusing to sleep alone.

His end of the line went dead silent. He and I had not spoken of the past since that day in the field. Now, I was on the phone telling him it was time to confront the beast head on, without warning.

I can't tomorrow but I will be there on Thursday. What time?

I was thinking five.

That's fine I will meet you at four in Durham and we can talk first.

By: Jeff & Kelly Halldorson

Erik I am sorry but I'm left with no choice.

You made your choice when we were kids. I made the wrong one.

Click.

Kelly comforted me that night as my heart pounded and my body quivered. I vomited until I had nothing left in me then continued to heave stomach acid. I wrenched in pain. I tore my throat and spat blood. None of it was a surprise to me; I had seen this before. Kelly held me, watching as my past purged out of me, physically tearing me apart. It wasn't the first time my emotions made me bleed. I had landed myself in the hospital once before with a severe panic attack; another time the thought of Jim couldn't be extinguished. The foundations to the walls I had erected around my darkest secret were eroding and the facade of strength that I worked so hard at was crumbling into black dust.

Erik and I met at the Store 24 parking lot in downtown Durham. When Erik said we should meet in Durham it went without question where I would find him. All through grade and high school Store 24, a convenience store, was the hangout and central meeting area in town. Kids would flock there like sheep looking for friends or fun.

I arrived before Erik, left to chain smoke and ponder. Thoughts and emotions drifted through my head like the smoke from my cigarettes. Swimming through a sea of fish unable to catch or hold onto one for long. With all things, time is what takes you to the next event in life.

Erik looked as rundown as I did. It was clear he had spent the last two days living in shadows of the past. I couldn't help but feel a little guilty knowing I had my Kelly at home and he didn't. It was written in both our tired, sad eyes...this was not going to be a walk in the park.

We left my VW in the parking lot and traveled together into the war that Susan and Jim had created once again. This time we went armed with each other. I was not looking for revenge or even vindication. I didn't need to be proven right. I always knew I was. So did my parents. What I wanted, what I needed, was to do my part to ensure the safety of my younger brothers.

Erik was fighting with his own conscience. In admitting the pain that Jim inflicted upon us as children, he was also admitting to strong-arming me into retracting my original disclosure. Forcing me to say I lied. It had been weighing on him for some time. On the ride to our childhood home Erik recounted to me what happened in that room with Susan back on the day of my original disclosure. On his return home from a local basketball game he walked into a nightmare, summoned to his pregnant mother's room. There he was hit with my actions of the day.

Susan gave him all the consequences first.

They are going to take you and Jeffrey away. They will put Sam in a foster home and will take the baby from me as soon as it is born. Your Dad will go to jail. They will take you away because I will be found incompetent as a parent.

After all that she finally asked a fifteen-year old boy, *Tell me Erik, did this happen?*

Per Susan, he then held the burden to the entire family structure in his hands. He had no time to see through the fog of deception that she was lying before him. Guilt was an effective tool in her bag of manipulations.

Erik was an old soul. His middle name, given at birth, Kahlil was a fitting one. Like his namesake, Kahlil Gibran the philosopher, Erik journeyed though life contemplating everything in search of deeper meaning. He overanalyzed the simplest of things. He was on an endless quest for answers to explain our past, some meaning that might make sense to him. But some things can never be explained or understood. Inevitably this would be his undoing. His relationships were affected by his lack of trust in women; something he openly expressed had everything to do with Susan.

She may well have had a more damaging effect on Erik's ability to love or accept love than Jim's betrayal. She would lie to us about such minor shit as children. She was never consistent when recounting facts, regularly warping them to paint herself in a more flattering light. Every now and then she would flat out lie for no discernable reason.

Her lies became truths to her and we were forced to accept them as such.

We drove on, headed to the home we were banished from, to confront a pedophile and tell a compulsive liar there was a good chance her young sons' innocence had been compromised. Our ship was sinking and we hadn't even set sail yet. Erik and I arrived to an empty house and a locked door. We took our respective seats. In good old time tradition, we waited to be let in by the first parent to arrive. We used the time to discuss a game plan. Erik started with the same question that was weighing on my mind.

What do we do if he shows up first?

I don't know. I was expecting her to be here.

Did you tell her we were coming?

No, but she is usually home by this time.

Well if he gets here first let me deal with him.

Fuck, if he gets here first I'll make him tell her himself.

That will never happen.

I sat frustrated, anxious, and trying to pretend I wasn't looking forward to finally getting it all out in the open. But horrified by the possibility Jim's dark-side may have revealed itself with his biological offspring. Part of me thought only of myself. I wanted Susan to know, without a doubt, that I had not lied to her. I told the truth and was punished for it. I wanted someone to apologize and give me back the two years I'd lost. I wanted her to stand up and lash out at him with the fury of a mother grizzly bear. I needed her to hate him.

Jim arrived first. His eyes showed us he knew exactly why we were there. He could not hide the fear. Color drained from his fat face. Six foot two with too many pounds for his frame, he looked so old. Years of self-destruction and vile actions had left him looking grim. Tired, aging skin oozed down his skull like melting wax. He wore his anxiety on his sleeve. No question, he wanted to run.

Hello boys. His voice cracked.

Erik took the lead. As if he had to prove he was capable of standing up to the man. *You know why we are here.*

Can we please take this inside?

He unlocked the door and led us into the kitchen. *What is going on?* He knew but he wasn't going to say it first. Maybe he figured he could change our minds or maybe he hoped we were there for some other reason.

Did you really think this day wouldn't come?

What day?

The day you had to stand up for raping your children. I don't know if it was out of pain but Erik was going to be blunt and cruel as possible.

I knew it would come. Some of the color was returning to his face. I could see the wheels turning. He was desperate to get out of this. He took to pleading. *I am sorry. I was a drunk. Didn't I give you a good home? We had good times too, didn't we?* He had to work fast…Susan's location and arrival time was unknown. *I was a drunk and you were hard kids. I didn't know what I was doing. Please…I have changed. I work hard. I help people and I don't drink and haven't for a long time. Please can we just not tell mom?*

There it was and I knew it was coming. The little push over the edge I needed and was longing for. I went at him. All those years of repressed anger and torment, funneled to my fists in one giant flurry of aggression. I got half way across the room before Erik threw me into the door of the refrigerator. I was more than willing to settle this argument physically. Let him explain to Susan why his son had shown up at random and beat the ever living shit out of him. Let them call the police. He could explain it to them to. Blood answers would suit me fine. He wasn't getting out of it this time. Erik wouldn't let it happen, although he came prepared for the possibility it could.

I fucking kept your shitty ass secret long enough! I'll gladly break you.

Please, Jeffrey it will kill her and the boys.

The Boys? The boys, been having a bit of fun with them have you?

No Jeffrey, I would never do that to my own children...

Erik lost it. Something went flying and smashed, sending glass raining all over the sink and floor. He unleashed on Jim. *Your children?! YOUR CHILDREN?! What the fuck are we? You chose us! You went out of your way to get us! You selected us...Your children? What were we, little fuck toys to you?*

NO! I didn't mean it like that ... I just mean -

It was too late for him to run. My mother stepped into the kitchen. Her presence announced by sounds of crackling broken glass under her feet. Any trace of color Jim had regained was now lost completely, a man facing down a firing squad.

Tension was baking in that kitchen. With broken glass at her feet, Susan stood stalk still looking upon her two eldest, their faces still hot from fury. Erik had driven two hours on a Thursday night. She must have wondered, why? Forced by circumstance she had to ask a question she didn't want an answer to.

What's going on? What is the matter? Why is there glass all over my kitchen floor? Erik why are you here?

I think that Jim has something to tell you.

Jim, what's going on? She was terrified yet somehow managed to exude some level of disgust and annoyance.

I felt both pity for her and anger at her. We were there to shatter her perfect little world. Built on a foundation of lies and deception, but it was still her world. Behind Susan, stood, two extremely confused little boys. They had lived to the ages of eight and six without ever seeing their parents - our parents - have a confrontation with their older brothers. I was just there two days before setting up their new beds.

It was as beautiful a day as anyone could wish in August of 1997, in New Hampshire. The sun shone brightly outside. It was almost exactly nine years from the day I told Grant the dark Halldorson secret. Those same neighbors still lived next door and we were standing in the same house. My truth would finally be heard and hopefully it wasn't too late to save my younger brothers.

Susan, please take the children upstairs and get them situated then we'll talk. Susan hesitated but did as Jim asked of her, leaving us alone with him again in the kitchen.

Please boys we don't need to do this. Really, please don't.

I spent two years locked away with your secret, only to have Mom call me years later to tell me that Sam can't sleep alone in his room. She asked me, of all people, to help put together bunk beds. So help me God if I find out that you touched those boys ...

Jeffrey you were sick. We were trying to get you the help you needed.

In a rehab? You knew I wasn't on drugs.

We just did what they told us was best... what Captain Golding told us you needed.

Oh you never thought to say to him, um, well I did sexually molest him all those years. Do you think that might have something to do with my problems?

You had all kinds of problems Jeffrey. We did the best we could. We don't need to do this now.

Erik interrupted. *We should have done it long ago.*

The tables had turned. Forces were shifting in our favor. All the previous battles and blood lost on the battlefield had led to what I thought was to be the Halldorsons' own private D-Day. Erik and I entered onto the beach, subjecting ourselves to possible slaughter only to come out victorious in the end. That is the way it should have gone. Unbeknownst to us, there was still a long fight ahead.

The three of us retreated to the farmer's porch and continued the discussion with Susan. It was overwhelming and I was having a hard time focusing on the task at hand. That ADD thing had kicked in and everything was became a bright shiny object. We sat on the patio furniture.

What is going on? I could feel the anticipation in her voice.

I asked Erik to come down because there is a situation that you need to be aware of. Situation, that was putting it mildly. But I couldn't summon the words to be any more direct. I didn't want to hurt her.

What is it? I don't like this one bit. I want to know what is going on now.

I think it is high time Dad does the talking.

Our attention shifted to Jim. I waited to hear the pain in his voice as he admitted to his wife of twenty-five years, that he had been sexually inappropriate with little boys. The little boys they had adopted together and promised to be loving parents to.

Well. His voice slow, he appeared to be working over every single word in his mind before he spoke them aloud. He was calculating. He was trying to find a way out. *Everything Jeffrey told Suzy was true.* The chicken shit tried to take the easy way out. He tried to run from the words. He couldn't bring himself to verbalize exactly what kind of monster he really was.

Everything he told Suzy about what? Had the conversation nine years ago had such little impact, she had no recollection of it? I doubt it.

Everything that he told her about me, and - and what I did. Devastated she sat. The color and texture of her face bore resemblance to Elmer's Glue.

What he means to say is that he had been raping us throughout our entire childhood. Apparently Erik hadn't turned off his blunt button.

She didn't cry. She didn't move. She just sat there doing nothing. I waited for her to her to scream, hit or cry. Anything would have been better than her silence. She just sat there looking at the son-of-a-bitch with a blank expression. I wouldn't have been surprised if she asked him politely to pass the salt.

Then it came. Her numbness wore off and the grizzly bear mother, I longed for, awakened.

You're not serious? Tell me this isn't true! You didn't, tell me you didn't!

Jim's look was as blank as hers had been a few minutes before. Coldly, he responded, *It's true.*

How!? When!? Where was I? What did you do to them? There was a pause. She shook her head, repulsed. *I'm going to be sick.*

Jim stood silently looking like a fool. He wasn't forthcoming with the answers to her questions. He didn't offer up anything.

Answer me!?

It just happened. I was drinking, I don't really know. Susan turned her attention to us. I for an instant saw a true mother within her, somewhere. I pitied her. I wanted to comfort her, to protect her.

How, please tell me how? What did he do to you? Please I am so, so, sorry.

Erik and I took turns tucking our mother back into our childhood beds.

It didn't matter if you were home or not. You were home most of the time. It happened for as far back as we can remember living with you. Jim would come into our rooms at night.

He would put his mouth on my penis. That sick man would take off his pants and rub his dick all over my body. I lay there and let him do it. He rubbed his DICK all over me!

It happened over and over and over again.

He would take my clothes off as I lay there pretending to sleep. He would rub his hands and tongue all over me then leave me there naked covered in spit and shame to somehow piece myself back together.

When he was really good and drunk he'd climb right up on the bed and jerk off. Then he went and slept next to you.

This is the way we grew up. That sick bastard coming into our rooms and violating our lives.

Sometimes you would come in and comfort us after when we were crying.

I can't even have sex with my girlfriend without him being in the room.

In a quiet whisper, almost inaudible, Susan had the grapes to ask ... *Why didn't you tell - me?*

Dumbfounded, I responded. *I did!*

Yes – but – but - you said you lied. You said it didn't really happen.

Erik responded. *I made him.*

What?! Why Erik? Why on earth did you ever do that?

I don't know. You were pregnant and Jim had stopped. I don't know why. Trust me I deal with that every day of my life.

Jim sat as still as a store mannequin. He said nothing. He didn't move, frozen as if he was the little boy in the bed this time.

My mother turned to him. *Is it true? Did you do this to them, to our children?*

Yes. It was all he said. No sorry, no nothing, just one word. *Yes.*

We could see the gears begin to turn in Susan's head. The thoughts were rolling visibly across her face. She started to put two and two together and didn't like at all how it added up.

The bunk beds, that's why you're here isn't it? You think it's happening to the boys. Oh my god, oh my god. You didn't, did you?

It was the first sign of tears. Right then and there I knew where Erik and I stood on Susan's pecking order. It was the fear for her, **own biological,** children that mattered. The grizzly had left to go defend the den.

No, I would never...they're ours...I don't drink. I couldn't do that to them.

But you could to them! You did to them! Why should I believe you? I have to know. I have to know now; I have to ask them.

Susan, please don't! They don't need to know. I'm telling you the truth, I am.

To hell with what you say I need to know. I need to hear it from them.

Her demeanor changed. She left the porch with purpose. I followed. Erik remained, at guard. There was no way we were letting Jim get away with it this time. What or if they discussed anything I don't know. I would wager they sat there in complete silence.

Sam was the first to be brought down. He was the older one and I believe that is why she started there.

Sam, it is very important that you tell me the truth. You are not in any trouble; you did nothing wrong, OK? Has anyone, even Daddy, ever touched you in any way that you felt was wrong?

She said it like she had just read it out of a brochure at the pediatrician's office. She looked at that eight-year old dead in the eyes and said it without emotion.

No. Tears started to build up in his eyes and his face went scarlet.

Are you sure? No one will get mad at you. You know that you can tell Mommy anything?

No. Why? Why are you asking me? Why is Erik here? What's going on?

I will talk to you more, later. OK? I love you. Now go upstairs and send Will down.

The gentle interrogation went down exactly the same with Will, although he was surely more confused. Susan questioned them until she felt content with the answers she had received. It was clear that if they had anything to tell it wouldn't be now, or to us. We returned to the silence of the porch to relay the results of the questioning.

Jim sat looking like a boxer losing his match and wanting the fight to just be over so he could retreat to the locker room. No such luck. For the next two hours we sat there and discussed everything that happened. Susan had a lot to say.

I can never let you alone with those children again. How can I trust you? You are truly sick.

I'll get help; I'll go tomorrow.

That's in no way going to be of any help. What about them and the help they need, what about that?

I'll pay for any counseling they want. I will.

What about our boys? You can't be alone with them. I don't think you should even be here now. What about the children I baby-sit. I am going to have to tell their parents. What about them?

Come on Susan you know me...

I don't know you! And it seems like I never have. You did that to them and then came and touched me in bed. How could I not know? How did I miss this?

It's not your fault Susan...

Yes, in part it is. Erik had chimed in. *We were defenseless little children and she is our mother. You can't sit there and deny that you didn't know something was wrong.*

The tears came back as she sunk into her pain with the realization of it all. I couldn't help but feel sorry for her. Her life was changing before me. I thought, for the first time, I would have my mother to fight with me. She was coming on to our team, leaving Jim to defend his fort alone. *I had no idea. I really didn't - know - it could possibly be this bad. I am sorry.*

The remainder of the time was spent putting together a plan for the rest of our lives. Susan was unsure that she would be able to have Jim stay with her and was insinuating that their marriage was over. She reassured us that in no way was Jim to ever be left unsupervised with our younger brothers. She had also laid out a plan as to how she was going to inform the families she baby-sat for. The boys would both get professional help to alleviate any concern we had for their safety.

Jim hardly spoke and showed next to no remorse other than parroting the occasional, *I'm sorry.* This was not all that shocking for as he had never been emotional throughout any of our upbringing. He vowed to take the next day off work and get himself into an aggressive therapy plan. He stated he understood all of our concerns and would agree to whatever Susan decided was best for the family.

Erik and I left their house feeling lighter, as if we had left the burden for them to deal with. We did our job and could now walk away without having to carry that evil secret any longer. We had freed a part of ourselves. Erik returned to his home alone and I returned to my little family.

The following weekend Jim took the boys camping, alone.

By: Jeff & Kelly Halldorson

Mother-in-Law Battles

(Kelly)

Jeff looked as though the weight of the world had been lifted from his shoulders.

How did things go?

The wait for him to return home was nothing short of excruciating. I put our boys to bed early in hopes they would be sound asleep when their dad returned. I wanted Jeff to have my full attention if he needed it. I most certainly wanted his.

Actually, it went okay. It was tough but it was okay.

What do you mean? What happened? Did Erik go? Tell me.

Yes, Erik was there. He admitted everything. He actually admitted it. He told her.

A weight was being lifted from me now, too. I could see the end of Jeff's suffering, of our suffering. Jim was going to be held accountable for the evil he perpetrated. For all the pain his actions had caused. All that pain. There had been so much pain.

Oh my God. Are you serious?

Yes Kelly.

What about the boys? Are they okay? Where is Jim? How did your Mom react? What did she say? Is she okay? Where is Jim? I couldn't stop. The questions poured out of me. He answered every one with patience. *What's next? Is she going to stay with him? How is she going to get by? Maybe we can move in and help with the kids? She must be devastated.*

It was something I had always thought about. I wanted to protect Sam and Will. I wanted to make sure they weren't being harmed but always felt so powerless. I was nursing my younger son and pregnant with my third child. Who was I to think I could do anything? The protectiveness that for years bubbled quietly under the surface seemed more like hot springs in Yellowstone with my hormones in overdrive.

Kelly, she wants us to come over in the morning to discuss everything. I think she's going to leave him. I really do. She said as much. The hours slipped by as the conversation continued. It proved to be a long night.

We arrived at Susan's just before lunch. We lucked out: our boys were fast asleep. Jeff's mother was out sitting on the porch. Sam and Will were inside playing video games. We opened all the car windows and left our boys cozy in their car seats. The driveway was literally a few feet from the porch, shaded by huge oak trees. If the boys so much as stirred we'd be able to see and hear them.

Susan looked as though she had aged fifteen years overnight. She never appeared particularly young, but had always at least looked her age. Not this day. I felt so badly for her. I had never truly looked at her as anything other than a victim. I was never convinced she knew about the abuse. I blamed her for locking Jeff up, but I figured she did so out of some misguided concern for his wellbeing. Part of me dismissed her actions after he was released from placement as some kind of tough love. I also thought she was a victim too. If Jim could hurt two little boys what might he have done to her?

How are you doing? It was all I could think to say. Jeff stood by my side and didn't utter a word.

Well, it's...it's, you know, difficult. I don't know what to say. I'm running on autopilot. It's all so...overwhelming. I...I called...he...he went to work and well we called his therapist. You know he's been in AA now for a long time and you know...well, the hardest thing is I know, now, why you wouldn't let Wolf and Griffin spend the night. You knew? You knew. She rambled on and on.

Sue, I...we want you to know we are here for you. Whatever you need, whatever you decide. We'll do what we can to help...

Jeff spoke up. *Yes, mom whatever you need.*

Thank-you, I appreciate it. You know we talked to his therapist. I talked to his therapist. He said...he said that things like this often come out after an alcoholic stops drinking. This is very common. I didn't know what to say but I knew I didn't like where she was headed, already. Nothing about any of this seemed normal or common. *Yes, he said...he said this happens all the time and we should not be surprised if more comes to the surface over the next few years.*

Um...okay......really?

Yes, all the time.

What are you going to do?

Well, I talked to our lawyer too.

Huh?

He said that the Statute of Limitations on this kind of thing. She didn't even say crime. I felt my stomach turn. *The, um, Statute of Limitations has passed. So, we don't need to worry about that.* I couldn't for the life of me get my head around the words that were coming out of this woman's mouth. Did she really just say she called a lawyer? Did she say we didn't need to worry? She must have seen the confusion and disgust on my face because her tone shifted ever so slightly to patronizing. *There is nothing the boys can do. He can't be arrested.*

What the fuck? It was all I could do not to scream. I shook my head, baffled. *You, ah, you called your lawyer? Did Jim stay here last night?* I knew the answers but I had to hear her tell me. I had to.

Yes, he stayed here.

Did he stay upstairs?

No, he slept in my bed. My jaw dropped. She continued. *Yes, he slept in my bed. I don't care. As far as I'm concerned the marriage is over so I don't care where he sleeps.* I looked at Jeff. He didn't seem at all phased. Did he hear what she was saying? By the look on his face he couldn't have. Could he?

One of our boys stirred. Jeff went to take care of him.

This couldn't be happening. She was going to stay with him. She was setting the groundwork for it all now. She was trying to prepare us. I ran my hands over my bulging tummy. I could never do this to my child. Not to any of my children. Was she for real? How could she call herself a mother?

You? You slept in the same bed with him? Part of me felt it was none of my business who she slept with. The other part was compelled to know.

Her tone got a bit defensive. *Yes, I told you. The marriage is over but I don't care where he sleeps or if he continues to live here. I'm going to go on with my life. We don't need to worry about him being arrested. He is in therapy. His therapist said this is common.*

What about Sam and Will?

They are fine. We talked to them. Jeffrey was there. Didn't he tell you?

I couldn't take it any longer. *Sue, I told you, Jeff and I are here for you if you need us. We don't have much money but...* Everything I had daydreamed about the days prior was all crumbling before my eyes. I thought she'd leave him and Jeff and I would be there to help care for the boys. It never crossed my mind that she might stay. I'd asked Jeff the question but I never really thought she would. I figured maybe I'd babysit the boys while she worked….God maybe we'd even move in to try and help her keep the house. I would get to be a big sister to the boys. Jeff would have his mother and brothers. It would all be Okay. It would all work out.

But no, that would be too easy.

We don't have much money but I…I could watch the kids if you need to work another job. Whatever…

That won't be necessary.

I wanted to leave. I walked into the house. Jeff was inside with Sam, Will and our boys. I picked up Wolf and hugged him. How could a mother do this? The thought kept repeating over and over in my head. The sight of Sam and Will playing so innocently was crushing. How could she stay with a man that might harm them? My head was spinning. I insisted we get the hell out of there as soon as possible.

The ride home I filled Jeff in on what Susan and I had discussed. *Jeff, she said she called her lawyer. She made that comment about the Statute of Limitations. Who would do that? I think she's lying. I don't believe her. You're only 23…there is no way she's right.*

I couldn't remember ever discussing the possibility of turning Jim in with Jeff. If we had talked about it, it likely was just a *have you ever thought of it* question on my part. It had most certainly crossed my mind many times but I never wanted to push Jeff. I felt he had already been through too much. Part of me felt extremely guilty. They had two other boys. She babysat. *Shouldn't I be pushing for him to be put away? I should have a long time ago. How could we prove it? What if Jeff was let down again?*

Life was hard, wonderful at times, but hard. We both came into the relationship damaged from our past. We were young, so very young. We dove headfirst into parenthood and marriage and had no idea what we were doing. At 23 he didn't know how to be a husband and at 24 I had no clue how to be a wife. Already we had two children with a third due in mere months. This was all more than we were ready for. None of that mattered, we were forced by life's circumstance to figure it out, best we could.

Jeff was unaffected by my recounting of the conversation with his mother. He seemed hell bent on finding nothing wrong with anything she said. It made perfect sense, to him, that she would call a lawyer. Once I realized, I stopped pressing. I ended the discussion. *I have to let it play out. I have to let him see for himself.* I didn't want him to blame me for damaging his relationship with her. A relationship, it was clear, he not only wanted but needed. He had been vindicated the night before, with Erik, and I damn sure wasn't going to rain on that parade. He deserved to feel good. He had done the right thing. *If she is lying, if she does choose Jim, we'll deal with it. Maybe I've got this all wrong anyway. Maybe it will still work out for the best.*

During dinner we got a call from Susan. Jeff spoke with her. She and Jim wanted us to come over to discuss *where we all go from here* and they both *wanted to put my mind at ease*. Susan knew I wasn't going to be easy to deal with. She knew I was going to be trouble for her. Jeff she could manipulate. He was desperate for her love. She knew that and used it to her advantage.

With our sons safely in the care of my aunt at home, we ventured again to the Halldorson household. Jim greeted us at the door with an awkward smile and ushered us into the living room while Susan settled their boys down upstairs. His size was physically intimidating. He stood nearly a foot taller than I and even in my condition he was more than twice my weight. Jim did his best to engage us. *Hi Kelly, we...ah... wanted you to know you can ask....*

I'll wait for Sue to come down.

Jim stood in front of the fireplace. Jeff sat next to me on the couch while Susan sat in a chair opposite Jeff and me. Erik wasn't there. It was only the four of us. We were told Erik would have his own such meeting but this one was for us. To help put our minds - my mind - at ease.

Jeff's mother spoke first. *Kelly we wanted you to come here so as to put any of your concerns to rest. If you have any questions we want you to feel free to ask.* The word *we* was spoken each time with emphasis. Their solidarity was clear. This was a meeting not to make us feel more comfortable but for them to demonstrate a united front. Jim wasn't going anywhere and neither was Susan. They were in this together and planned on keeping it that way, no matter what.

I shot a concerned look at Jeff. He was pale. It was sinking in. He rested his hand on my knee and I turned to Jim. *What is she talking about? What do you mean, do I have any questions?*

We want you to know that you can speak freely and I'm getting help. I'm not drinking...

Okay. You know what, I don't have any questions...well maybe I do but first I have something to say.

Please, say it. It's okay, you can say anything.

You are disgusting. What you did was disgusting and wrong. I have always wanted to say that to you....and you are NEVER to be alone with my children. I don't want you to even be around my children at all.

Yes, yes, I, I completely understand. I know. I know. You're right. You're within your rights.

Okay. And you know I – I do have a question. Why? No sooner than the words parted my lips did I wish to take them back. It didn't matter why. Did it? He did it because he was a fucking sicko. I finished the thought regardless. *Why did you do this? To them? To these two boys that needed a father?*

Um, I don't know. Well, you know, they were so much more difficult than we expected them to be. And - and they were such hard kids that... I didn't know what to do. I felt like I had taken a knife and stabbed the love of my life square in the back. Why did I ask that question? I knew Jim wouldn't give any kind of real answer. Of course he would be defensive but to blame it on Erik and Jeff's behavior? What?

Stop. No. You're saying you did this to them because they were tough kids? No. No. You did this because you are sick. It wasn't their fault.

I – I wasn't saying it was their fault. Really I wasn't.

What about Sam and Will? What about them?

I would never do that to my own boys. I wanted to crawl into a hole and die. I just kept making it worse. I wanted to comfort Jeff but I was failing miserably.

What? I had to change the subject. It was going nowhere. He was taking no responsibility and making horrid excuses for ruining his sons. *What is this help you're getting? You realize it doesn't matter to me. You are still not going to be around my children.*

Yes, yes.

I don't even think you should be around your children.

Susan jumped in. *Okay, why don't we talk about where we go from here?* Her voice was cold and had an air of condescension. *We want you to feel comfortable. Nothing has happened to Sam and Will. Jim is in therapy and hasn't been drinking. We know you two are struggling. You're living in that tiny two bedroom apartment. You both are working. Jeff is working two jobs. You are about to have a third child, a* daughter. *Where is she going to sleep?* I didn't have a clue where she was going with this. What the hell did it have to do with what was going on?

Ah – yeah.

Well, we just want you to be okay. In some ways we haven't been helpful to you both. You know my mother left me money. I want to use it to help you to get into a home of your own...

I was still confused.

...And we understand you are having a hard time getting ahead, as young as you are - and Jim and I would like to help with that.

With these last words there was no question where she was going. I couldn't hide my repulsion; she turned to Jeff. He was wide-eyed and eager for any help from them. He was searching, searching for anything positive. There was no doubt he realized at this point that she was staying with him. Fuck, what a way to find out. I began to loathe her. My emotions were on overdrive, not the least bit helped by my blustering hormones. I did my best to try and find some good in her, not for myself but for Jeff.

The conversation continued in the same direction. Susan did all the talking. They asked us how we were doing financially. They questioned us about our debt. Did we just have the school loan? Did we have credit card debt? Jeff answered all their questions. I sat dumbfounded. What was happening? No, I knew what was happening. They were doing their damnedest to buy our silence.

We left that night with the agreement Jeff would return in a few days with all of our bills and they would do what they could to *help us out*. I felt so dirty. I voiced my concerns with Jeff on the way home. They fell on deaf ears. *Kelly, your family has helped us out before. This could be good. We could get out of our hole. We could take this really bad thing and it could be good.* I wanted nothing to do with it.

I didn't blame Jeff at all. He had been through hell. He was working two jobs and doing his best to keep our little family afloat. Why wouldn't he embrace any help he could? *They are stepping up, they are being parents.* No matter how hard I tried, I just never saw it that way.

After everything she was staying with him. Sam and Will would still be living under the same roof with that monster and I didn't think there was a thing I could do about it. I wanted to scream from the rooftops - *Jim Halldorson is a child molester!!* I couldn't prove anything and according to Susan it didn't matter the Statute of Limitations had expired. I might alienate Jeff and potentially destroy the relationship with his mother he was so desperate for. What about my kids? I had two boys and daughter coming in a few months. I didn't want to drive him away. I didn't want to be without Jeff and I didn't want my children to be without their dad.

I did the only thing I knew how to do. I loved Jeff.

By: Jeff & Kelly Halldorson

Broken Promises

(Jeff)

My mother did little to keep up her end of the bargain. I had hoped she would protect her children, young and old, from anymore pain. I wanted her to shower her children with love and cut all ties with Jim. It didn't happen.

Within a month everything was lost. Not just swept under the rug but lost. Gone. Susan threw the revelations of that night down the toilet, flushing twice; to make sure the plumber himself would never find a trace. It only compounded my belief of how little I mattered to the Halldorson family.

Susan falling short on her promises was a major turning point for Erik. He had held his head above water, best he could. Now he was drowning. It became increasingly clear that he had, understandably, lost all faith in humanity and started his withdrawal from society. He had graduated college with a bachelor's degree in Chemical Biology and took a job in Portsmouth, NH. He moved back to the town of Durham to share a house with old high school friends.

Erik took an opportunity to get off the dayshift and onto nights. He began working from 7pm to 7am four to five days a week. Erik took every holiday shift available claiming it was for the money. I believe it was because it left him without having to be alone or go to some other family's gathering. This only withdrew him further and he started to live with a completely different perspective on life. Essentially Erik became as destructive, to himself, as I had in my younger years. There was little I could do but sit and watch my brother, the only person I had known my entire life, self-destruct.

The wear and tear became visible in Erik's face and body. Standing an impressive six foot seven, Erik towered over most of the world. He took to slouching to lower his stature. He became pale and emaciated. On days when sleep was impossible for him he would retreat into creating music in his dark sun-starved room. Weeks would go by when the only sun that blessed his skin would be on the way to or from work. Within no time Erik far surpassed my destructiveness. I took my anger out on the world; he took it out on himself. I wasn't privy to all that was going on, often it wasn't until the end of a relationship with a woman would she inform me of just how low Erik lived in his homemade dungeon. He had sentenced himself for the crimes of the past, living out his life on house arrest.

Erik and I were walking down entirely different roads. Until the day Susan betrayed his heart, Erik and I drove through life on the same highway, traveling in different lanes. That day Erik got off at his exit, parked his car and began to wait for death to take him. He was living in a state of constant depression. Randomly he would talk to Kelly or I about suicide or his long thoughts on the concept of death and possible afterlife. He became lost to us. Lost to even himself. We often took rides on Erik's personal rollercoaster, becoming more concerned for his wellbeing with each drop.

I was living with some guilt regarding Erik. I truly believe that, although painful and sad, rehabilitation played a major role in how I coped with life as an adult. The help I received and tools I was given at IFLL, a little lost for some years, were embedded in the way I dealt with my life. I wish that he had received the help he needed when he was young. He was overlooked, and any cries for help were stifled by our parent's incompetence.

After Kelly and my meetings with Susan and Jim, they cut off nearly all contact with us. The two families split until the birth of my daughter.

On the night before Kelly was to go into the hospital to be induced into labor, Susan called. She called for one reason and one reason only.

Kelly and I had decided to make a gesture to our mothers as soon as we found out we were having a girl. We planned to use Sue-Ann, Sue for Susan and Ann after Kelly's mother, as the baby's middle name. To Kelly's side of the family this was no small act; the last six girls shared the middle name Marie. Part of the family's Catholic heritage, it had become somewhat of a tradition.

Susan called that night to tell us that we didn't have to name our daughter after her and we would probably regret it if we did anyway. It was completely out of the blue. Quite honestly she didn't have any reason to think we were still going to do it anyway. We hadn't discussed it with her or even mentioned it since well before the disclosure and the fallout from it. This wasn't some attempt at concern but a direct dig at Kelly.

From some twisted sense of abandonment I was still trying hard to repair a relationship with Susan. Somewhere down in my soul I wanted a mother so badly that I was willing to settle for this woman that stayed with an abomination. She even confessed to Kelly that at one point in her and Jim's marriage that Jim had to be screened for sexually transmitted diseases because he was sleeping with so many other women that she was afraid he would bring something home.

This woman had left me to the wolves, fed me to her husband and thrown me out to make room in her house. I had been kicked, stabbed in the back, and ruined. Yet, I was so lost for someone to call Mom that I went back to get kicked again.

To make matters worse, Susan and Kelly weren't even on speaking terms. To begin with, Susan had called a couple of weeks after the disclosure to talk with Kelly. During the conversation the subject of Jim came up.

Kelly I want you to know you can talk to me. Really, say anything you'd like. It's not going to offend me. Is there something else you need to say? Are you upset with me in some way?

Well, no...it's just...I guess I'm just disappointed in you.

That was putting it mildly but Kelly still wanted to make sure that she didn't interfere with my relationship with my mother. She did her best to treat Susan with respect whether she deserved it or not.

What do you mean? What did I do?!

You...I thought you were going to leave him. How could you stay? I'm just disappointed.

That was all it took. Just like Susan was looking for the perfect excuse to cast me out when I broke into the house for my clothes, she was doing the same with Kelly now. She wanted anything that might justify her cutting us off. Kelly was her scapegoat.

What?! You told me you would support me no matter what! You stood on my porch and told me it would be okay whatever I decided to do!?

You're right. I'm sorry. I misspoke. To be perfectly honest I never dreamed you would actually stay with a man that could do that to your children, a man that molested your children. And even the idea of being near him sickens me... so I can't understand how you could manage. I thought you were stronger than that. What I meant when I said we'd support you was that...

She didn't give Kelly the opportunity to go on.

I knew it. You know, it is none of your business. My marriage is my marriage it has nothing to do with you or Jeffrey. I am really upset about this. I love your children. I tried to help you when Jeffrey left you. I tried to be a good grandmother. You both have your own problems and I've always been supportive. Jeffrey is not perfect as you know and neither are you for that matter. It's my marriage. I'm so upset. This is how I'm repaid. I'm so upset. I need to go.

After that conversation Kelly had no more patience for Susan's lies and deceptions. She said she would continue to have a relationship with her for me and would do her best to be civil but wouldn't dance around the topic of Jim anymore. Susan wouldn't even give her the chance. Susan became hostile toward Kelly even to the point of writing me a letter to tell me how much Kelly had insulted her and the Halldorson name. That she would never have talked to Jim's mother the way Kelly had spoken to her and she had no intention of continuing on with a relationship with her. It became a feud that I was caught in. For some sick reason I felt compelled to mend things with Susan even though she was putting in no effort herself. If anything she was intentionally pushing in the other direction. I was trying to fill a hole by shoveling hope into the bottom of a latrine.

This woman slept in the same bed with a man the same day she found out he had sexually molested her children. She allowed the same man to take the younger two boys on a camping trip the weekend after. The Halldorson family crest was already well tarnished with shit and it wasn't Kelly's fault.

We had made our boundaries clear to Susan. We were not in any way interested in having Jim near our children. Not that we thought he would be sexually inappropriate, we were always there. He was just a creepy old child molester and who would want that around their kids? Plus, I didn't want him to have the joy of being a grandfather because he didn't deserve it.

I saw what a grandfather was in Bob, Kelly's stepfather. He was a real granddad. He loved my children. With no biological children of his own Kelly and I were the closest he had to offspring. He poured his life and love into our family. He gave our children his heart. He hugged them. He played with them. He cared for them. With Bob and Ann as my children's grandparents there was no way I would bestow that honor on Jim. Simply put, they were good people. He was not. I wasn't sure that Susan was even worthy, after seeing how Ann unconditionally loved our children; with Susan there were always conditions.

All this and she still had the nerve to call the night before Kelly was to be induced. She still supposedly thought we'd be naming our daughter after her. Conflicted and caught up in the desire for the birth of our daughter to be a happy time we still gave her name to our daughter.

On the day of Zoë Sue-Ann Halldorson's birth I invited Susan and the boys to come to the hospital. She refused to come without Jim. How could I have the audacity not to invite my father to such an occasion as bringing another Halldorson into this world? Spineless, I let her bring him despite pleas from Kelly not to.

I had that SOB standing there in front of my wife, exhausted from labor, ogling over our beautiful daughter. I didn't seem to be able to stop the longing to have these two horrific human beings in my life. I wanted to prove my worth to them and was incapable of cutting the umbilical cord. I even subjected poor Kelly to them on such an important day.

For the next few months I made feeble attempts to hold together what was left of Susan's and my relationship. With her love and devotion to Jim heavily defined. She had made her decision to back the pedophile and adulterer over her sons. We were never going to be what I longed for. I was destined to go through this life motherless. Accepting that was hard but out of my control. We parted ways for the next few years.

I began to wonder what my other options were. Susan didn't seem to care about what happened and I began to feel like Erik and I were entitled to some form of justice. Anything at all would have appeased me. Susan gave me nothing but more hurt. I went to see a lawyer. I chose the law office of Bill Shaheen, the husband of former New Hampshire Governor Jeanne Shaheen. I chose him because he was the judge that emancipated me and set my mother straight all those years ago.

I sat in his office waiting room sweating with anticipation. I wanted so much to tell him exactly what Jim had done. Then he would know why I was sent away.

What is it that I can do for you Jeffrey? He met me with a firm handshake and all that sticky sincerity you get from a used car salesman.

Well, I was hoping to find out what my legal rights are, if I have any, as a sexual assault victim. I know there is a lot involved with that statute of limitation and all.

Well, that is not my usual line of work, but this is a big office and we have many lawyers in this practice. Why don't you tell me the situation and we can go from there.

I spent the next hour telling him my story. He asked many questions about times and Jim's actions.

So you want to sue Jim in a civil court?

I don't know what I want to do. Can I press charges? Can I sue him? I was hoping that telling Susan would bring some form of closure but it didn't.

Does Jim have any assets or money to sue him for?

Well he has money and the house, a camp up north. I just want some kind of justice to be served. He walked away with no real consequences for his actions.

With that he led me to the door.

I don't have the answers for you right now but I will. Give us some time and we will see what we can do for you.

I left feeling a little lighter. I had told Bill the real story and I hoped that my injustice as a teen would help to fuel him in his search for answers.

It was about three weeks before I heard back from him.

I have spoken with some of my colleagues and we would like to set up another appointment with you so that you can speak with them directly. I have to be honest it looks like it would be a hard case to go after.

We made the appointment and said our goodbyes.

Once again I sat there in the waiting room, this time I was not nearly as happy to be there. I sat in Bill Shaheen's office with two other lawyers and once again went over the whole ordeal that was my past. It was decided by all three of them, that too much time had lapsed and there was nothing left for me to do.

I am sorry but the statutes are not in your favor. There is nothing that you can really do legally. You only have so much time to press charges after your 18th birthday and you are just too old now. If you had pressed charges and won then, you could have gone after him civilly. I will look into some other avenues but I think there is nothing for you, I am sorry.

I left there believing Jim had gotten away with all his crimes and would walk a free man for the remainder of his days, confirmed for me by a call from Bill's office apologizing that there was no more they could do.

Kelly and I continued to raise our family with little to no contact with the other Halldorson family. I would drift in and out of my younger brothers' lives. Susan and I did not speak and there was no way I was going to apologize for any of my wife's or my actions. Susan was losing her hold on my maternal need. Kelly's family completely and warmly embraced me.

Kelly's extended family gave me what I had been longing for my entire life. Never turning a family member away; they also extended warm welcomes to Erik on the rare occasion I could get him to a family gathering. I was no less a part of their family than anyone else. The same went for my brother.

Holidays were spent in the tradition of a Norman Rockwell painting. Children by the fire on Christmas Day at Aunt Donna and Uncle Andy's with four generations gathered to celebrate family and friends. Grampy, the great grandfather to my children, adorned with a Santa hat would disperse gifts to the children as they waited with bright smiles. There was nothing more anyone could ask for. I had found the true magic of family at last and I was embraced as part of it.

Every family has its problems and dramas. They were no exception to this. Though, however bad it got, they remained determined to not give up or simply walk away from a problem or family member. They always struggled to work things out and help each other.

With all their love and acceptance of me there was still that latrine I was trying to fill. I couldn't seem to shake it. I needed to accept that I was going to go through this world with a sporadic brother and an in-law family. I had to wake up to this and see it for what it was, a whole hell of a lot more than some people have. It was with this attitude that Susan and the Halldorson family would re-enter my life.

In 2001 we decided to send our children to the private Christian school that the Halldorson family was deeply rooted in. We knew that going there would, to some degree, bring the families together. This was not our intention. We simply liked the school and its proximity to us. We weren't religious but cost was a factor. The school cost considerably less than the alternatives and we were not putting our children into public school, so this proved a good option for us.

My two younger brothers had attended the school their entire academic upbringing and Susan was vested in the school system. She ran the book exchange, lunchroom and often substituted classes. With the death of her mother, Susan honored her by donating money to build a nurse's office and help pay a salary for a full-time nurse. Her mother had spent her entire career as a public school nurse. Even until the day she died she volunteered as a nurse at the retirement home that was her residence. My grandmother was to me, a great woman. She saw people for what they were.

To Kelly and my surprise we found a different Susan than we had expected. She wanted to continue a relationship with our family void of Jim. To her recount, things were not good in their marriage, such that they slept in separate rooms and hadn't been intimate in years. Jim had replaced his sobriety with prescription pills. She also told us he had sold the house in Durham and purchased a house in Dover without even consulting her or the boys forcing them to move. He spent the money from the house sale on a summer home over three hours away in northern Maine, again without any input from Susan.

Jim had quit his job at Converse which had, of course, filed for Chapter Eleven. He found a position in at a large printing press manufacturer from Germany with a plant in Dover. He ran the Human Resources department. I had friends with my father's signature on their paychecks. It would seem that it took a financial strain for Susan to turn on Jim. Within one year of their move to Dover, Susan had to work a fulltime job to make ends meet. Within two years of the move, she was working both a fulltime job and a part-time job. The boys were generally left to fend for themselves around the house.

Susan and I never spoke of the past. Most of our conversations pertained to her ever growing distain for Jim. He was getting worse with his new hobby of popping pills. She withheld no punches, constantly complaining about the family economics and how he had lost their life's savings, spending all their money on drugs from Indonesia. It was hard to see the financial burden looking at their enormous Victorian home complete with in-law apartment and three-car garage but, she insisted it was there.

Jim's driving got increasingly worse too. They purchased an old Isuzu Trooper because he couldn't stop hitting things and the bills on their good cars put a big dent in the wallet. I did my best to stay clear from Jim. I wanted nothing to do with him and didn't hide the fact from anyone. Kelly and Susan let bygones be bygones and were cordial to each other. I spent time with my younger brothers and Susan became Grammy Sue.

Erik was still finding life challenging. He continued to spend endless hours locked away in his homemade dungeon working on his music withdrawn from the family and from me. I often didn't see him for weeks without word. He was slipping further from me and I became concerned.

With my two younger brothers now in their teens and very into playing music themselves, I had what I thought was a brilliant idea. I had a ten by twelve storage shed with power where I lived. I convinced Jim that it would be good for all of his boys if he invested some money into it and turned it into a makeshift home recording studio.

He agreed and paid for the materials and some music equipment. We were now wired for sound. It became the place we could play. Being an avid guitar player I found it a great outlet. Erik would now spend long hours into the night recording his music outside his home. The younger brothers came often to see us. Local musicians came and we jammed until we were too tired to stand or the neighbors got fed up. We called it the Dog House and rightfully so. It put me in it with Kelly. She spent countless nights with only the computer for company and was left to tuck the kids into bed alone. The novelty of the Dog House didn't last long.

Things changed on the home front too. I embarked on a new venture. I opened the Dover Brick House, a music club in downtown Dover, New Hampshire. This put a major strain on my family, financially and emotionally. Taking a page from Jim's book, I did it without consultation of my wife or kids.

My business partner, a friend of mine, and I acquired a building to rent. The layout of the building and location were perfect. The fact that the homeless and pigeons had been the only occupants for the last thirty-two years wasn't. Looking up from the basement, two levels above, you could see the sky. It was my job to build the place and my partner's job to run it. The next five months I rarely saw my family. I was the only carpenter among all the people that came out to help. We had to build it all: bathrooms, bars, the stage, kitchen, everything. I orchestrated the electricians, plumbers, flooring installers, roofers and other subcontractors to get the building built and all with next to no immediate financial compensation.

In the final months the time I spent with my family was while we worked at the Brick House. Kelly and I would spend long hours into the night putting our artistic abilities to the test to make the place come alive. While we worked side by side our children slept on the stage that was to be the heart of the entire project. I began without the consent of Kelly, but in the end, she was not only on board but helped sail the ship into port, dock the damn thing and tie it to the moorings.

We had our Grand Opening in September of 2004, only five months after the start of the project. The place was a hit.

Kelly, the kids and I moved to Dover, the town Kelly grew up in. We found a modest Victorian house to rent with more room than we could use. It was close to the bar and right on the main artery into town. Susan and Jim now lived only a stone's throw from us, less than a quarter of a mile away.

Within days of moving in, Kelly got hit with a surprise visit.

Uninvited Visitor

(Kelly)

It was late afternoon and Jeff was working at the Brick House. I heard the doorbell. The kids yelled up to me that someone was at the door. I was upstairs unpacking and hadn't a clue who it could be. We had only been in the house a short time and hadn't yet had any friends over. I ran downstairs and got a glimpse of the tall grinning man through the front door window.

Go upstairs.

Why? Who is it?!

Please, just go upstairs guys, PLEASE.

I could see his eyes on the kids through window.

As I approached, his smile grew. My hand shook as I unlocked the dead bolt and opened the door. I left the chain latched so the door only opened a few inches. He stood with the storm door open ready to hop in.

Hi Kelly! His tone was genuine delight and excitement. *I – I just wanted to stop by and see if you needed any help. I could move some boxes for you. Is there anything I can do?*

Ah, no Jim. I'm all set. My voice quivered.

Are you sure? I thought I could help you move or unpack - whatever. You know seeing as we are neighbors now.

I hadn't spoken to Jim since his visit to the hospital for Zoe's birth. My heart was racing. I thought, what the hell is he doing here?

No, I'm quite sure. I'm all set.

In the years past I had grown more confident in my resolve to have nothing to do with this man. I wasn't the confused young woman I had once been. I was a mother first and I wasn't going to allow any sicko to ogle my children.

You can leave now.

Oh, I'm sorry. I – I just wanted to - to - see if I could help.

I don't need your help, please leave.

I closed the door, locked it and picked up the phone to call Jeff.

By: Jeff & Kelly Halldorson

Talk with Sam

(Jeff)

He what? You're fucking kidding me! Don't worry, I'll take care of it.

But...

I said, I'll take care of it. I love you, bye.

Okay, I love you too.

Click.

Jim knew he wasn't allowed anywhere near my family. Livid doesn't even begin to describe how I felt. I called Susan.

Hi Jeffrey.

Where's Jim?

I don't know.

I have to talk to him. What's his cell number?

Why?

Just give it to me.

I didn't leave her any time to speak. She gave me the number and I called him, still enraged.

Hello?

Jim, you went by my house!

I was jus -

Shut the fuck up, don't ever go by my house again.

Click.

Within fifteen minutes Jim, clearly high on something, showed up at the Brick House raging about how angry I was on the phone. He claimed to only be trying to reach out and be friendly. He said he was my father and had every right to stop by my house unexpected as a well wisher. I had him thrown out by the bouncer. We were no longer on speaking terms.

I expressed my anger to Susan yet. She explained there was little she could do about him. His behavior was grossly unpredictable. I didn't blame her for the incident and we continued on with our relationship as though nothing had happened. I employed Will at the bar as a dishwasher and we all spoke often.

I didn't remain in the restaurant business long.

The plan for the Brick House had been for me to do the building and my partner Chris was to do the managing of it. I did not like the way he ran it. I ended up spending a good chunk of my time there and away from my family. At first I enjoyed it. There was a novelty to it. I was in charge and I didn't have to swing a hammer. Everyone wanted to be my friend and I got plenty of attention from men and women alike. It was a nice escape from the pressures of a domestic life.

Problems arose when the bar didn't bring in anything to speak of financially, certainly not enough to support my family. Kelly could only work so much to supplement while still caring for the kids. I was forced to continue working as a full-time contractor during the day while working nights at the bar. Needless to say working in a bar was not conducive to a family lifestyle.

In December of 2004 I left the Brick House, giving up my interest in the business, and returned to work full-time in the construction field.

Jim continued in a downward spiral. Over fear of losing his job in Dover, he quit and took a position an hour away in Portland, Maine working for Mercy Hospital. His drug use continued. Although he was able to carry on functioning, as an alcoholic, for many years he wasn't able to maintain that same control while on the prescription drugs. He crashed the Isuzu, forcing him to use a rental while it was repaired. On the way to return the rental car, he crashed it into a guardrail, totaling the vehicle. Behind him was a State Trooper. This particular Trooper was in charge of assessing what drugs DUI drivers were on. It was determined Jim was under the influence, and illegally prescribed drugs were found in the rental car. Jim lost his driver's license.

With Jim no longer able to make the drive to work he decided to get an apartment in Portland. He spent weeknights in Maine and returned home, courtesy of a ride from Susan, on the weekends.

Susan wanted a divorce. She told Kelly and me one day while visiting, that she had consulted with her lawyer. He told her it was not in her best interest financially. She had decided not to pursue it and instead asked him to simply remain in his apartment in Portland from then on. Their relationship in shambles, it became clear, at least to us, that the less money Jim brought in and the more money he cost the family the less Susan wanted him around. She just wanted him to go away and even said to Kelly and I that it would be nice if he would just *disappear* or better yet *die*.

As a result of my work on the Brick House, I garnered some attention for my talents as a contractor. Work was steady and in the summer of 2005. Sam joined on as a laborer. He wanted to save money for school. He would start his first year of college that fall. I was thrilled to have him around. I was proud to see the good, strong man he was becoming. It truly was a win/win for both of us. He was able to make money and have time off when he wanted, and I got to spend time and connect with him.

Even though things were good at home, for the most part, I convinced myself that I was in a rut. Go to work, pay bills, go to work, go to sleep, pay bills and so on. I didn't handle the lifestyle like I thought I would. I told myself that was all I wanted, but when I came down to it I didn't handle the structure of it well. It would be my family that I would start lying to in order to cover my own destructive actions. I was slipping further from reality. I wanted to be free, but free from what?

On one long term jobsite I became acquainted with a young woman, Julia. She was a tenant at one of the apartments I was doing a condo conversion on. She was friendly and started hanging around the jobsite and talked with us while we were working. She had a sad story. She said she needed work but struggled because of medical problems including some debilitating kind of arthritis. I took a liking to her and hired her to clean the units when I was done with the conversions. I didn't find her at all attractive. She was heavy and awkward so I thought nothing of spending time with her in a work capacity. I kind of started to look at her as *one of the guys.* I even talked with Kelly about trying to help her out. She met Kelly and the kids a number of times when they would stop by for lunch to see me.

Then one night at another jobsite everyone else had left except Julia and me. I was finishing up some trim on a closet and she was cleaning the unit. Out of the blue she walked up to me, cornering me in a closet and started to try and kiss me and grabbed me inappropriately. I pushed her away and told her I didn't want anything of the kind. Shaken, I went on with my work and she left me alone for a bit. I should have walked right out or told her to get the fuck out. I didn't. Instead I went on working she must have taken that as a sign I was interested because she came on to me again pulling me into a bedroom of the unit. The second time I didn't protest.

Like my father before me, I lived two lives: one that was a husband and a family man, the other a free running delinquent with no responsibilities, taking breaks from my workday schedule for rendezvous. My sexual relationship with Julia ate away at me. The guilt was overwhelming and I would go home lash out at Kelly and the kids, as though somehow it was their fault. Yet throughout it all I was compelled to continue with the recklessness and destruction. It wasn't even an attraction for Julia. I reveled in the wretchedness of it all. I even thought, if she says anything to anyone I can just say, *are you kidding? Look at her?* When she wasn't around on jobsites I often joked about how unattractive I found her with the other men I worked with. And while with her, I complained about my wife and my mundane life.

One afternoon on the jobsite, Sam and I sat in my van; it must have been during lunch or coming back from picking up materials. The conversation between Sam and I drifted onto the topic of Jim, something we normally avoided. We spoke about the past and who Jim was as a father in general.

Mom and Dad are not talking and it sucks to be around him. I think they are headed for divorce. I'm glad I'm leaving soon. I don't want to come back. Period.

I don't think that she'll ever leave him.

She's not happy.

If she hasn't left him by now, do you really think she's going to? The man sat there and told his wife that he sexually molested his two children and she let him spend every night in the house after.

But they told us that wasn't true. That you guys had made it up.

What?!

Mom and Dad came to us and told us after you left that night...that you and Erik were crazy and were jealous because we were their biological children. You guys were on drugs and were going to beat him up if he didn't tell her that. Mom said it happened before you were adopted and you were confused because they were both named Jim. (My biological father's name is also Jim.) She said you lived in a house full of gay guys.

Fucking bitch! This happened that night? She is such a liar. This happened that night?!

Yeah and she told me that one other time when I was older too. So, we always just believed it didn't happen.

Mom really told you this?

Yeah.

*Did **she** tell you? Or did **he**?*

She did. He was never really a talker, you know.

I can't believe she said that. We sat there and Jim told her everything. He admitted to everything. She was right there. She heard it all. She cried. We even talked about it afterwards with Kelly. Just so you know it's all true. We were afraid it was happening to you. We didn't lie about anything.

It never happened to me.

What did Jim say? He must have said something.

He did say you were going to beat him up. That he had to say it. He was afraid. He said he would never do anything like that to any child.

He said that? That night?

Yeah.

Fuck! Those fucking liars - we didn't lie, Sam! Just so you know...we didn't.

The rest of the day we didn't talk much. I called Kelly and Sam left work early. I told Kelly everything Sam had said. That Jim told all of them he lied about molesting us that day on the farmer's porch all those years ago and he had only admitted to touching us because we said we would beat him if he didn't. And he did so with Susan by his side...not only corroborating his every word but even taking the lead. Sam and Will really had no choice but to believe their parents.

Kelly helped bring me back down to earth enough to finish the day at work. Little did I know, after hanging up the phone, she would do a bit of truth seeking of her own.

My life past and present was constantly surrounding me. I had to shut the lies of my affair out so that I could continue to use Kelly as my support. Julia and I had a meaningless affair, meaningless to Julia and I but in the end devastating to my wife and children. I risked my family for nothing, yet at the very same time continued to emotionally drain Kelly, the person who was holding it all together.

Even knowing right from wrong I was compelled to throw myself down a path of destruction. There wasn't a strong need sexually or even emotionally for Julia. I just didn't seem comfortable or even able to maintain a normal life. I needed some sort of chaos, even if I had to create it.

Statute of Limitations

(Kelly)

Hello, Durham Police Department

Hello, yes, I...I am calling for...well...I am curious about the Statute of Limitations on child sexual abuse.

Okay. Are you the victim?

No...no...it wasn't me....no...um...

Some part of me started to panic. I was opening a huge can of worms. I hadn't anticipated them wanting any information from me. I naively thought they would just answer my questions.

...it...it was my husband.

I thought oh my God! Did I just say that? They know where I'm calling from. They'll know who he is. Could they call back to try and reach Jeff? All of these seemingly absurd thoughts began to run through my mind. I felt like I had betrayed Jeff.

When did the abuse occur?

It was when he was young. It was...ongoing...a number of years. He is now 31.

Overwhelmed, I couldn't even manage the simple math in my head.

So, I guess it was in the ... 80's? It wasn't me. It's hard. I don't...

It's okay. Really, it's okay.

She spoke calmly and I began to regain my composure and felt a certain degree of relief. Maybe I had done the right thing.

Yes, so I'm calling because I wanted to know what the Statute was and whether he could do anything about it.

Well, the Statute itself is complicated ... it -

Yeah, I know. I looked it up online a few years ago and it didn't seem entirely clear to me.

Yes, well, the Statute is complicated as I've said but basically your husband has until he is 40 years old to come to us.

I knew it! I just ...

I'm sorry?

I knew ... it's just we were told something different.

By us here?

No, it's a long story. So...what is the next step? Does he talk to you? Does he go to the DA? If I tell him and he wants to do something...what should he do next?

You can tell your husband that he should, he can come right down here to the Durham Police Department and we can start from there.

So, that's it.

Yes, it's that simple. Tell him it is okay, he's not the only one. We've handled cases like this before.

Thank-you. Thank-you.

Did I answer your questions?

Yes, yes you did. Thank-you so much. I ... I guess that's it. Hopefully you'll be hearing from him soon.

I hung up the phone and walked upstairs. The kids were playing with Legos in Griffin's room. I just stood in the doorway and watched. How did we get here? Where might this lead? What will it mean? To Jeff? To Erik? To our family life?

When Jeff came home after work I wasted no time telling him what I had found out. I wanted him to know she had lied. I wanted him to know he could do something if he wanted to.

They said all you have to do is go down to the station and they would go from there. They said you still have time. You don't have to do this right away. You have until you're 40. There is still time.

I don't know. I don't know what to do. What about Sam and Will? Think what it would do to them? How it would affect their lives. I don't know if I can do that.

I know. I understand. I just wanted you to know, that it is up to you. There is a lot to consider but it's your call. It's your life too. I love you.

We didn't speak again about my conversation with the Durham PD for a while. I had told him. I didn't need to belabor it. He had enough to think about. Our discussions focused mainly around his frustration with the entire situation. How Jim and Sue had lied to the younger boys and how much it hurt and angered him. I just listened. It was out of my hands now even if I had gone to the police myself about it. An investigation would go nowhere without Jeff and Erik supporting it.

Jeff was once again left to carry the burden and all I could do was be there to talk him through it.

Jim's Driveway

(Jeff)

Kelly told me about the Statute and her conversation with the Durham Police Department but I wasn't ready to take that kind of action. An action that might result in such a permanent consequence and would have such a serious effect upon so many lives; not just Jim and Susan but Kelly, Sam, Will, Erik and my children. Nonetheless I was infuriated. My vindication was a fallacy. Susan and Jim just faked their way through it, laughing behind my back. I wanted to do something. I needed to do something. I just didn't know what that something was yet.

I had a short conversation with Susan about it. I wasn't forthcoming about my conversation with Sam. I found it hard to sit in the same room as her.

I am tired of the past following me around. I know that you and Jim are walking on rough ground.

Well things aren't easy that is for sure.

Did you know that I can press charges on him until I am 40?

No, I thought that the statutes of limitations were up.

Nope. I have to be honest I have given it some thought.

Well, Jeffrey if you do decide to go ahead and press charges please let me know before you do so that I may get my finances in order.

I had to check myself. Did she just say what I think she said? Get her finances in order.

I called Erik. I told him I was thinking about pressing charges against Jim. I explained to him that if I did his name would come up. I asked him if he would be able to handle going through something like that. Erik told me he was behind me 100% with whatever I decided to do. He did like the idea of Jim being held accountable but he also said he wasn't strong enough to do it himself. He would, however, do anything I needed to help. That was a relief but I still had the boys, Kelly, and my kids to consider. Not to mention my affair with Julia.

The next weekend I found myself in the driveway of Susan and Jim's house, standing toe to toe with Jim. I wasn't going to go easy on him. I wasn't a timid little boy in the dark. It was Man to Man this time. I was older now, stronger; we looked each other in the eye. I was now the bigger, meaner, hate-filled man that the man before me had created. This was the day the victim didn't sulk into some shadow of fear.

Can we please go in the house?

No. I'm not going to be here long. I've got to tell you, Jim, you pulled a good one. Here I am thinking all this time you and Sue really wanted to change your tune, but no.

The words were passing through gritted teeth of anger. I knew he could see the loathing written on my face and portrayed in every movement of my body.

Jeffrey - Jeffrey!? What do you mean?

Jim you fuckin' wormed your way out of that whole business with what you did to Erik and I didn't you? You and Susan told the boys that what you did never happened. You fucking piece of shit. You made me out to be a liar again! I didn't lie! You asshole - I didn't lie!

Jeffrey – please -

I don't care about you or her any more. I'm not going through life as a liar. You did this; this is your fault. I had better find out that you cleaned this mess up. I want them to know everything, all of it. Every last fucking detail or I will, so help me God. Do you want those kids to hear it from me? I won't be nice about it, not this time. This is it Jim. I don't want any of that "I did what Suzie said I did." shit. I want you to go in there and tell them you raped us with your mouth over and over again, that you killed the innocence in two little boys. You know what? You had better fucking do it. And you know what else? It's not too late for me to go to the police and I have every fucking right to.

I did not let him respond I turned and walked away.

Jeffrey - Jeffrey please!

I kept walking without turning back. I hate that name Jeffrey. They were the only ones that called me that. I was Jeff and Jeff didn't want to hear anything that son of a bitch had to say. I was done. I was going to take back my life one piece at a time, one piece from him, and one piece from her, and so on. Until I was as whole as I could get. It was either that or I was going to destroy myself and everything around me, everything I loved. As it was I knew that I was never going to be whole. I was never going to be solid. I was going to have to try to get as close to that as I could.

Let him stand there with his guilt and fear. I didn't care. He knew I meant every word of it and that what I had to say was final. He knew it was time to tell the boys the truth. That was a piece I was taking back.

Why was I doing this? What did I want? Why now?

Because skeletons don't sleep, they sit in the closet and rot. The stench can't be ignored. I wanted to forget about it but every time I tried to close the door on my past those boney fingers would wrap themselves around my leg and pull me back until I was forced to face him. It was time to give the fucker a proper burial. I just didn't know how yet.

The horrible thing about it was, I was piling my own skeletons in a completely different closet. I was stealing a page from my father's book. I was a cheat and a liar. I was part of what I hated so much about my parents.

Just like their secrets, my secrets were only temporary.

By: Jeff & Kelly Halldorson

Jeff's Breakdown

(Kelly)

It was mid-September in 2005. Jeff and I really needed a break. He seemed preoccupied. I assumed it was the stress of the situation with his father and mother. I had no clue he was seeing another woman. He had made his share of mistakes in our marriage but infidelity was one thing I truly believed was not in his character despite his actions before we were married. In hindsight this may have been naive. But when we married, I chose to trust him again because I believed, at the time, it was the only way to have a successful marriage, to trust the other person implicitly.

In addition I had met Julia. She had met my children. I had the feeling she was interested in him but I have a tendency to give people the benefit of the doubt. Generally, I think better of people. I was nothing but kind to her yet she purposefully and willfully pursued my husband.

That is not something that reconciles itself well with my value system or any part of my being. She gave no thought to the lives she would be affecting, most significantly, my three children.

As far as the situation with his parents, Jeff didn't seem sure what the right thing to do was. I was still reeling from discovering some indication of Sue lying about the Statute. I had grown tired of living somebody else's lie. Sue and Jim and their failures to their son had had a rippling effect upon the life of our family. The pain, the lies and the suffering carried right on through the generations to our own children. It may not have manifested itself in the same manner but it was and continues to be there at times.

Gary Hoey, a rock guitarist, was playing at the Brick House with his band. Jeff and I decided it might be just what we needed, a night out together without any family pressures. I made childcare arrangements and Jeff called his former business partner Chris to be sure we could get into the show. The plan was to put all the stress that had been going on with Jim, Sue and the boys aside, relax and enjoy each other's company.

I put on my Saturday night best, complete with short skirt and tall black boots. Jeff cleaned up nicely too. When my aunt Linda arrived to take care of the kids we said our goodnights, informed Linda of our itinerary and walked into town. We lived only two blocks from the Brick House and it was a beautiful New England fall evening, the perfect night for a walk.

We arrived at the Brick House well before the show started and Chris made sure we were treated like rock stars. I introduced myself to Gary Hoey, he complemented me on my boots. I had a photograph I had taken of him at a show years ago that I asked him to sign. I spent a good twenty minutes talking to him about life, family and New Hampshire.

Jeff wasn't content standing in one place. While I talked with Gary, he made the rounds. Chris introduced him to some new faces and he said his hellos to the old ones, sharing a toast with every one of them along the way. By the time I caught up with Jeff he was already on his second or third beer. Jeff is no big drinker and it didn't take much to put him under.

It was no big deal, I told myself. Jeff deserved some time out, he worked so hard. It had been a rough few years. We ran into a friend of ours, Steve, who had worked with us on the Brick House project. We shared a table with him. We talked with him about girlfriends, life, and his job – all the everyday chit chat. Jeff once again got restless. He got up and went off to find Chris while I stayed at the table with Steve.

About the third song into Gary Hoey's set, Jeff returned completely lit. He was taking full advantage of the bar and its limitless offering thanks to a little help from Chris. I was caught off guard by Jeff's level of intoxication. I had expected a fun night out with my adult 31 year old husband. Instead I felt like my seventeen year old boyfriend, who was captain of the football team, had just ditched me to hang out with his teammates and the cheerleaders.

Are you okay?

Ah - yeah - everything is great. I'm just having a little fun. Chris showed me the new Jaeger cooler - I'm - just great...

Do you want to go home?

Oh - no -why would I want that? No, I'm having a great time. Aren't you?

Yes, I'm fine...

What was I supposed to say really with Steve, my company for the night, sitting right there.

... But I'd like to see a little more of you.

We have all night. I'm just talking to a few people.

Okay, just please slow down a little.

With that he happily staggered off to meet back up with Chris and his other friends of the moment.

Our night out had turned into my night of babysitting a drunk. More than an hour passed without so much as a hello from Jeff. I was beginning to feel sorry for poor Steve stuck talking to me. I excused myself from the table to go look around for Jeff. No luck. So I went back and sat down at the table. Another twenty minutes or so passed and Chris came by the table.

Hey - Kelly - I - um - You have to get him out of here.

What? Where is he? Why?

I'm sorry - If it were anyone else - I - I would have had him thrown out an hour ago.

Seriously? Where is he?

He's up by the front of the stage.

Okay. I'm sorry. I'll get him out of here. I'm so sorry. I had no idea.

I nodded goodbye to Steve, grabbed my jacket and headed over to the front of the crowd. I found Jeff straddling a piece of the band's sound equipment on the edge of the stage. I walked over patted him on the back. He turned and looked up at me a little taken aback...almost as though he didn't expect to see me. I kissed him on the cheek.

Oh, Hey - What's up?

Hun, I think it's time to go.

What? Why? Aren't you having a good time?

No, I'm fine. It's okay we just - we really have to leave.

Then why do we have to go? I'm having a good time.

Jeff, Chris asked me to come and get you. He said we needed to leave.

What the fuck? Why? Where the fuck is he? I built this fucking place! I can stay here. What the fu...

Jeff it's no big deal. Really come on. We have to go. I'm tired of being here anyway and you promised me a little nookie tonight. Remember? You're not going to let me down now are you?

Alright...let's go.

He stood up almost knocking me over in the process. He turned toward the band, stumbling, waved and shouted....

IT WAS NICE TO MEET YOU! You liked my WIFE's BOOTS right!?

Fortunately, I think the music was too loud for Gary or his bandmates to hear but he probably got the gist of the situation. He nodded and smiled a goodbye as we left.

I managed to maneuver Jeff down the stairs and out of the building. The cool night air had no effect on Jeff's level of sobriety and two blocks never seemed so far. In fact the more we walked the more difficult it proved to be.

I labored to keep him standing and moving. He leaned on my small frame with what felt like his entire body weight. I have no idea how we made it even ten feet. I wasn't drunk but I only weighed around 105 pounds at the time. I had two, maybe three drinks and hadn't eaten dinner so the alcohol certainly had some effect upon me. Jeff was heavy and I was exhausted.

To top it all off Jeff started to babble incoherently and kept stopping to sit, once attempting to do so in the middle of a crosswalk. His speech was slurred and was making no sense.

Jeff what is going on? Are you going be okay? How much did you drink?

I was at a loss. He got louder and louder.

I – bad - it's so bad - WHY?

What are you talking about?

Suddenly, he started crying. No, not crying, sobbing.

I have to – sssttop – I – I -think I'm...

What? What do you mean? Can you hold on? We are just around the corner from the house. Seriously, JEFF - we aren't far, see? Look between those trees...

I pointed just across over the tops of the trees if you looked closely you could see a tiny corner of the house.

See? We aren't far if you just hang on.

I didn't think I had any chance of making it home if we stopped to sit down anywhere. We had been together for twelve years and I had only seen him get sick from drinking once. I'd seen him drunk but never anything near what I witnessed that night.

No, no. The demons...the demons...

What?!

With that I realized exactly how serious of a situation this was. There was a church a few feet ahead of us with a little stone bench in front of it. I figured if we could just make it there. I could sit him down and figure things out. He made it to the church alright but collapsed on top of the drying flower beds. I was so thankful he landed on something soft.

He sobbed and wailed. *It's so bad. The demons they keep haunting me. Why?! Why?! I'm sorry. It's bad. I'm such a bad man. I hate them. I really hate them. The demons - WHY? The nightmares! I'm no good. Why are you here? Why are you with me?*

He started retching. I rubbed his back and did my best to try and bring him back down to reality.

Jeff, I love you. You are not a bad man. It's okay. I love you. I LOVE you. Breathe...we'll be home soon.

The wailing and sobbing continued. He lay on the ground, half-heartedly propped up on his arms, like an infant in the beginning stages of crawling. I sat next to him and took off my boots. When he stopped vomiting I was able to coax him up to a sitting position. He leaned his head on my shoulder and cried.

I'm no good for you. They were right. I was never any good.

I love you. I love you. It's okay.

No. You shouldn't. They didn't love me either. The demons...the demons...

He was getting louder again.

Jeff, let's try and get home. Okay?

He replied something inaudible.

Jeff, come on. Let's go. Get up, honey. Let's get you home to our nice warm bed.

No. I'm going to stay here. You don't want me. Nobody wants me.

He's in my dreams. The demon....

The irony of Jeff wailing about demons and vomiting in the flowerbeds on the front lawn of a church was not lost on me. I started to get a clearer picture of what was happening, or so I thought.

What demons Jeff? Can I help you get rid of the demons? What demons?

All of them. Him. James. He raped us. Why? I was just a little boy. A little boy.

I'm sorry. I'm so sorry. I love you. Let's get home.

He stood up.

And she let him. She didn't love us. They picked us.

He staggered in the direction of our house and I did my best to keep his steps straight. Walking barefoot, I held my boots in one arm while using my other to steady his steps.

His sobbing and wailing softened to sniffling and whimpering.

We walked into the house. I turned to Linda who was reading on the couch. All the kids were tucked in asleep upstairs.

Sorry, he's just really drunk and upset. It's okay. Just let me get him upstairs and I'll be right back down.

I walked him upstairs and left him sitting up on our bed and went back down to talk to Linda.

He's just - he's really not doing well. There is a lot going on with his family and work. He's tired...I'm sorry. Thank-you so much for coming over to...

There was a crash upstairs.

You okay Jeff? I hollered up. I heard a groan in reply.

Do you want me to stay?

No, thank you for watching the kids - I - I love you. I'll call you tomorrow.

Linda saw herself out and I ran upstairs to find Jeff crawling toward the bathroom presumably to continue what he had started back on the front lawn of the church.

I helped him over to the tub. I figured it was much better than him hanging over the toilet and probably a lot safer too. I was starting to get very concerned about him possibly having alcohol poisoning. I regretted telling Linda to go ahead and go home.

Having thrown up everything in his stomach, the dry heaves began. With the dry heaves I saw the return of the wails and pleading.

Why? He loved us. He must have loved us? She lied. She told Sam - she told him that we lied. Do you fucking believe that? He thinks I'm a liar. She was supposed to love me!

It was all I could take. I snapped. What I had envisioned as a fun and romantic evening had turned into nothing even close to that. I cried.

Jeff, I love you. I'm here. I'll be here. I'm so sorry she did that to you. I know you're not a liar. The boys will see that too.

She...she...made that up about the Statute...

I know, I know. I'm sorry.

I don't deserve you. Kelly, I don't. I'm no good. They were right. I'm no good. Why? Why are you here?

It was heartbreaking for me to see Jeff in this condition. I felt guilty. I should have stopped him from drinking so much. I should have spent more time trying to engage him at the Brick House. I should have done *something* different. I so wanted to help. I think I was searching for something to blame, besides myself. I didn't have to look far to find it. The next words out of Jeff's mouth were an inspiration to me.

We were kids – Kelly, we were kids?! She's a fucking bitch - she...

You're right Jeff. I'm sorry. She did hurt you. You didn't deserve any of it. You were just a child.

It was just after midnight but I decided that I had something to say to Sue. I had watched and bit my tongue long enough. Witnessing Jeff break into pieces on the floor of our bathroom was the final straw.

I grabbed the phone and dialed Sue.

Hello?

I didn't waste any time.

Do you know where your son is?! Do you know what he is doing right now? My voice was shaking. *He's drunk and he's crying, sobbing on our bathroom floor.*

Silence on the other end.

Do you know why he's crying?

I was too fueled by my frustration, sadness and anger to see how ridiculous I was being. Of course she had no idea why I was calling her in the middle of the night.

You ruined him - both of you - you broke him.

What are you talking about, Kelly? We took them in. We accepted you as family...we...

I'm talking about Jim molesting Erik and Jeff. You are married to a fucking pedophile.

I unleashed on her. In the twelve years I'd known her I never swore in her presence, much less at her. I said everything I'd been thinking for years and I was not nice about it.

I have sat back and watched you protect that man for years, for years you have chosen him over those boys. You promised them that things were going to change, you promised him. You lied and said they couldn't go to the police because the Statute had expired. I knew you were lying about that. I just knew it. So, you know what I did? I called the police department. They <u>can</u> go to the police and after this I think Jeff will. And that *help* you provided us with after Jim told you about the molestation - when we thought Sam and Will were in danger -that was just your way of appeasing them wasn't it? Money to keep quiet...

Wait just a minute, that wasn't hush money! We knew you needed it – we – we - just wanted to help – we...

Oh sure - and you were helping by telling Jeff the Statute had expired?

That is what I was told by my lawyer. It's not my fault if I was given information that was wrong.

That's right! You called your lawyer. You found out for sure your husband molested children and you went to find out if he could get arrested! Who does that? Your husband admits to...

Wait just a minute, he didn't admit anything.

What the fuck?! Are you serious?

No, Jim didn't say anything about molesting Jeffrey or anyone else.

You brought me over to your house to discuss it...remember you wanted **to put my mind at ease**. *You...*

He didn't admit to anything. Jeffrey and Erik came to the house and threatened...

It was a waste of time. She wasn't going to hear anything I had to say. She was in panic mode and I really shouldn't have been surprised because I had put her there. I told her we knew the Statute hadn't expired; I told her I thought she tried to hush Jeff and Erik with money.

She had plenty of reason to be nervous. But I know if I continued on with the conversation she was going to have more ammunition to use against me. I had seen that she had no qualms about lying and twisting things to suit her own best interest. What would stop her from doing that against me, again?

I'm done. I interrupted then hung up the phone, still out of sorts from my expectation of a relaxing adult night out. Jeff had been so distant and withdrawn that all I wanted was to spend some good time with him, happy. Jeff was haunted by more than demons of his past. I only saw Jeff a victim. No matter what had happened between us I really didn't ever see him as the bad guy, always the tortured hero. I had no idea how far he had fallen and how deceitful he had become. I always trusted his fidelity, naively.

I checked on the kids. They were all still sound asleep. I was exhausted. There was no way I was going to move Jeff onto our bed. I conceded defeat to whatever force of nature was doing its damndest to destroy *my* night out, put a pillow under Jeff's head, grabbed a blanket and curled up next to him on the floor in the doorway of the bathroom.

Running my hands through his hair I talked to, him in his sleep.

I love you Jeff. You are worthy. They were cruel. I am so sorry you've had all this pain. You ARE loved. Don't lose sight of that. You can do something about all of this. It is within your power.

By: Jeff & Kelly Halldorson

Detective Tarrants

(Jeff)

The seat was hard and the room was warmer than it should have been for the time of year. I waited anxiously for the officer to join me. I felt the perspiration rolling down my rib cage inside my shirt and became self conscious of both my appearance and odor. Did I stink? Would I look like a bum in my work clothes?

On October 3, 2005 I sat in the Durham Police station waiting. The lady at the front desk was kind and ushered me into a room after I explained that I was there to press charges on my father. She didn't ask for any details. I just had to sit in that hot room on a hard chair. I looked around. It wasn't the police station that I had frequented in my youth; it was new and had a sterile feeling. Covering the walls were pictures of things that meant nothing to the average Joe. Yet if they hadn't been there I would be staring at the blank off-white walls.

I sat at the table in the room and waited. I had an ass-quivering feeling. Kind of like being at a job interview that I knew I was under-qualified for. I had no idea what was going to come through the door and anticipation was a killer. The sweat continued to roll, cold and unpleasant. I wanted to sniff my arm pits but figured if I did it would be the precise moment the officer would walk in.

I was having a hard time staying in my rock of a chair. This was not any place I wanted to be. It was, however, the place I needed to be. I had made the decision to stop pussy-footing around the shit that was my past. I would no longer be victim to it.

I knew if anything like what I'd experienced happened to any one of my children there would be hell to pay. I would rip the life from any person who hurt my children. I would not stand for that kind of pain being brought down on someone I loved. But I had. I had never stood up for my brother. He had been hurt too. Wasn't it fair to bring the full force of the law down on the man that hurt my brother in the prime of his innocence? Why wouldn't I stand up for him, much less myself?

It was always easier to dismiss the actions against me and deal with life as it came. Not anymore. I wasn't willing to be a victim; I wasn't willing to let Jim walk free while my brother and I remained trapped in a cage of his actions. I wanted out of the shadow he cast. I wanted Erik free and vindicated, allowed to live life without having to see that filth walking freely down the street, suffering no real consequence for the evil he perpetrated and the he pain he left in his wake. As Judge Shaheen said to me the day my childhood ended, *There comes a time when enough is enough. This is that time.* Kelly had given me information to make it happen.

The door opened. To my relief in walked a man in street clothes, not cop paraphernalia. There was no gun and fifty pound arsenal strapped to his hips or bright shining badge pinned to his chest. Nor did he appear a stuffed suit with a clipboard.

Detective Tarrants stood about my height maybe a little shorter, dressed in clothes that distinguished him as a member of the police force but from a distance didn't scream COP. He was clean cut to army specs, with short brown hair and stocky build for his job. But the way he carried himself didn't ooze of arrogance or authority. He did have the clipboard though.

He politely introduced himself and sat in the other hard chair, corner to me at the table. He seemed comfortable in the position he was in. I am sure this wasn't the first time he took down a statement from an adult his own age. Regardless of what I was going to tell him he was prepared to do his job.

What can I help you with today?

I sat there wondering what it really was he could do for me.

Well, I have some questions and I don't really know where I am going with all of this.

Well, that is easy - we can start with the questions. There is no harm in that is there?

My main question - I think - I am pretty clear on but I wanted to be sure. What is the statute of limitations are on sex offenses, specifically child sexual molestation?

The laws on that changed in the early '80s. If the offense happened after that, the victim can bring forth charges up until their fortieth birthday. They are a little more specific but that's it in a nutshell.

He was soft spoken and appeared to be listening. He looked at me when he spoke and didn't pay any mind to his clipboard. He was listening to me, focused on what was happening at the table.

Oh, well I don't know what to do.

If you want to tell me what happened off the record, to start, we can go with that for now. Know that I will recommend to you that if it's as bad as I think it might be that I am going to recommend that you proceed with charges.

Well, in the late '70s to the late '80s my brother and I were molested by our adoptive father.

Was it here in Durham?

Here and in New Jersey.

Well it ultimately is your decision whether or not to press charges. In a late disclosure, as yours would be considered, it really comes down to if it can be proven or not. It can be hard and in order to get a conviction it has to be a rock solid case. What about your brother will he come in?

He said he would.

Then it is up to you as to the next step we take. Do you want to put this to paper?

To paper, that is what would come next if I so chose to do that. Here was a man I did not know and had never seen before willing to listen to me, not run off and forget about it in a week. He was going to hand write whatever I told him and take it as fact for now. He was prepared to take my statement and then go off and try and prove it. Prove me right. Prove that I was not a liar or a junkie and all I had to do was say yes.

There was a long pause as I hesitated. I sat, in silence, like a deer in headlights. Then I said it. I committed myself and my family to seeking justice for crimes long since past. *Okay.* I told him.

With every scratch on his yellow legal pad my words became final. They might as well be etched in stone. There was no undoing them. I was there to do a job and that is the way that I approached it. This wasn't my childhood neighbors Grant or Suzie Armstrong I was talking to. This man wasn't going to forget about what I was telling him and I wouldn't be able to take it back!

The perspiration quickened as I went into details about my victimization. Detective Tarrants sat with me, interrupting my flow of words only when necessary for clarification. He never rushed me or looked at his watch. I had his complete attention. He listened; never doubting nor judging.

After I was finished recounting Jim's actions, Tarrants calmly explained the next step in the process.

Jeff, we are going to have to schedule a forensic interview at the Strafford County Attorney's office. There you will be interviewed and we will have to go from there. Is this something you are willing to do?

Yes.

We can go forth without it, but the interview will make our jobs a lot easier.

Yes, of course I will.

Do you think that Erik will be willing to come in and give a statement?

He said he would, and I think he will. I did tell him that I was planning on doing this. I'll let him know I came in today. The rest is up to him.

Durham Police Department

Incident Narrative Report

Accident/case Number D-2005-02173, Det. Gabe Tarrants

On 10/03/05, Jeff Halldorson came to the police station to report a series of sexual assaults perpetrated on him by his adopted father, James Earl Halldorson. Jeff told me he and his brother, Erik, had been adopted by James and Susan Halldorson when Jeff was 3 and Erik, was 4. He said that between the ages of 4 and 14, he was sexually molested by James. Jeff said he knew Erik was also molested during that time because they would talk to each other about it. He said he was trying to help Erik decide to come to report it as well. Jeff stated his father had admitted to the molestation several times to the rest of the family.

I explained the Strafford County Sexual Assault Protocol to Jeff, who agreed to participate in the forensic interview. The interview was set up with Carolann Jensen for 10/18/05, at 1330 hrs.

I walked out of the police department into the crisp autumn New England air. I felt the coolness drying the sweat from my shirt. There was no release, no weight lifted.

I put on a brave face though inside I was scared shitless. The date was set for my forensic interview, October 18, 2005. Two weeks. The first of a year-long series of waiting games had begun. I let Erik know I had pressed charges on our father for sexually molesting me as a child and advised him to do the same. He agreed to contact Detective Tarrants, but regardless, I was doing this. I was moving forward with the charges and hoped Erik would follow through I knew he needed this even more than I did.

Erik lived life on the fringe of battle every day. He wanted to fight but was reluctant to draw first blood. With my visit to the Durham Police Department he no longer needed worry about that. I desperately wanted to end it all, the years of lies, and was ready to make my last stand. If Erik needed to be spectator on the sideline of the battle it was fine with me. In the end the results would be the same. In the end there would be no question as to who the liars were and it would be a matter of public record.

My biggest fear was what the impact was going to be on my younger brothers. I knew that they could end up hating me for what I was doing and there was a good chance that they would be lost to me, forever. I love them dearly, but they as much as everyone else needed to be freed from the past our father had created.

Kelly put it to me this way... In the future they would be grown men with families of their own. Then, when they look upon their own children, they will know...it was the right thing to do. I could lose them for a time but the lesson they would learn would be the greatest gift I could ever give them. Hopefully then they would be able to forgive me.

I also had another fear. I was afraid someone would find out about my affair with Julia and try and use it to discredit me. Show the public that I was really a liar and a cheat. If that happened, I thought, the whole case could be lost and I would be embarrassed. I resolved to keep my secret and hope no one asked those kinds of questions. I started working toward ending it with Julia and asked her to continue to keep quiet about our relationship.

Carolann

(Jeff)

One o'clock on Tuesday, October 18, 2005 I pulled into the Strafford County Attorney's office parking lot. I had about twenty minutes to wait before meeting Detective Tarrants. He had called me the day prior to make sure that my feet hadn't gotten cold since we last spoke. I assured him I would be there and had no intention of backing out. Relieved at this, he expected me there at 1:20, ten minutes before the interview.

A new momentum began to creep its way through me. I knew I needed to see this through. It was time for justice.

Det. Tarrants met me at the front door and we entered together. He led me through the winding corridors and staircases to the room. He walked with a purpose, yet was incredibly polite. I have to give it to that man; he truly treated me on a professional and yet personal level. He was never once was condescending or patronizing. He looked me in the eyes when he spoke, a simple gesture which had a calming effect on me. It eased the stress of what I was going through.

We entered the office where the interview was to take place. It was there that I met Carolann Jensen. She was a pretty woman, somewhere in her thirties. She was small but her handshake demanded respect instantly. She was also cold. There was a defined line with Carolann that I had not encountered with Det. Tarrants. She was there to do a job and had no time for pleasantries.

The two of them walked me through the forensic interview setup. They led me through a tight corridor to a small room. The room was just big enough for a desk which had a video monitor and recording instruments.

This is where I will be during your interview, explained Det, Tarrants. *I will be handling all the recording, both video and audio. I will meet you after you and Carolann are done, okay?*

I nodded understanding and followed Carolann into the next room. It was set up much differently. I felt like I had walked into a waiting room of a pediatrics department. The walls were painted in flowery colors. It was surely designed to comfort a child. There were two chairs, side by side, in the center of the room.

Carolann confirmed the room was also used to interview small children. She pointed out the video camera and the microphone and started right into the interview.

For the record please state your name and address.

There was no emotion in her voice. She was cool and to the point. She looked me straight in the eye, as if staring me down. It was intimidating to have such a fragile looking woman putting the grips to a hardened man.

Please start from the beginning and tell me everything.

And so I did. She often cut me off only to quickly ask a question. We covered everything. There was nothing she didn't ask and there was nothing I didn't answer. I found myself once again recounting the story of my childhood nights this time to a video camera in a sterile room.

You will have to excuse me if I seem to be lacking in emotion. It has become a story that I have told so many times that that is just what it has become to me, a story. I have had to tell complete strangers, such as you, horrid details of what happened to me. I have detached myself from them in order to just get them out. I don't fear them because I know inside that none of this is my fault, but I still feel like I should be crying or something. I just don't because this has become a job to me.

That is fine you don't have to explain.

On went the questioning. It ran in circles, it was the same group of questions asked in many different ways. She talked me in, around and over. She worked me over as she worked her profession to a tee. I would tell the story as she wrote down notes and I was brought back to those stale conversations I had with the suits in therapy as a child.

In the midst of a completely different part of my tale she would ask me a question that seemingly had no bearing on what we were currently discussing. I knew what the game was but I had no intention of playing it. I let her lead the way. I only answered with truth to her questions. I knew she was digging for the truth and I had no problem helping her shovel it out.

For two hours that felt like eternity, I gave Carolann the answers she sought. It was hard, partially because she was a woman and I had to tell her intimate details about sexual encounters with the pig that was my father and partially because there was no emotion in her voice or actions. No empathy. She was like a machine, well-oiled and all business.

After every last gruesome detail, each and every nasty act I could remember was covered, the forensic interview concluded. I was exhausted, completely physically and emotionally taxed. With the end of the interview, Carolann's entire demeanor changed within the blink of an eye.

Thank god that's over I am sorry if I came off as a bitch but that's part of my job.

She laughed almost instantly, as if to ensure herself that she still could. Life that wasn't there before blossomed, as did her personality. I was floored. It had been an act she executed flawlessly.

We left the interrogation room and entered a room I had yet to see. On the wall was a mural of Harry Potter.

How fitting. I said.

Why?

I love Harry Potter. I think it's fitting that you have him here on the wall.

Why do you think that?

Well, you bring children in here to ask them questions about the life they live. Most of those lives have severe issues. I myself longed to be a Harry Potter, to have someone show up and tell me that I was more than just a boy living in my own cupboard under the stairs. I daydreamed of someone showing up to tell me that there was a major mistake and that my birth father was a major rock-star and he never wanted me to be taken away. I think it is just fitting.

I never thought of it that way. I guess it is.

Carolann and I met up with Det. Tarrants and we started the walk back to the main entrance. Carolann informed me of the role she would play in what was to come.

I am here to answer any questions you have. I will be going through the whole process with you and your family from beginning to end. If there is anything that you need you can call me any time. I will work with you and the prosecutor to make sure that your interests are protected and all of your needs are met.

With that we parted ways. True to her word, Carolann would be the greatest advocate that Kelly, Erik or I could possibly expect.

Durham Police Department

Incident Narrative Report

Accident/case Number D-2005-02173, Det. Gabe Tarrants

On 10/18/05, at 1320 hrs., I met Jeff at the Strafford County Attorney's Office for the Forensic Interview with Carolann Jensen. The interview began at 1330 hrs. Jeff began by saying that his father is a pedophile and assaulted he and his brother for 11 years. Jeff said he and his brother had separate rooms and the incidents always happened at night. It started when he was 4 years old in Wisconsin and continued when they moved to New Jersey and he had finished the second grade. Jeff said they then moved to Durham where he repeated second grade, making him about 7 years old.

He said the incidents would always involve his father performing oral sex on him, then sometimes he would rub his genitals on Jeff's body. Jeff said sometimes his father would have to change Jeff's position in bed, in order to perform the oral sex act. He said he would just keep still and silent, like he was asleep, until it was over and his father would leave the room. Jeff said there were never any words spoken during the incidents. He said he remember smelling the alcohol on his father's breath. Jeff also said the incidents would occur whether his mother was home or at work.

Jeff said he knew it was happening to his brother Erik as well. When they were younger, they never talked specifics about an incident but would simply ask each other, "Did it happen to you last night?"

And each would either answer yes or no. Jeff said he remembered the last time it happened was when he was 14 years old. His mother had sent him on a bus to Boston, MA., where he met his father after work and they attended a Red Sox baseball game against the Oakland A's. Jeff said they left in the seventh inning and went home. He remembered going to bed shortly after returning home and soon after that his father entered his room and performed oral sex on him. He remembered his father leaving the bedroom door open when he finished and left.

Jeff said he had told a neighbor friend, Grant Armstrong, what was happening. Grant told his mother Susan who confronted Jeff's mother. Jeff said he was then threatened by Erik to tell their mother he had lied about the molestation. According to Jeff, when he told his mother he had lied, she briefly cried then it was "business as usual for her" After this incident, Jeff said his father took him for a walk and apologized for what he had been doing to him. Jeff said the molestation never happened again after that.

Years later, Jeff and Erik were moved out of the house and their parents were raising two boys of their own, ▮▮▮▮▮▮▮ and ▮▮▮▮. Jeff said his mother told him that ▮▮▮ didn't like to sleep alone, so Jeff thought that his father might have been molesting him as well. He said he told Erik they had to confront their father and let their mother know what really happened. When they confronted their father, they asked him how he liked little boys and if he was doing the same thing to ▮▮▮▮▮▮ and ▮▮▮▮. Jeff said his father told them he would never do anything like that to his own kids, but did admit to them and his wife that he had molested Jeff and Erik and that everything Jeff had told her years ago was true. Jeff said his mother asked the father how she could trust him with ▮▮▮▮▮▮▮ and ▮▮▮▮. Jeff said he and his wife, Kelly, talked to his parents about a year ago where James again admitted to molesting Jeff and Erik in front of them.

The Wiretap

(Kelly)

After Jeff's forensic interview the state felt they had enough evidence to request a warrant for a wiretap.

Durham Police Department

Incident Narrative Report

Accident/case Number D-2005-02173

On 10/21/05, I received a One-Party Intercept authorization from Assistant Attorney General Karen Huntress. This allowed us to record a phone conversation that was going to take place between Jeff and his father on 10/24/05 at 0900 hrs. The time frame authorized was for 10/24/05, from 0700 hrs to 1900 hrs., and allowed us to place the call from Jeff's residence in Dover, NH and call James's office at Mercy Hospital in Portland, ME. Investigator Hart from the Strafford Country Attorney's Office was conducting the intercept.

The morning of the phone intercept Jeff asked that I be there so I made arrangements for my aunt to take the kids.

Detective Tarrants and Investigator Hart were personable, empathetic and professional. First Tarrants introduced himself to me and then introduced Investigator Hart to both Jeff and I. Investigator Hart explained the process to us. Basically, they hooked up a special phone to our phone which had a recording device. Investigator Hart would listen in on the conversation and try to coach Jeff by writing notes on a legal pad, mouthing words and/or hand gestures.

I had to run out and pick up a corded phone because all we had in the house were cordless phones. Both Jeff and I had been under the impression they would bring a device with them and we just needed to have a phone outlet. We were mistaken.

When I got back everything was set up. Ins. Hart and Det. Tarrants had gone over the list of specific information they were looking to get out of Jim, with Jeff. All that had to be done was plug the new phone into the recording device.

Within minutes they made the call to Jim at Mercy hospital. Since I had missed a good chunk of the explanation on how it would all work, Det. Tarrants sat with me attempting to explain everything as Ins. Hart and Jeff got Jim on the line.

Jim answered on their first try. Tarrants and I could only hear Jeff's side of the conversation and it was too difficult to read the notes from Hart. They needed to get Jim to confess to specific acts of sexual assault. They needed frequency and they needed him to admit that he did this to both Jeff and Erik.

Jeff was masterful.

It was hard listening even just to Jeff's side of the conversation. I'm not sure how I would have held up had I been listening to both sides. I had never heard Jeff discuss exactly what his father had done to him. Nor had I ever heard him speak so bluntly about it. I fought back tears as I listened. Jeff struggled, trying to keep everything straight and not accidentally clue his father in on what was going on. He would glance over at me shaking his head, as though he was in complete shock. He seemed to be asking. *Is this really happening?*

I just mouthed the words, *I love you. You're doing great. Keep it up.*

Jeff was able to get every piece of information out of Jim they were looking for. Each confession Jim made, Hart would smile and write frantically on the legal pad for Jeff to get a bit more...then Hart would nod his head in approval as Jim dug his own grave, divulging more and more with each passing moment.

Once it was over Hart told us it was the best (in regards to information obtained) one-party intercept confession he had ever been part of.

The following is the actual transcript from the one-party intercept.

> Introduction by Investigator Hart:
>
> ...2005. The time right now is 9:20 am. My name is Tom Hart. I'm an investigator with the Strafford County Attorney's Office. Last Friday, Karen Huntress, and Assistant Attorney General for the Attorney General's Office, State of New Hampshire, gave permission for a one-party intercept to take place today's date between 7:00am and 7:00pm. Permission was gained through the Durham Police Department, the investigating agency of lead by Detective Gabe Tarrants, who will be present for this one-party intercept this morning. We will be calling and making contact with a James Halldorson in Portland, Maine at ███-███-████, and that would be at the Mercy Hospital in Portland, Maine.
>
> (Dialing phone)
>
> <u>KEY:</u>
>
> "A" represents responses/statements by James Halldorson
>
> "Q" represents response/statements by Jeffrey Halldorson
>
> <u>BEGIN TELEPHONE CONVERSATION</u>
>
> A. This is Jim.

Q. Jim, it's Dad. Dad, it's Jeff.

A. Right.

Q. I'm sorry to call you at work. I don't have another number for you.

A. It's okay.

Q. Listen, uh, I hate to talk to you at work but I gotta – I got some shit going on with Erik.

A. Yeah?

Q. And I just wanted to talk to you if you have a few minutes?

A. Yeah, It's okay. Yeah. Of course.

Q. Um – You um – You went down and talked to the boys?

A. Yes.

Q. What did you tell them, cuz they won't talk to us?

A. I – I talked to them and I told them it was true and then we just had a discussion, so.

Q. Cuz ah, you know, they won't return our phone calls. I mean the whole fucking reason I did this is because, you know, I wanted to have a normal relationship with them. You know?

A. Jeff – Jeffrey, I did not say this to contact them at all. That's their own personal decision.

Q. Well, yeah Dad, but it's kind of a fucked up situation.

A. Jeffrey, I did not tell them anything about their relationship with you. We had a discussion. They're dealing with it. I have no idea. I gave them no direction whatsoever. So, please, don't – don't put that back on me. I gave them no direction. Sat there with the boys and Mom and I said exactly the discussion you and I had in the driveway. Okay?

Q. What? I don't –

A. Well, I said that I – I said, "I'm not going to hide behind the fact that I was drunk. It happened." Okay? And (INAUDIBLE)

Q. But what did you tell them? I mean did you just sit there and say the same thing that you said before about what Jeff told Suzie was true? I mean cuz you know, that's what Mom's falling on, saying, "Well, you know? I don't know if" – I'm just – I'm fucking tired of this.

A. Yeah, well.

Q. Why? Why did this happen?

A. Jeff, I don't understand. I can't explain it.

Q. You know, I'm sure you're probably sick and tired of me calling you at work about this stuff but –

A. I'm not sick and tired, Jeffrey. I love you; you're my son.

Q. Then why would you do this? I mean – You know, I think the hardest thing is that I'm having a hard time dealing with it is because, you know, I'm watching my fucking kids grow up.

A. Jeff, you're my son.

Q. I'm your son, but dad, you fucking raped us. I mean cut and dry you wrapped your fucking mouth around my dick. Why? What would posses you to do that? I mean I'm looking at my kids and I – There's no way I could do that to them.

A. I don't know, Jeffrey. I don't know, Jeffrey. I got – I got treatment – You told me – the day you and Erik came to the house you said to get help. I – The next day I drove down to Shrewsbury to the EAP program and I've been getting help for ten years.

Q. Did you tell them what was happening?

A. Yes, of course I did.

Q. You told them that you – that – that- that you molested your children and they – and they – and they helped you with that? Or did you just tell them you were an alcoholic and –

A. No, Jeffrey. I'm not going to go into details. I got – I told them what happened.

Q. Yeah. But dad, -

A. Jeffrey –

Q. – throughout our lives man, what – what – what you say happened to us and what you say happened, are two different stories, and that's what I'm having a hard time with, man.

A. Jeff, (INAUDIBLE)

Q. I mean it happened for years, dad. It wasn't just like a one-time thing.

A. Jeffrey, -

Q. I'm not – I mean we've had this conversation.

A. Yes, we've had this conversation and, you know, I do love you. I can't explain – I can't explain anything I do. I have no logical explanation for it. You know, we had a lot of good fucking times thought when you were a kid. I took you guys a lot of places, and I'm sorry. I did more stuff with you than I did with the little kids, as a father and son. I took you to baseball games, I took you to hikes, I took you –

Q. Dad, Dad, Dad you took me to a baseball game. The last time you took me to a baseball game was the last time you raped me. We left at the seventh inning because of that, because you had to get home, cuz you didn't want to sit in traffic.

A. I – Well, -

Q. I mean –

A. – we lived in New Jersey; we went to the library every Saturday, we went on hikes, we did all kinds of cool stuff. Okay? I tried to be the best father I could. I can't explain it. I want to get – You know, I want you to get healthy. I tried – I – I – I – I – I – I got counseling; you told me you were getting counseling.

Q. Yeah, but what about Erik?

A. I – I – I have to talked – Well, what's going on?

Q. Have you seen Erik lately?

A. No.

Q. I mean that's – that's the whole – I mean – It seems like I'm the driving force behind this but – You know? It mean it seems like – no – that – You know? It seems like this happened with me a lot more than it happened with him, and I don't – I don't understand why he's such a fucking mess and yet I have to go on with my life.

A. Jeffrey, -

Q. I don't understand how – Yeah, okay, maybe it's not fair that he gets to be dysfunctional and I have to be so fucking responsible.

A. Jeffrey, he – Jeffrey, he obviously has – he obviously has; this is not an excuse, but he has some inherent mental problems that - that – that – that – that – this is – I'm not – I'm not laying it all on this but it's complicated by the fact that he obviously has mental problems. You know that. Jeffrey?

Q. I just –

A. You know this, don't you?

Q. Yeah, I do but –

A. (INAUDIBLE)

Q. – don't you think that – I mean –

A. Yes. I'm not – And I'm not – I'm not – I'm not copping out on this but that's where – that's the difference is, is that I think no matter how he was raised, he has mental problems that are going to pop up anyway. You know? And I'm just being honest with you. It doesn't help that he takes – he's been taking drugs for so many years. I mean – And I can understand why. I mean Christ, I used to use drugs. Talk to me Jeffrey. Don't be silent.

Q. I don't know what the fuck to say, dad. You don't have to deal with him. I mean – You don't have – You know what? I've gone and I've let it go, and every time I fucking let it go and I try to go back and see my brother, all he talks about is how – I mean is this shit that happened. That's – That's seriously. I go over there and he's like, "That man did this. That man did that." And I mean it's just – I mean how – I mean were you – Was it more predominant with him? I mean did you – Did you – Did this happen more with him than me? I mean what – what – how is it?

A. I don't know, Jeffrey.

Q. I mean do you remember anything? I mean is this just – I mean is this just – Are you just - You just get to escape without the memories of what happened?

A. I don't escape with it. I mean –

Q. Do you really get to get away without having to remember what happened?

A. I don't get away with it, Jeffrey. I don't get away with anything.

Q. No. I mean do you get – do you get to go on with – I mean –

A. Do I get to go on?

Q. – do you remember any of it? Do you remember – maybe that's it. Maybe – Do you sleep at night or do you think about it – Do you remember any of what happened, like the physical act? Do you remember any of that?

A. Yes. Yes. And it makes me sick because I wish it never ever happened. I wish – I tried my hardest to be a parent to you guys. And, you know, there were a lot of good things and we moved to Durham so we could get you in the best school system. I hated my fucking job. I did my job so that I could provide a house and – You know? I – I fell down and I did something sick and I can't explain it. And – And I want to do everything in my power to – I don't know how I can make it up to you but I've tried, Jeffrey. I've tried it every way. You came to me and asked to build a studio and I – Cuz you said that it would be therapeutic for Erik.

Q. Oh everything I fuck – You've got to understand, I've been through all this *for* Erik. You know what I mean? As twisted and sick as it sounds, man, I just want my brother to have a fucking normal life/

A. Right.

Q. He can't even –

A. And that's why you came to me and asked to build a studio –

Q. I know and that doesn't fucking help. Nothing helps. Nothing helps. Nothing helps. And now – Now what am I supposed to fucking do? I gotta - I just gotta go back to being – And you know how – I mean it's somewhat – It's – It's somewhat – It's somewhat comforting knowing that you actually remember some of it happening.

A. Oh, yes I do, Jeffrey.

Q. Because, you know what, you've been –

A. It's torture. It's torture. Alright?

Q. Good. You fucking deserve it. Cuz you know what, we're tortured.

A. Okay. Well, can we work together to – to – to – to – to deal with this? And the kids, I did not give any directions to – Hold on a second. Let me close my door.

Q. Did it happen to the boys?

A. I did not give any direction to ▇▇▇▇ and ▇▇▇▇. And – You know? You know, Kelly ripped Mom's ass apart and I'm really kind of upset about that. When she ripped apart about Mom's house, her decorations and everything, and that really devastated her.

Q. No. Fuck. Fuck. Jim, stop for a second. You and I – Alright, and I'm going to go off the record with this and if you repeat this to Mom I'll fucking deny it. Mom's a fucking – Mom's a compulsive liar. Don't you know that? Don't you know that? I mean, give me a little bit here. She's – She's not exactly the most sane woman, and you have to admit some of that. {BEEP} You know what I mean? Jim? {BEEP}

A. Why – why would she make fun of –

Q. I'm sorry, there's just – there's somebody else calling in. Forget it. I mean you have to give me a little bit on that one?

A. Why would she make fun of Mom's decorations in our house? That really –

Q. What I'm trying to say is that never fucking happened.

A. That never happened?

Q. No. We love that house. We envied that house. Jim, that is what we fucking strived for is to have that damn house or a house like that. That's the kind of life we want -

A. That never happened? Mom made that up?

Q. Dude, I – Jim, haven't you figured out the crap that Mom makes up to turn people against east other? She sat there and told ▮▮▮▮▮ that Kelly was saying, "Oh, Kelly's have these parties and all" – I mean that not my call, but – but, yes. Yeah. Mom makes up shit, Jim, in case you haven't figured that out.

A. Well, she said that you and Kelly were drunk that night when Kelly called her.

Q. No. Kelly wasn't. I was. But anyway.

A. But Jeff –

Q. The reason I'm calling – The reason I'm calling is because I just need to – this has to – this has to be the last fucking conversation. I can't continue doing this... I need to – My boys just had their birthday. Alright? And we had all the grandparents over. And you know, there was something fucking missing, Jim, and that's always going to be missing. Okay? And now I need to get one with my life and just accept that. In order for me to fucking do that, I just need this to be done and I'm – and I'm – and – I got – You know what? I have – I'm gonna have to say, you know, I don't know if I'm going to be able to deal with you, I don't know if I'm ever going to be able to deal with Mom on a normal basis. So, what I'm – what I'm calling you for is I got to figure out what to do about Erik. Alright? It's no – It's no longer about me. It's about what I'm going to fucking do with Erik. It's no – It's no longer about me. It's about what I'm going to fucking do about Erik. You're not going to do anything about Erik; Mom's not going to do anything about Eirk. I'm the one that's stuck with him.

A. Well, what –

Q. No. Well, just listen to me. So, what – what I need to know is, I need to know whether I need to go ahead and do something serious, you know, to get him some serious help. I mean –

A. I fucking –

Q. Why me and Erik? I mean why me and Erik? Why – I mean did it happen to anybody else, Jim? Be honest for this – for the fucking love of God.

A. No. It did not happen to (INAUDIBLE)

Q. Why? Then why just me and Erik?

A. Jeffrey, I don't know. I don't know. I've been dealing with this for ten years (INAUDIBLE)

Q. I mean what does your therapist tell you? I mean honestly how – You know? I mean, did it happen more with me or did it happen more with Erik? I need to know cuz I need to know if that's what is driving him fucking crazy.

A. Ah –

Q. It's a tough question to answer, Jim, I understand but I need to know.

A. Probably – It was probably split.

Q. I can't hear you.

A. It was probably the same. Even. I'm guessing.

Q. How – How – I mean how much, man? My little fucking twisted minds messed up, Jim.

A. Jeff. Jeff, you know what? I can't – You know what?

Q. I know this is going to fuck up the rest of your day as much as it is going to fuck up the rest of mine.

A. No. No. No. This – This – No. I want to talk about this. I want to talk about this because it's fucked up my life as badly as it's fucked up your life. Believe me. Because I don't know why it happened. I'm a – You know? You're going to laugh but, you know, otherwise I'm a decent person. I have a mission here. I – We – I have a – I – I am responsible. I am two steps – I am two steps down from the chairman of the – the CEO of this hospital. I'm responsible for – We're a charity hospital. I'm responsible for hiring and maintaining and paying the best clinical staff here, so I'm on a mission. I'm doing a good deed. I'm trying my best to do something decent with my life. And we take care of charity patients, we provide pre-medical care, and I'm trying to – I'm trying to – I'm – You know? That doesn't mean shit to you in your little – and the problems you have. But I'm trying to do something decent with my life. And quite frankly, I can't afford to live separately. It's – It's – It's – It's draining every dollar we have.

Q. Jim this happened to me every week for a long time.

A. I know, Jeffrey.

Q. And you need to help me.

A. I'm helping. I want to help you. I want to be as close to you as I can. So, this is a good conversation. It bothers me. It bothers the fucking shit out of me as badly as it does you. It tortures me every fucking God damn fucking day, because otherwise in my life, I have been a good person. I served my Country in the Air Force during Vietnam. I did all that shit. You know?

Q. Ah, -

A. I tried to make it up with ▇▇▇▇▇ and ▇▇▇▇ and send them to good schools, too, and to be there. And you know what? I was never as close to them as I was to you and Erik as little kids.

Q. You were clo – Jim, come on, back down a second here. I mean -

A. Jeffrey, we had a lot of good times when you were kids. You don't remember?

Q. We did. We did, Dad, but every – but the days – the days were fine. It was the nights we had to worry about.

A. I know.

Q. Were you – I mean –

A. None of us can keep torturing ourselves with this.

Q. Uh, ha, ha, ha, it's not something we do by choice.

A. I know, Jeffrey. I'm not –

Q. I mean I have to ask –

A. I'm not trying to be (INAUDIBLE)

Q. I mean were you violent with Erik? I mean did –

A. Violent? Never. I was never violent with Erik. Never.

Q. Well, I mean was it just the same – the same thing as with me?

A. Yes. Yes. Yes.

Q. So, it was just oral; nothing else?

A. Yes. I never –

Q. You didn't violently rape him?

A. Never.

Q. Cuz that's the – that's the way he lives his fucking life.

A. No! Jeffrey, -

Q. Okay. Cuz that's the way –

A. Jeffrey, -

Q. Well, you have to – Slow down. You know, I'm not the one that's on trial here. I'm not the one that did anything wrong. Okay?

A. I never penetrated either one of you. Never. I've never done that to anybody in my life. I've never done that.

Q. Yeah, but you sucked my dick.

A. Yes.

Q. And Erik's. And this is what we have to fucking live with every day. And now – but – but I have to live with Erik who acts like he's been viciously raped repetitively and locked up in a little – I mean that's what he acts like , Jim. It's like he's fucking lives in a closet and he's been raped and beaten and sodomized, and that's the way he lives his life. He lives his life like a fucking lunatic. I don't know- I mean – and he can't even – and now he's trying to – now he's trying to be in another fucking relationship. And you know what, it's starting all over again with him. And that's what I deal with. That's what I deal with. I deal with my brother being alone for the rest of his fucking life because of you. I mean this happened - a hun – This happened to us hundreds of times. What can we do about it? I mean what are we going to do? What am I supposed to do?

A. You know, it was very – You know, you – You kids did not bond with your parents the first three years of your life and that – that didn't help the situation. Again, I'm –

Q. So, that's why you did –

A. No. No. No. No. No. No. That is part of the formula. That is part of the formula that makes it very difficult from Erik, and he has a genetic – He has an inherited mental problem that helps – I didn't – You're right, I didn't help the situation but he has a inherited problem as well. I did not penetrate him. I did – I Jeffrey. –

141

Q. What about me, man? I mean I've been fucked – You know, I've been – You guys had me locked up for two fucking years and I think – You know what, sometimes I think that's what saved me, but.

A. You've got a lot to live for, so. Man, you've got beautiful kids. You did a great job in that Brick House. I am so proud of what you did there. I brag on you all the time. Let's not all live as prisoners. Let's get –

Q. Listen.

A. Let's get healed.

Q. Listen. I got to –

A. Let's get healed, (INAUDIBLE)

Q. Are you going to be in you office today?

A. Yeah.

Q. Cuz I've got to go do lunch with fucking Erik and I just cannot – If you'll be in later, I might call you back; I don't know. I got to – I got to do something with this kid. I love him to death and I just can't have him fucking falling apart. So, I don't know if I'm going to for, you know, try and do something with guardianship and have him placed or what. I just don't know. He's – He need – He needs something I can't give him.

A. He's still working, right?

Q. Yeah, he's still working.

A. That's a – That's – That's incredible that he's held that job. That is the best thing for him.

Q. Um hmm (affirmative). You need help. I hope you're getting it.

A. Yes, Jeffrey. I – I got to the therapist's every week. I've been going to therapy for ten years.

Q. At least one of us has. I got to go.

A. Jeff. Jeff, let's all get healed and get –

Q. Some day.

A. Jeff, we need to move on with our lives (INAUDIBLE)

Q. I'm moving on with mine. I'm not calling you cuz of me anymore. I've got a wife and three kids, man. I'm pretty lucky. It's my – It's the – the one thing that – that – that – that – holds this thing together is that I can't have a normal fucking relationship with my brother cuz he can't get by the fact that this happened. And every time I think it's over, every time I think I can move on, I get drunk. So, I stopped drinking. Okay great. So, no I gotta – Every time I want to fucking go see my brother, the only person I've know my entire life, I gotta live – relive everything that happened to me. And – and – and I gotta decide how I'm going to go about fixing that, cuz I've fixed my life. I'm lucky. I'm lucky. I could walk away from you tomorrow and be fucking fine, because I have my family. Erik has nothing. I mean you did this; not me, and now I gotta clean it up. Jim, you take care.

A. Jim – Jeffrey?

Q. What?

A. Call me.

Q. What?

A. Please call me. Don't. I – The boys had no direction whatsoever from me at all. They're just dealing with it. Okay? It's very hard for them to digest.

Q. You know, I took ▓▓▓▓▓▓▓▓ in all summer, took care of his every fucking need, and now I can't even get a phone call back from him. I did everything that I could do for that kid. I took ▮▮▮ and I worked and I tried and I tried and I tried. He's just a lost soul, Jim. This all happened. – I mean this –

A. No. No. No way. Don't – No way, man. Don't – Don't go there, Jeffrey.

Q. Don't go where?

A. You took ▮▮▮ in?

Q. No. I mean I fucking – I – I spent – I used to call him every week, we used to get together, he used to come over for dinner.

A. Yeah. Well, you did something to really anger him cuz he wouldn't call you back all summer.

Q. Yeah. You know what I did? I told him his father was a fucking pedophile. That's what I told him. That's exactly what I told him. And I said, "You know what?" Cuz, you know, when you moved out it was the first time I could actually have a relationship with these guys. I could bring my kids over there. We could ride – I mean I live a stone's throw away from that house, and my kids and I could ride our bikes over there and we could go see Grammy Sue and we could see, you know, ▮▮▮ and all those guys. And we used to go over there and we used to hang out. But you know what? There was talk of you coming back and I told ▮▮▮, I sat there. I said, "Your father's a pedophile, and now he won't talk to me?" I mean I didn't tell him anything that wasn't true, did I? And he didn't believe me. And now you went and told him the truth, right?

A. Yes, I did.

Q. And not they still won't talk to me. So I lose. Why did this happen to me? Why? I was just a fucking kid, Jim. And it's harder now cuz I've seen my kids; they're the same age, and I don't – I don't get it. You said that you were sexually offended?

A. Yes, I was.

Q. Then why the hell would you want to put that on somebody else? That's the last thing I want for my kids.

A. Okay.

Q. Why do you think you are never going to see them?

A. I don't – I – I respect that.

Q. I gotta go. I'll talk to you later. I'll call you after lunch with Erik.

A. Okay.

Q. Bye.

A. Bye.

PARTIES HANG UP

What that transcript didn't reveal...

Imagine, for a moment, talking to your father on the phone. It is a serious discussion that requires a great deal of attention on your part to follow. Three people are in the room with you watching you talk. One of the people is telling you what to say to your father. You can't let your father know that someone else is listening and you have to try and get him to discuss decades old secrets about his inappropriate sexual encounters.

Now imagine your entire future, the future of your kids, your father and so many others resting on you keeping it all straight and getting the information needed out of your father.

Jeff was truly remarkable.

By: Jeff & Kelly Halldorson

Jim @ Mercy

(Jeff)

The case against Jim was building. They had a recorded confession and Erik was doing his part cooperating with the investigative team. Everything seemed, at least at this point, to be moving pretty fast. I decided it was time; I needed to cut off the sexual relationship with Julia. I didn't want to get caught. My time for being reckless was over. She agreed never to discuss our relationship with anyone. I didn't, however, sever all ties with her.

With the ammunition of the wiretap in hand, Det. Tarrants went to the Mercy Hospital in Portland, Maine, ready to meet the accused head on. Alongside him was Detective Bilodeau, a new member of the campaign to bring Jim to justice.

In the office of the hospital they came face to face with the man they wanted to put behind bars. They brought the battle onto the enemy's territory. Sitting at the same desk where he had been confronted by his son on the phone only three days prior; Jim looked across to two Durham, NH Detectives.

Jim you have been advised that you do not have to speak to us. You do understand that, correct?

I do.

May we record this conversation?

No.

Regardless, the interrogation began. Detectives Tarrants and Bilodeau took turns leading the questioning, playing off each other flawlessly.

There have been allegations brought against you by Jeff and Erik stating that you have sexually assaulted them in the past. Is that true?

Let me start by saying that I am not a pedophile, I have never touched my two younger sons and I have no desire to have any sexual contact with children.

Did you ever perform any inappropriate sexual acts on Jeff or Erik?

I cannot remember any ever taking place. I however was a blackout drunk at that point in my life. Since then I have been in counseling and have ten years of sobriety.

So did you or did you not have inappropriate sexual contact with the boys as children?

There is a possibility that something inappropriate happened. I was a black out drunk as I told you.

The longer they spoke the more his story changed. The more questions asked the more things started to take shape. And finally the truth emerged.

Yes, I did. I entered their rooms as they slept and I did. I did...

He was tired of fighting, tired of hiding from his actions. Actions he couldn't make sense of himself. The detectives saw the relief in his eyes.

Okay. Do we have your permission to audiotape?

Yes. Yes, you do.

The following is the interrogation transcript.

<u>INTERVIEW BY DETECTIVE TARRANTS:</u>

Q. Today is October 27th, 2005. It is ten minutes past 11:00 in the am. This is Detective Tarrants in here with Detective Bilodeau, and sir can you state your name for us?

A. James Halldorson

Q. James Halldorson. We are here at Mercy Hospital in Portland Maine. James, Dect. Bilodeau and I are going to ask you a couple questions. Just answer as truthfully as you have. And I guess, first of all, we're here: we're here talking to you about some allegations made by your sons, Jeffrey and Erik. Some things that happened years ago when you lived in Durham.

A. Um hmm (affirmative response)

Q. On - What address that you lived at in Durham?

A. Nine Tirrell Place.

Q. Nine Tirrell Place. And you moved to Durham?

A. About 1980. June of 1980.

Q. June of '80.

> Detective Bilodeau: And to interrupt real quick. You know you are not under arrest right now?

A. I understand.

Q. And you can tell us to leave at any point?

A. I understand.

Detective Tarrants continued with the questioning.

Q. We've asked you if there had been any kind of inappropriate acts that took place between you and Jeff and Erik while you lived in Durham?

A. Um hmm (affirmative response)

Q. Your answer to that?

A. My... My statement is

Q. Statement.

A. -- is that approximate - Well, my answer is that approximately eight years ago I arrived home from work one night in Durham. I can't remember the exact date. It had to have been more than eight years ago because ▮ was probably about six, so I would say twelve years ago. I arrived home from work and I found Jeff and Erik on the porch of the house. Um - Went inside. They were in extremely agitated and, oh, belligerent modes, and they said, "We understand from Mom that ▮ has had trouble sleeping," which is not uncommon in this child. We lived right off of route 4; it's very noisy. And they said, "We came to find out if you were molesting the children since"... They accused me of molesting them as youngsters. My wife came home, approached me, they, they threatened me that they would beat the crap out of me.

I think Jeffrey said he would hold me down and Erik would beat me. Erik was 6'7". My wife came home, brought the children down in front of Jeffrey and Erik and said " children" being ▮ and ▮. ▮ was born in 1986. ▮ was born in 1988. And she brought them down individually and said," Has your father ever touched you in an inappropriate way?" And they both totally denied it and said; "I have no idea what you are talking about." And we had a long discussion. After that, I tried to appease the situation, because this is the first time that it had ever come out in the open, and briefly said to my wife " It may have happened." And Jeff... Jeffrey's parting words to me is, "I hope you get some good help."

The following day, I drove down to Shrewsbury Mass. to a very good friend of mine who is president of an employee assistance program, who's an RN and a counselor, and who had also been involved in an intervention to get me into a rehabilitation program for alcoholism in Hempstead Hospital. And not to put him in a difficult position where he would have to report it to the police, I presented it to him theoretically of, "What if this happened, what if that happened?"

Finally he said to me, "You know, Jim, we're friends going long back. Just tell me off the record." And I said, "Well, my sons accused me of this."

Q. What did your sons accuse you of?

A. I believe...I can't recall the details but I believe of sexually molesting them was - was the "terminalization" - I don't believe there was any details that they specified. So, Jim said, "The best for you... for Jim Halldorson to do is to maintain your sobriety program, working through AA, and see an individual counselor," Which I have done off and on for ten years.

After this was brought to my attention, it was at the top of my mind and thought it through and through and said, " I have no desire to go after young children, look at pictures on the internet or anything like that." It's just - I like sexy women. You know? I'm not sexually attracted to youngsters. So, I have - I have gone through counseling ever since and I stopped drinking, which was over ten years ago. It's probably twelve now. Um - The incidents that - that ah - Detective Tarrants jarred my memory on is that Jeffrey did say something to our neighbor, Suzie Armstrong. I had kind of forgot about that, and she reported it immediately to my wife and, um, my wife, um, did; and I don't recall the timeframe, did tell me about it. She had also done some babysitting; and this is something that I didn't discuss with you earlier, for three different women, and she felt that an obligation just to report it to the women that this had been reported to her.

This was either after this incident with Suzie or either after the incident with then the boys came to the house. Ah, it was Mary or Bonnie, I don't remember her last name; she lived in Rochester, and our next-door neighbor. And they all said" Well, we know Jim doesn't have any contact with children and we have complete faith in you and we would never believe this about Jim."

So she did do her due dil..due diligence in covering her bases. To this day, she tells me she doesn't believe that I would ever do anything like that. And, ah, in her mind, she has said to me, "I don't understand, because once Kelly accused you of being," Kelly being Jeff's wife. "Kelly accused you of being a pedophile." Using the word "pedophile" over and over. Those words don't necessarily come from Jeff and Erik that I recall. And my wife says, "Well, once you're a pedophile, you're always a pedophile. It's an incurable disease"...

Q. Right.

A. "unlike alcoholism, which has treatment through stopping drinking, AA, and spirituality." And she says, "I know you boys know you've never..." being ▄▄▄▄▄▄▄ and ▄▄▄▄▄▄▄, " have never tou- You've never touched them and they don't believe Erik and Jeffrey. And you know it never happened anyplace else."

Incidents where I have helped Jeffrey financially after my wife and I inherited some money, we were totally voluntary and there was never a discussion of, "Well, this is quid pro quo for us not reporting you to the police." That never came up.

Q. Right.

A. The only thing that ever came up is when Jeffrey ask me for about $4,500.00 to build a recording studio, where he thought that it would be therapeutic for Erik, and he said, " I blame you for what happened to Erik." That was the only time it ever came up. And it would be a good opportunity for the four boys to play music together.

Subsequent phone call a few weeks ago when Kelly was drunk in the middle of the night and called my wife, she accused our financial aid of being hush money, and there couldn't be anything further from the truth. I've never approached my adoptive children and said, "The intention of this money is to keep your mouth shut. Um...

Q. And, and your sure of that? Another thing that we're sure of is that nothing inappropriate ever happened between yourself and your biological sons.

A. Yeah, that's absolutely correct.

Q. "That's correct." Going back though to when you first moved to Durham, there were some inappropriate actions that you recall between yourself and Erik and yourself and Jeffrey; is that correct?

A. Yes. Hazed by my deep alcoholism, that vague recollections which are hard to decipher when there was a blackout... Well a blackout drunk to use harsh words. But I was a blackout drunk, but if I was blacked out, obviously, I couldn't perform anything but I would have been severely inebriated.

Q. Right.

> Detective Bilodeau: Discuss what you did, opposed to what you didn't do to the boys?

A. To my recollection, it would have been going into their rooms when I believed they were asleep and, um, performed oral sex; never to the point of ejaculation, never asking them to touch me or do anything to me because I always thought... I mean if they had turned the light on or asked me what I was doing, I would have left the room promptly. In a phone conversation with Jeffrey the other day, he used the word "sodomy" and I know from my own personal sexual preference, that is something that absolutely totally disgusts me and I know that I would never do that to anybody, even a hot-looking young babe I wouldn't even do that to.

Q. And you said " Never to the point of ejaculation," that was Erik and Jeffrey?

A. That's correct.

Q. Would you ever...

A. No, sir.

Q. – ejaculate when you were doing that to them?

A. No, sir.

Q. "No," okay.

Detective Bilodeau: And to make it clear, They never woke up?

A. If they would of woken up, I would have left the room.

Q. No words were spoken?

A. They... They... They must have feigned sleeping. That's all I can say. No, words were never spoken.

Detective Bilodeau: Now, how many times do you recall doing this? I know we discussed it earlier. Would it be one to ten; ten to twenty? Somewhere in between?

A. Somewhere in between.

Detective Bilodeau: Okay. So it's clear to say somewhere between one and twenty?

A. Right. Now Kelly- Kelly did say to my wife, I believe, it happened hundreds of times, I don't believe it.

Q. And , Mr. Halldorson, you've sought counseling -

A. Yes.

Q. Like you said before, for alcohol and -

A. And life counseling.

Q. "Life counseling" okay. On choices that - thing that you might have done in your past?

A. Yes. And mar- mar- marital issues. We had couple counseling and that. We went as far as we could on that, and I worked on myself as an individual. Um, so, I have been un... I have been under counseling on and off, you know, the last ten years. I'm under counseling right now.

Detective Bilodeau: Let me ask you this: When was the last time you recall performing oral sex on either Erik or Jeffrey, or what were the circumstances that made you stop?

A. Um, I would have I-I-I can't put an exact date or even a year on that, and I would have to say when our younger children were born in '86 and '88. Um, my... I got better, I stopped drinking and, um, those children brought a whole different dynamic and dimension in my life. Um, Erik and Jeffrey were very difficult children to raise. There was almost daily issues from the Oyster River School System. Um, teachers would um, say" They're difficult children in the classroom," particularly Jeffrey. We had to go to Judge Shaheen to have the Oyster River School System... the state mandate the Oyster River School System send him for A.D.D. treatment, which the oyster River School System didn't have the resources for. Ah, Captain Golding was totally involved all along the way, ah, with this. We sought his counsel on getting alcohol treatment for Jeffrey because some of our neighbors reported that - that he had wood - alcohol in the woods. Ah, and he was such a problematic child. Ah, Captain Golding was wonderful to my wife and I - as far as giving counsel.

Um, the other disturbing thing is, is that when my wife was pregnant with ▓▓▓▓, which would have been in the early part of 1988. Jeff was at - supposedly a Boy Scout meeting: I found out he wasn't there, but I went to pick him up because I had just discovered a candle under the vanity in my wife's bathroom when she was pregnant with ▓▓▓▓ and that nobody else was in the house. And the only person that could have possibly have "litten" it would have been Jeffrey. We believe there was an intention to, ah, inflict bodily- to kill my wife and unborn child and burn the house down.

Q. Now, this was possibly still during or near the end of the acts -

A. It would have been after.

Q. - or after the inappropriate acts had occurred?

A. Yes.

Q. And we're saying it was - they all happened between when you moved from Durham in 1980 to between 1986 and 1988?

A. (INAUDIBLE)

Q. And it's clear... made clear to us by you that this is something that you have struggled with every day since '88?

A. Yes. And I believe that's one of the things that Jeffrey seems to struggle with, is that he believes that, I am blasé, but I struggle with it daily and I would and - and I had hoped when we had that meeting, when they came to our house, I don't know, ten years ago, that everything was out in the open and that - that -

Detective Bilodeau: Who was at that meeting about ten years ago?

A. Ah, Jeffrey and Erik as I said, were at the door waiting, and they confronted me, and then my wife came home and then the boys came - the little boys came home.

Detective Bilodeau: Now, you guys all sat down together, you your wife -

A. Ah, no initially it the two older boys and my wife.

Detective Bilodeau: "two older boys" being?

A. Erik and Jeffrey. And then, obviously, when she spoke to the younger boys, I was not present in the room.

Detective Bilodeau: Okay.

A. She didn't want me - Or you know, she just wanted to find out the truth. Ah, my wife also babysat for three different people, Mary in Somersworth, Bonnie, I can't think of her name in Rochester, and the next door neighbor Jane, who all had young boys, and she immediately said, "These allegations were made." She thought it was due diligence to do so, and all three of those women said, ah

Q. What's -

A. When – when - One other point when Jeffrey, after Captain Golding suggested, when Jeffrey appeared to have substance abuse problems, he was around 16, he suggest a program called STRAIGHT, which is in Canton Mass. or somewhere around there, that we participated in. And then he was eventually transferred to, I believe it's Brookside or Brookstone hospital in Nashua, New Hampshire. Ah, in one of those counseling sessions, it did come up and the counselor did say...

Detective Bilodeau: What came up?

A. Ah, something about being sexually abused as a child. And She said, "You know, it's my obligation as a therapist that I have to report this to Social services." And we - My wife and I never heard anything about that after.

Detective Bilodeau: And that was in Canton, Mass.?

A. No. This was at Brookstone or the Brookside Hospital in Nashua New Hampshire.

Detective Bilodeau: Okay. If we can go back to Durham, were Jeff and Erik sharing a room at that point when you would go into that room?

A. Ah, they had separate rooms in Durham.

Detective Bilodeau: Okay. Is there a specific room that you would go to? Would you go to Erik more often than Jeff?

A. I can't - I have no recollection.

Detective Bilodeau: Okay.

A. I believe... I can say that Jeffrey and Erik, um, we adopted them when they were three and four years old. They were abandoned by their natural parents, passed around amongst foster homes and other families. I think when children don't bond –bond- have a bonding with their parents or an adult at that age, it manifests itself – ah - with them, in particular, when they became adolescents and there was a great deal of acting out. I can remember Captain Golding saying Jeffrey was the most difficult children he ever dealt with in his whole professional career.

Q. Now, what were the ages of the boys when you adopted them?

A. Three and four.

Q. "Three and four." And you were - where in Wisconsin were you living?

A. Ah, Trenton, Wisconsin.

Q. Okay. Did - did it start there or did it just start taking place when you moved to Durham, that you remember?

A. I don't remember. I would say Durham, but... Jeff, Jeff's recollection to Kelly was that it might have happened over a period of ten years, and I have...I have no... I don't believe it's true.

Q. As far as you can recall, it was... the acts only took place while living in Durham?

A. Right.

Q. Okay.

A. Um, It was my - I would like to state my desire. I said to you gentleman that I have sought out a career in an institution of compassion, charity and spiritual guidance, and I would like nothing more than, while I believe in justice, than to ah - heal, more than anything else. And Jeffrey did ask me on the telephone and has asked before "Why did this happen?" And I would say, "I can't answer that I have no idea." But I can unequivocally say that, um, the diagnosis of a pedophile is being somebody that's incurable and I strongly believe that - I know for a fact that ever since I've been sober, the thought never crossed my mind of having any desire for any children; nothing of the nature.

Q. Okay. It's 11:33 and this will conclude the interview.

END

Jim took no responsibility for the anger of my youth. It hurts knowing he primarily blames it on the abandonment of my "natural parents". I fill with tears as I hear him try and justify his actions and discuss how difficult we were as children. Maybe, just maybe, if he loved us as a father should love his sons then I wouldn't have been so hard to deal with.

I was a little boy. Fat and awkward the first time he slipped in to my bed. I wasn't a problem. I thought I was in heaven living with two people who had saved me and become my mommy and daddy. Jim helped create the problem within me. Just as he told me on the phone about Erik, it is part of the formula. James Halldorson was a part of the formula that made me who I was, who I am.

Erik

(Kelly)

After the one-party intercept with Jim, Jeff called Erik to let him know how well things went. And asked him again to go to go to the Durham P.D. and speak with Det. Tarrants. He headed over on his way to work.

Durham Police Department
Incident Narrative Report

Accident/case Number D-2005-02173, Det. Gabe Tarrants

On 10/25/05, I spoke with Erik Halldorson at the police station. I explained where we were with the case to that point and asked I he would be willing to participate in a forensic interview like Jeff had. He said he did not wish to take part in a forensic interview but would answer any questions I asked and would give a written statement after. I asked him if he could remember any incidents between he and James when they lived in Durham. He said he could completely recall incidents where James performed oral sex on him. At that point, Erik said he would do a interview with me, but still did not wish to go through what Jeff went through in his interview. We set a date of 10/28/05, at 1300 hrs., for that interview.

On the same day Det. Tarrants interviewed me briefly and requested I provide a written statement, regarding some specifics we had discussed.

My written statement, 10/25/05

Durham Police Department Voluntary Statement

We had a meeting at Jeff's parents that included James, Sue, Jeff, and I. The purpose of the meeting was to "clear the air" and discuss the coming out of the molestation. A sort of "where do we go from here." It was also to be an opportunity for them to put me "at ease" them being Sue, Jeff's mom and Jim and for me to question them/him. My first statement was that my children would never be around Jim. They responded that they "completely understood" and wouldn't expect anything else. Next I questioned James as to "why would he molest" these two boys (Jeff and Erik) that he had taken in. His response was that he "wasn't prepared for how difficult they were" There was no denial. So I asked again, "Why would you do this? Because they were too difficult?" He again responded without denial and said that Jeffrey and Erik were much more challenging than he was "prepared for."

Also, through this whole meeting Sue kept saying Jeff and Erik could not press charges and they were trying to move forward. James was going to counseling and they wanted to work things out.

Durham Police Department
Incident Narrative Report

Accident/case Number D-2005-02173, Det. Gabe Tarrants

On 10/25/05, at about 1050 hrs. I received a written statement from Jeff's wife, Kelly Halldorson. This was reference to the meeting her, Jeff and Jeff's parents. According to Kelly, the meeting was for James to put her mind at ease. Kelly said she told them that James was to never be around her kids. Jeff's parents said they understood. She then said she asked James why he would molest the boys he had taken in. James said he had not been prepared for how difficult they would be. Kelly again asked why he molested the boys. James said they were much more challenging than he was prepared for. During their conversation, Kelly said Susan was claiming that Jeff and Erik could not press charges and that everyone should just try to move forward. This was the last time Kelly had a conversation with them about the molestation.

Although Erik originally objected to going through the videotaped forensic interview, in the end he agreed and did so just three days after his initial visit to the Durham Police Department.

Durham Police Department

Incident Narrative Report

Accident/case Number D-2005-02173

On 10/28/05, at about 1300 hrs. Erik Halldorson came to the police station and agreed to participate in a Forensic interview with Carolann Jensen. In the interview, Erik made statement consistent with those made by Jeff. He said he remembered incidents when his father entered his room while he was sleeping and performed oral sex on him. He said the incidents always involved oral sex by his father and that he would sometimes lick Erik's face. Erik said he could remember he and Jeff asking each other if their father had gone into their rooms the previous night. Erik said that his father stopped molesting him when he was 11 or 12 years old (1983 or 1984), after his father showed him a magazine cover of homosexuality and asked him what he thought of it. Erik said he told his father he thought that he (father) was a homosexual.

Erik said he remembered an incident that happened a few years later where his mother was made aware that Jeff had told a neighbor that their father was molesting them. He said his mother, who was pregnant at the time, made him feel guilty about the stress it would cause and told Jeff to tell her it was not true. Erik also spoke of the time that he and Jeff confronted their father several years ago when they were told by their mother that one of their younger brothers was having trouble sleeping. Erik said his father denied ever touching their younger brothers but admitted to molesting he and Jeff.

The support and cooperation from Erik went a long way for Jeff. It seemed to create a ripple effect. For the first time in a long while Jeff seemed as though he might be happy.

He looked at me with fresh eyes. He would talk me up endlessly to Carolann and the Detectives.

She is my best friend, what more could I wish for? I have a wife that loves me and stands by me through all this shit.

The pieces were coming together. Detective Tarrants would stop at nothing to make sure Jim was brought down and Carolann was there to make sure we were all protected.

Jeff's anxiety was replaced with anticipation for the next step. It turned out after the major information gathering period (the wiretap and forensic interviews) there was a lot of waiting we hadn't anticipated.

For both Jeff and I the next part couldn't come fast enough. I wanted to be able to finally put it all behind us. Most importantly I wanted to end Jeff's suffering. I wanted him to be able to prove to the world that he was not a liar. That his father, his mother - the two people that pledged to love and care for him - had wronged him in such a cruel way. I really believed putting Jim behind bars would be the means to end it.

Jeff embraced the process with a newfound purpose. *His* purpose and focus became Erik. He would put the man that hurt his brother behind bars and bring Erik some much needed peace of mind and in the end bring himself vindication.

Susan & friends

(Kelly)

After the forensic interview with Erik, Det. Tarrants gave Susan a call.

> **Narrative Title: Tarrants Supplement**
>
> On 10/28/05, I spoke with Susan Halldorson on the phone. I advised her of the investigation and she agreed to speak with me at 1530 hrs., on 11/01/05. On 10/31/05, she called the police station and advised she had decided not to speak with me and did not want to be contacted again.

Throughout my entire relationship with Jeff and his family, I have been the most confused by his mother. We are all filled with contradictions; but Sue's contradictions seem much more profound. At times I feel she must be evil, while other times I'm filled with sadness and compassion for her.

I have so many issues with her. One of the most serious is that she continued to babysit children, sometimes overnight, while Jim was home after being told that her husband had molested Jeff and Erik.

The following are statements and/or investigative reports from friends of Susan, the mothers of the children she babysat. Some of the statements were given after the arrest but it makes sense, I believe to have it all grouped here.

Title: Tarrants Supplement – Jane ▮

On 11/01/05, I spoke with Jane ▮, a former neighbor of the Halldorsons on Tirrell Place. James Halldorson had told us that his wife used to babysit for ▮ near the time that Jeff and Erik first accused him of molesting them. ▮ said Susan Halldorson advised her of the accusations and assured her that they were false. ▮ said that James never had contact with her child, that she trusted the Halldorsons and never saw anything that would let her believe the accusations to be true.

I find it so disturbing how in each instance of Sue "informing" the parents of the children she babysat she also tells them how it's not true anyway. Here, my sons said this happened...but it's not true...but I had to tell you...just so you know. Then she was able to come to all of us and say, "I told the people I was babysitting for."

She was very close to all of these women. She put them in a position to choose between a good friend and her troubled son. Who would you believe?

Title: Sue Armstrong – Tarrants

On 12/05/05, I spoke with Sue Armstrong from her home in ▮. She was very shocked to hear the recent turn of events. She remembered Jeff telling her that his father was molesting him. She said she spoke to Sue Halldorson about Jeff's allegations. According to Armstrong, Halldorson began to cry and told her nothing like that was happening in her house and the boys must have been confused with incidents that happened in their first home. She said the allegations were never mentioned again and she never noticed anything strange coming from the house.

Durham Police Department

Voluntary Statement, Mary ▮ 02/16/06

Approx 9-11 years ago Sue Halldorson came to me and told me her older son had accused Jim of molesting him. She wanted me to know since she watched my children at her house and at her home. We were together with our children at the time. A that time I had no problem with Jim being around my children. He drank and was a womanizer but it did not affect my children. We remained close. Sue watched my children.

I'm left with this, would you continue to have your children watched by this woman, in her home? I don't think it's as simple as you might think. This sort of thing happens all the time. I am guilty of letting Susan continue to watch my children. Yes, I was careful and was sure to be sure not to let Jim near them...but it was still a risk. When we don't confront skeletons head on we all take chances.

All of these woman should, have done something other than what they did. What really did they have to lose? A friendship? What did they have to gain? They could have protected children.

I should have done something sooner, too. We all should have.

By: Jeff & Kelly Halldorson

The Arrest

(Jeff)

Det. Tarrants called us to let us know that an arrest warrant had been obtained and they expected that within the next few days James would turn himself in.

> **Entered By: Gabe A Tarrants, on 11/3/2005**
>
> Title: Arrest- Tarrants
>
> On 11/02/05 at about 1600hrs, James E. Halldorson, accompanied by Attorney Tim Harrington, reported to the Durham Police Station to answer to two arrest warrants for Aggravated Felonious sexual Assault. The warrants were signed by Judge Gerald Taube on 11/01/05. Halldorson was processed and posted a $25,000.00 cash or bond bail and was released. His arraignment date is 12/01/05, at the Durham District Court. James was advised of his bail conditions, refraining from having any communication with Jeff, Erik, Kelly Halldorson and his wife Susan, who appeared at the station with James. I served Susan with a Grand Jury Subpoena, requesting her testimony on what she knew about admissions James had made in front of her. I explained to her that she was going to be a witness for the prosecution; therefore, she could not have contact with James.

That turned out to be exactly what happened. Carolann called us to let us know.

I had a feeling that Susan was finally listening now. Between the recorded phone call and Jim giving his statement at the Hospital, there would be little left to prove. They had arrested Jim on three counts of Aggravated Felonious Sexual Assault. We were told this was just to get the ball rolling and there would be more charges to come.

STATE OF NEW HAMPSHIRE

COUNTY: STRAFFORD

COURT: DURHAM DISTRICT

ARREST WARRANT

TO THE SHERIFF OF ANY COUNTY IN THIS STATE OR DEPUTY, OR ANY POLICE OFFICER WITHIN THE STATE.

WHEREAS, THE COMPLAINANT, _Detective Gabe A. Tarrants_ OF THE DURHAM POLICE DEPARTMENT IN THE COUNTY OF STRAFFORD HAS

EXHIBITED TO ME _GERALD TAUBE_ A JUSTICE/JUSTICE OF THE PEACE IN THE COUNTY OF STRAFFORD, HIS COMPLAINT UPON OATH AGAINST THE DEFENDANT, _James Earl Halidorson_ OF _#56 Summer Street, Dover, NH 03820_ IN THE COUNTY OF _Strafford_ FOR THE CRIMES OF _Aggravated Felonious Sexual Assault_ (RSA) 632-A:2

WE COMMAND YOU TO TAKE THE DEFENDANT, IF FOUND TO BE IN YOUR PRECINCT, AND BRING HIM BEFORE THE DURHAM DISTRICT COURT.

DATED THE _1st_ DAY OF _November_, 20_05_

_____
JUSTICE/JUSTICE OF THE PEACE

RETURN

STATE OF NEW HAMPSHIRE)
)
COUNTY OF STRAFFORD   )

I HAVE ARRESTED THE DEFENDANT AND NOW HAVE HIM BEFORE THE COURT AS COMMANDED.

_11-2-05_
DATE

Gabe Tarrants
NAME OF OFFICER

Detective
TITLE OF OFFICER

When I saw it on the Nightly News it really hit me, hard. The magnitude of what Jim's arrest meant was overwhelming. If only they had listened when I was young I wouldn't have to explain to my guys on the job site in the morning why my Father was all over the news. Overnight it was everywhere in my little world. It was on the TV and in all of the newspapers. Not huge, but little snippets here and there.

"Local man arrested..."

"...Sexually assaulting two boys in the '80's..."

"...James E. Halldorson turns self in to local authorities..."

I chased Jim's story around and became obsessed with finding every article I could, on the Internet. It was the same article just worded a little differently. From Boston to Vermont it was out there. Not on the front page, but if you looked for it you could find it.

Jim was released on $25,000 bond pending his arraignment. He was to have no contact with me, Erik, my mother or Kelly. He was required to continue living in Portland and could not possess any weapons nor was he allowed to drink or do drugs.

After Jim's arrest and release on bail there was little for us to do other than wait and wait some more. Carolann kept us abreast via phone calls, emails or letters. We were forced to focus on the everyday happenings. Kelly and I talked about it, but not as much and Erik was just happy to see the *Son of a Bitch* was getting what he deserved.

I had walked into the Durham Police Department on October 3[rd,] and through their diligence the Department had him singing his guilt and arrested by November 2nd. In addition, during that timeframe, both my sons had their birthdays and I ended an inappropriate sexual relationship. It had been one hell of a month.

As fast as the ride began it also seemed to come to a screeching halt. Only little bits here and there popped up.

Susan
(Jeff)

On November 2, 2005 Susan Halldorson was issued a Grand Jury Subpoena.

The State of New Hampshire

Grand Jury Subpoena

TO: SUSAN HALLDORSON

You are required to appear at the GRAND JURY, to be holden at Dover in said country, at 9:00 am in the forenoon on THURSDAY, the 17th day of NOVEMBER A.D. 2005, to testify what you know relating to a case then and there to be heard and tried betwixt State of New Hampshire, Plaintiff, JAMES HALLDORSON, defendant,

HEREOF FAIL NOT, as you will answer your default under the penalties prescribed by law.

Apparently that got her attention and she agreed to be interviewed by Det. Tarrants.

Entered By: Gabe A. Tarrants, On 12/2/05
Title: Sue Halldorson – Tarrants

On 11/15/05, at about 1500 hrs., an audio recorded interview took place between myself, Inv. Hart and Sue Halldorson, at the

Strafford County Attorney's Office. Several days earlier, Sue had been served with a Grand Jury Subpoena, in order to retrieve her testimony about anything she might have known about the sexual abuse. Sue said she heard nothing of the abuse until she was approached by her neighbor, Suzie Armstrong. She said she called James at work and he denied the allegations. When she asked Erik if any of the allegations made by Jeff were true, he said they were not. When she asked Jeff about it, he told her she was just going to believe James anyway. After the conversation, she called her mother who was a nurse and asked her if there were any physical symptoms to look for. Sue said the topic was never discussed again until years later.

Sue said that eight years later, she returned home from work to find Jeff, Erik, Kelly and James at the house. Jeff and Erik said they needed to speak with Sue so they headed out to the porch. As they went outside, James told Sue that "Whatever Suzie said was true" (meaning Suzie Armstrong) Sue said that on the porch Jeff and Erik said they had been molested by James and they were afraid the same thing was happening to their younger brothers. Sue said she asked ▮▮▮▮ and ▮▮▮▮ and they both denied being molested by James. According to Sue, after Jeff and Erik left that night, she decided to sleep on the third floor, away from James. They had a brief conversation where James asked her to talk about the allegations. When she told him she didn't want to talk about it at that time, he said he only admitted to doing it because he was afraid of Jeff and Erik. Sue said she called an attorney a few days later to see what the statute of limitations would be on the assaults. Shortly after that night, she said James started going to Life Counseling. Sue said they never spoke of the allegations again.

Susan was interviewed by Det. Tarrants accompanied by Det. Hart, the same officer from the wiretap. Tarrants had his work cut out for him. It took time and incredible patience to decipher what the hell she was talking about and work through her web of lies and distractions. Her complete interview is more than three times in length and about ten times more confusing than Jim's interview and confession at Mercy Hospital.

Here are just pieces of it.

INTERVIEW BY DETECTIVE TARRANTS:

(Investigator Hart: Go ahead, Gabe, if you want to introduce yourself.)

Q. It's November 15th at 3 O'clock. Where at the Strafford County Attorney's Office, Tom Hart's office. This is Detective Tarrants from the Durham P.D., Tom Hart from the County Attorney's Office and could you state your name for me please?

A. Susan Halldorson

Q. Mrs. Halldorson is here today to talk about what she knows about an incident, incidents pertaining to her husband Jim and their two sons, Jeff and Erik. Mrs. Halldorson, were you ever made aware of any allegations made by Jeff or Erik toward Jim?

A. I was contacted by my neighbor in 1988, in the spring. Her name was Suzie Armstrong. She lived next door to us in Durham. She came to me and said that she had been approached that she and her husband Bruce had been approached by Jeffrey, that he was being molested. I said, "Do you know who it's by?" And she said, "Yes, and Jeffrey said it...that it is his father Jim."

Q. Okay.

A. That was the first indication that I had any knowledge of anything going on. Um, I immediately called my husband who at the time in Massachusetts and he said he didn't know what I was talking about. He denied it. My son Erik was at home at the time, Jeffrey was on the boat with Bruce Armstrong and his children so that Suzie could come talk to me. Um, and I asked Erik and I said "Have you ever been touched by your father in an inappropriate way? Have you ever been molested by your father?" And he said his father had never touched him and that he thought that Jeffrey had lied and made it up.

Q. Now, in the spring of '88, you were pregnant; correct?

A. I was pregnant with my second biological child.

171

Q. The second, which is?

A. ▇▇▇▇

Q. Okay.

A. When Jeffrey came home I asked him because I thought it was a pretty serious allegation.

Q. Um hmm. (Affirmative response)

A. And his basic response to me was "Well, you always take his side it doesn't make any difference what I say. Forget it." And we went from there. It wasn't brought forth again. I did call, um, I was going to take him to the pediatrician and have him examined, although it probably wouldn't have done any good because I'm sure that there was no physical evidence. And I did call, ah, my mother, who is a registered nurse and say, "What do I look for as far as signs" -

A. Um hmm. (Affirmative response)

Q. - ""if there is something that I need to be aware of?" But it was dropped at that point. When Jeffrey said, "Never mind. Forget it."

That was it. That was the defining moment when Susan didn't act as a mother should. She said in her own words that she dropped it and with that choice my mother made it possible for Jim to enter my room once more.

Q. When you found out about the allegations and you talked to Erik, did you hint around at all to how stressful that would be on your pregnancy or anything like that?

A. I don't think I did because I was - I wasn't really thinking about the pregnancy at that point. I had had a very - it had been stressful since the beginning because an episode earlier in the year when Jeffrey tried to burn the house down when he first, ah, found out I was pregnant.

Q. Okay.

A. So, I had already had stress. I don't think I would have brought it up again to Erik. He knew that things were pretty conflicting with Jeffrey and, and his parents during that year.

Q. So did the allegations die down after that?

A. It was never brought up again.

Q. Never brought up?

A. We never - I talked to my neighbor. I should also put in there that my neighbor was not aware that Jeffrey and Erik were adopted. And when -

Q. This is the Armstrongs?

A. The Armstrongs. So, um, I said to her, "By the way, I just need you to know that Erik and Jeffrey are adopted, they are not our biological children, and they come from an abusive background. And we have it in writing that they have witnessed homosexual activity from the social worker in Wisconsin, but were only verbally told that they may have been molested but there was no proof."

Q. This was - So they were how old?

A. In Wisconsin. Ah, right before they were put into foster care, which would have been when they were, I want to say three and four.

Q. Okay - and you didn't hear anything else about any molestation until years later; correct?

A. That's correct. We didn't hear anything else. It was seven years later. I believe they were 22 and 23 years old. My son ███████, who is now 19, was probably around 9 at the time was having trouble sleeping. He was never a good sleeper.

Susan went into evasive mode dancing around the questions and the two detectives did their best to keep up with her. Susan would not admit that she knew anything unless it was dragged out of her.

> Q. So seven years later when Jim said to you, "What Suzie told you was true..." Again no specifics...
>
> A. Nothing, no specifics.
>
> Q. Suzie told you there was molestation and he said that it was true?
>
> A. That's correct.
>
> Q. Okay.
>
> A. That's correct. And still, at this time, did not know that Erik was involved at all. The only two questions I asked when they came over that night was you know, "Why, why wouldn't I have known?" Because I was living in that house with two babies, I wasn't working, and I'm a very light sleeper. And, um, they basically told me it happened when I wasn't in the home.
>
> Q. Didn't you- did you work at -
>
> A. I didn't at that time.
>
> Q.- - outside at the mall at all at that time?
>
> A. I didn't at the time. No. When ▇▇▇ was born, I was no longer working. I did... I stopped working when ▇▇▇▇ was born, um, and went back during the days to train a replacement for six weeks.

On an on it went in twisting circles.

> Q. Were there ever any other conversations after the one where James told you what Suzie said was true?

Every question had to be spelled out in order to get a straight answer, if that was at all possible.

> A. Not – Not with me. Oh, you mean between the two of us?
>
> Q. Between you and Jim and Jeff and Erik or Jeff and Kelly?
>
> A. No. Not between me and Jim or Jeffrey and Erik and Kelly. The only other conversation came when Jeffrey told me he had to have a meeting with ▮▮▮▮▮▮ and ▮▮▮▮.
>
> Q. Um hmm (affirmative response)
>
> A. And I was not present at that one. That was between the boys and their father. I cannot tell you what was said at that meeting.

She even seemed to be confusing herself.

> Q. There wasn't one between you and Jim and Jeff and Kelly where –
>
> A. Absolutely not.
>
> Q. - - where Kelly was asking Jim questions about it?
>
> A. Absolutely not.
>
> Q. No?
>
> A. No.
>
> Q. Okay.
>
> A. No. I have never had a conversation with Kelly and Jim about what – anything at all. I've never discussed this with Kelly.

Apparently she was the only one that didn't remember the conversation and meeting. If she did she was clearly not ready to admit it.

They moved on.

> Q. Okay. Do you remember the baseball game that Jeffrey took the bus down to Boston and met Jim when he got out of work; they went to a Red Sox game?
>
> A. No, I do not. No, I do not.
>
> Q. I guess Jeff was about 14, do you remember that?
>
> A. I don't have any recollection of that at all. I'm sorry. I don't.

Again they move on to question about the Statute of Limitations and her call to the lawyer after the porch disclosure.

> Q. Okay that's fine. As far as emails you said that Kelly emailed you several times prior to the investigation started?
>
> A. Yes. Yes.
>
> Q. What did those contain?
>
> A. Okay. It's basically about hush money and um, um, that I had lied to them about the statute of limitations.
>
> Q. Um hmm (affirmative response)
>
> A. And you know? I was set straight on that recently because I – When the – When they came to the house the second time when they were 22 and 23.
>
> Q. Um hmm (affirmative response)
>
> A. I did call my lawyer, cuz I found it kind of interesting that they waited so many years to come and tell me this. So, I called – At that time....

She went on for a bit in attempt to explain her thoughts on the whole statute of limitations issue....just more circles.

Q. Why – why were you calling about the statute of limitations back then?

A. I was interested to find out why they came at that time to the house to make an accusation, and I wanted to know, you know, why it was so close to the statute of limitations, which I had been told was seven years; if they were just like waiting until the statue ran out to come out and make the second charge. I was confused.

Q. How – Now, you said this in 1988,

A. Right.

Q. - - it was first disclosed to you?

A. Right.

Q. Now, when did you talk about the statute of limitations?

A. Not until they came the second time

That part of the questioning leaves…well…some more questions for me. Did she originally discuss the Statute of Limitations with her lawyer after the first disclosure?

The discussion circled back around to the second disclosure.

A. He said, "Whatever Suzie Armstrong said was correct." And that was Jeffrey.

Q. Was there a conversation about Jeffrey and Erik during that?

A. No.

Q. It was just a conversation about Jeff?

A. It was just – just Jeffrey. Yes. He was the one that Suzie came and told me about.

Q. Because I thought that Erik and Jeff were there, ah, sitting there with Kelly.

A. I'm talking about the first allegation with Suzie, was just about Jeffrey being molested.

Q. Right.

A. The second one, yeah, the second time.

Q. The second there they were all seated together?

A. Kelly, Jeffrey and Erik came, yes.

She didn't even remember who was there. **She couldn't even remember who was there.**

Q. Okay. And at that point, the second time –

A. Yes.

Q. - - both were saying that they were molested by Jim?

A. Yes. Yes.

Q. And you approached Jim and asked about just Jeffrey; not Erik?

A. No. No. No. No. No. No. No. No. The time I approached Jim was when it was – it was first brought to my attention was when I just talked about Jeffrey. The second time that the allegation was made and they came to the house, I never asked Jim. The boys came to us and told me that it was true for both of them. Jim and I never had a conversation that night when the boys were there. Jim was not in the conversation in the beginning; just Kelly, Jeffrey and Erik and I were sitting on the porch when they told me.

Q. Okay. And when they told you, they both told you that they were molested, Jeff and Erik did; correct?

A. Yes.

Q. Okay. And then you had a conversation after with your husband Jim?

A. Yes.

Q. And how soon after, that night, the next day?

A. No. That night.

Q. That night?

A. That night?

Q. In person or I thought you called him?

A. No. No. No. He was – He was –

Q. I guess we're going to have to start right from the beginning on the second time.

A. Okay. Okay.

Q. The second time –

A. Yes.

Q. – when there was a disclosure of this information, Jeff, Erik were at your house where, in what town?

A. In the kitchen.

Q. Okay. And your husband Jim was there, present?

A. He was – he had just come home from work, is my understanding. I was not in the home when they arrived.

Q. Okay. And Kelly was there?

A. I believe, yes, she was there with them.

Q. Okay. So then, you arrived?

A. I came home.

Q. And then you learned that there is a – a second disclosure at that point of Jim molesting Erik and Jeff:

A. Just that – Yes. Okay. Yes. Yeah. They didn't actually tell me right out. What they said was, "We're here because we're concerned that ▇▇▇▇▇▇'s not sleeping through the night. We'd like to go and speak to him." And I went upstairs and asked the biological children if they had ever been touched by their father, with Erik and Jeffrey present.

Q. Okay. But prior to even going upstairs, -

A. Right.

Q. - - there was conversation about them being molested?

A. No. Not until – Not until we went upstairs and they asked the boys first. Then when we came downstairs - there was conversation about the molestation on the front porch.

Q. Okay. So, Jim had to be there for that; correct?

A. He did not go upstairs with me when I asked the biological children.

Q. When you came back down and when you had the a conversation –

A. He was in the kitchen. He was in the kitchen.

Q. Okay. So, you were all together at one point when there was a disclosure in front of him with you present and - and Jim?

A. I would have to say yes. I honestly don't remember where he was but I would have to say yes.

Q. Okay. And the disclosure was that they were both molested.

A. Yes.

Q. Okay. And Jim said that that's true?

A. He said, "What Suzie Armstrong said was true." He never admitted to Erik, to my knowledge.

Q. Okay. But they're both sitting there –

A. That's correct.

Q. - - in front of him saying that he molested them?

A. That's correct.

Q. And isn't it true that he said he was going to get help for this?

A. He had a conversation with Jeffrey. I did not have a conversation with him. I believe he and Jeffrey had a conversation about getting help.

Q. Okay.

A. I was not present at that conversation.

Q. Did they refer to what type of molestation took place?

A. No.

Q. Okay. And did –

A. They did not give me details.

Q. And at – at that point, obviously, the first point, from what I'm understanding, you didn't believe the allegations in 1988?

A. That's correct. Cuz, Erik told me that Jeffrey had lied and made it up and that his father had never touched him.

Q. Okay. And I'm assuming at that point, hearing from him, the kids, and Jim at that point, you believe it, that it happened?

A. I believed that something may have happened, yes.

Q. Okay. Well, in fact, something did happen because Jim said it happened; correct?

A. He did say that. "What Suzie said was correct." That's right.

INVESTIGATOR HART: Okay. Jeff and Erik were there when Jim told you that; right? Was he in their presence?

A. I'd have to say – I'd have to say probably yes. I honestly – You know? I honestly don't remember where Jim was. I have to tell you the truth, I don't. I'm not going to lie about it, I don't remember where he was. But I would have to think that he would have probably been in the kitchen with us and then he – I don't know whether he came out on the front porch with us or not. I honestly don't remember. All I remember is sitting on the front porch with Kelly, Jeffrey, myself and Erik. I don't remember where Jim was at that point, to tell the truth.

That never happened. There was never a time where the four of us sat and talked about this on her front porch. It's no wonder she kept confusing herself and the investigators. Not only was she juggling lies, but she had merged three separate meetings in her mind. One with Erik and I disclosing in front of Jim, second being Kelly and I visiting her the next day on the front porch and the third being our meeting with myself, Kelly, her and Jim.

They circled back around to the Statute.

Q. Okay. So, when you called a – lawyer about the statute of limitations, -

A. Um hmm (affirmative response)

Q. - - that was – was that back – If I'm understanding that right, just forgive me if I don't understand that.

A. No. That's okay.

Q. The first time?

A. No.

Q. Was that the first –

A. No. The second time that I called.

Q. It was the second disclosure when the group was together?

A. Right.

Q. And why were you calling on the statute of limitations?

A. I wanted to know why they had waited the number of years that they did, that they didn't come back before then. And I was curious. I knew that there was such a thing as a statute of limitations and I was just trying to find out if they were waiting – that they didn't want to do anything about it, were they not coming in time to make charges. I was confused as to why they had waited to come the seven years.

Q. Okay. I mean I – I'm not trying to be sarcastic but –

A. No, that's okay.

Q. - -I guess, does it matter? Did it matter, the statute of limitations?

A. I was curious. I just wanted to know. I wondered why they had waited the amount of time they had.

Q. Yeah.

A. That's all

Q. Okay.

A. That's all. There wasn't anything other than I was – wondered why they had waited the number of years that they had. And that Erik had never come forth with any of this.

Q. And did Jim talk to you about this after this?

A. No. He didn't talk to me about it. He just said that he didn't – He said that he admitted that he did it because he was afraid they were going to beat the crap out of him. That's all he said to me.

Q. So, he only admitted that he did it because they were going to beat the crap out of him?

A. That's correct.

Q. So to this day, do you believe the allegations?

A. Ah, I have – I have some questions.

She had some questions. I wonder what exactly those questions were.

Q. And you – you even have questions that the boys went in front of Jim and Jim said it? I mean there a – was there some type of force shown in front of Jim the day that you were there and there was a disclosure in front of you that would make him say this?

A. Not to me because I wasn't there when it – when they confronted him in the beginning. I wasn't home.

Q. Di d you have a conversation with Jim after about this?

A. No. We talked –

Q. – and never talked about it again?

A. No. We talked about it. He said that they came in and they grabbed him and they told him that if he didn't tell me truth, they would beat the crap out of him. That's what Jim told me.

Q. Okay. And did – did he say he was getting help for it, and do you know what type of help he got or that?

A. He went to some gentleman by the name of ▮▮▮▮ who referred him to I don't know who.

Q. Okay. And it was for the sexual assaults, the molestations?

A. I honestly don't know. That conversation was between he and James and I didn't have any contact with ▮▮▮▮.

Q. How long were you with, ah, Jim after the disclosure, I mean together?

A. I have always been with him, until a year ago.

Q. Okay. And this conversation never came up again after that disclosure and what he was doing for help or was there any concern in your mind with him about what was going on?

A. No. Because the children that were living in the home said that he had never touched them, and the older children were no longer living in the home.

Q. Okay. And did – Isn't that how that originally started out in '88, that they just said, "Forget about it" and – I mean back then, he – he – he lied to you and said nothing happened; correct? And then now he's saying, seven years later, that it did happen. I mean is that true?

A. He said it happened.

Q. - - the way that went?

A. No. He said it happened, yeah.

Q. And did he seem sincere with you about it or did he seem frightened? I mean I'm trying to get a gist of how this conversation took place. I mean if he was frightened and he – and he – and you felt like he was forced into the statement, I guess you were there and that's – that's what I'm asking you about.

A. I don't think he was frightened but I think he felt (forced) into the statement, yes.

Q. Why would – Why do you think he'd go all the way to Massachusetts for counseling if he was just agreeing with Jeff and Erik at that day because he was scared of them? Do you think he would have gone all the way to Massachusetts for counseling?

A. I don't think he knew where else to go. This is somebody that he was referred to from his company. He asked for a referral when he was working in Massachusetts. So I don't think he knew where else to go.

Q. But would he have really had to have gone to the counseling if there, in fact, hadn't been a reason to go; if he was just saying yes to satisfy them?

A. Well, there were other reasons he went for counseling. He was also an alcoholic.

Q. Was it an alcohol counselor or was it a - some sort - of overall life counselor?

A. I think it he's a – I think he's an overall – I think he's an overall life counselor. I don't think he's – he's in a specific area. I don't know him. I really don't know what his expertise is. I don't know him.

Q. Okay. Are you aware of the allegations to this day of what's going on?

A. I'm sorry? Yeah.

Q. You're aware of everything that's going on to this day?

A. No.

Q. You're not?

A. No, I'm not.

Q. Okay. And has Jim had any conversation with you since the allegation's come out?

A. No. I haven't seen or talked to him or had any contact with him.

Q. Okay. So to this point, from that conversation that everybody had together, you still have doubts in your mind about this; is that what you're saying?

A. I do, to some degree, yeah. You know? I find it difficult because my husband is a womanizer, that I find it difficult that he – that, ah, he would – he's a sexual predator.

Q. When I spoke to you on the phone he first time, -

A. Um hmm (affirmative response)

Q. - - I think I had called you at St. Thomas.

A. Yes, you did.

Q. I hadn't talked to your husband yet.

A. Um hmm (affirmative response)

Q. Then when you called me back to say that you weren't going to hold to our meeting that next week, it was after I talked to Jim –

A. Um hmm (affirmative response)

Q. - - and you had spoken to him –

A. Um hmm (affirmative response)

Q. - - after my meeting with him. What did tell you?

A. The –

Q. Did he tell you anything about the meeting?

A. No. No. He didn't talk to me about the meeting but he said – The reason that I said that I didn't want to have a meeting with you was he said that he had talked to Jeffrey and said that he was upset that had been confrontational with his mother, with me.

Q. Um hmm (affirmative response)

A. And had some things, you know, "I don't care if you attack me but I don't want you to attack your mother" And Jeffrey said, "Well, she lies to put herself in a better situation We all know that but if you hold me to it, I'll deny it." And then he said he had a conversation about his brother ▇ and he said, "Well, ▇ isn't talking to me and I don't know why." And Jeffrey said that ▇ wasn't talking to his father because he told him he was a sexual predator and that's not true. He and Jeffrey had had a confrontation over the summer and they had stopped speaking because ▇ is only 17 and he wanted an apology for – from his brother because he said some things to him that he didn't like, and so they were just not speaking. It had nothing to do with his father. And that's why I said I didn't want to speak to you because I was upset that he had brought this up, that, you know, he had told ▇ that and they hadn't had – ever that conversation. And I felt like it was an attack on my character to, you know, say, "Well, she lies to put herself in a good situation"

On and on it went. She forgot this or couldn't remember that. The one thing she stood firm on was that she knew nothing about what happened. That they had never discussed it other than those two, brief, exchange of words, nearly a decade apart.

Q. Okay. Then why don't you just start right from the beginning of that conversation (at the house), exactly how it started and what was said.

A. Ah, I can't tell you verbatim what was said. Um, I can only tell you that I came into the house with the two children. And the – Jeffrey and Erik and Kelly were there in the kitchen and they said, "We need to have a conversation but we want to see the little kids first." We understand that ███████ is not sleeping through the night and we want to have a conversation with him." And so I said, "Okay" And I said, "Can you tell me what it's about?" And they said, "Well, we want to know if Dad's molesting ███████ or ███," because he's not, you know.

Q. Okay

A. And I said, "Okay. We got to go upstairs and we'll ask the boys." And so, Erik and Jeffrey and I went up there, Kelly did not come with us. Upstairs I asked ███████ and ███, had they ever been touched inappropriately by their father or in any way shape or form. And they both denied it and immediately began crying. And you know, then we went downstairs and proceeded to go out on the porch and have a conversation about this. And that is when I learned that Erik said that he had also been molested by his father.

Q. Okay. And what did Jim say? What was his response'?

A. There was no response from him at this point. I... I'm trying to tell you, I don't remember where he was at this point. I can only remember that it was the boys, Kelly and myself on the front porch. I honestly don't remember Jim being in the conversation at that time.

Q. Okay. At what time was he involved in the conversation?

A. I -after he - After he said in the kitchen when he said, "What Suzie told you is true." That's the only thing I remember him saying to me that night.

Q. So the only thing he says that night you remember is, "Whatever Suzie said, that's true"?

A. That's correct.

Q. And he wasn't present during the time that Erik said he molested him?

A. He may have been I honestly don't remember. I'm not trying to be dishonest with you. I just honestly don't remember other than it was the boys, myself and Kelly on the front porch.

It is hard to imagine forgetting anything that happened on the day that her two oldest kids tell her that her husband was molesting them. To wash away that memory must have taken a lot of effort, or lack of caring.

Q. Okay. And I'm not trying to be difficult with you either but -

A. No. I understand.

Q.- but you've got to understand something.

A. Okay.

Q. You - You were there and part of a conversation that I'm sure that they went there and their whole purpose of this is to bring the family together to disclose this information; not to have someone in one part of the house and in another of the other house and I - I honestly think that they were together and there was a disclosure said in front of him. And I think that there was more said than, "Whatever Suzie said was true." I don't know how someone could get together like that and make such a disclosure, approach your other children- and then come back down, and he never said anything else. I - I find that hard to believe. That's what I'm having a hard time believing.

A. I understand that and I'm trying to be honest with you. I don't remember other than that comment. There may have been conversation but I am telling you that I don't remember. I have no reason to keep it from you. If I could – I'm not going to make something up that I don't remember.

It was clear that there was little to be gained. Either Susan had washed her hands of the whole thing or she wasn't going to tell.

Q. And I don't want you to make anything up.

A. I don't remember. No, I'm trying –

Q. And I think you're – I think you're a relatively intelligent person and – and I –

A. And I am not trying to keep anything from you. I honestly don't remember, except for the boys and Kelly and myself being on the front porch. Was Jim there? I honestly cannot remember.

Q. And Erik, you do remember Erik and Jeff saying that Jim molested them?

A. I remember that me asking Erik if he – Erik saying to me – I said, "Why are you here?" And Erik saying to me, "Because Dad molested me, too"

Q. Okay. And then at some point, you talk with Jim, individually?

A. Not until after the boys had left. The boys went home.

Q. So they –

A. The boys and Kelly left.

Q. So, they went home.

A. They went home.

Q. They went home after that?

A. They went home after that.

Q. And then what did you say with Jim?

A. I went upstairs and I asked him, I said, "Is it," you know, "you're telling me that what Suzie said is true, and not you're telling me that was because the boys were going to beat you up?" And he said,

"I have nothing more to say," you know, basically. We didn't discuss the conversation anymore.

Q. He was upstairs at that point, in the bedroom?

A. No. He was in the – I was on the third floor and he was in the – in our bedroom. I was up on the third floor. We had a third floor. I was not in the room with him. I wasn't going to spend the night with him.

Q. But you went down to that bedroom to – to speak with him?

A. He came up to the third floor to speak to me.

Q. He came up.

A. He came to me. I did not go to him. He came to me. I needed some time to just collect myself, cuz I still had two small children in the house that I had to take care of.

Q. Exactly. Exactly.

A. Yeah. So, I needed to collect myself, get the boys organized, you know, get them dinner and bed and son on and so forth. So, I basically took care of the little kids and got them in bed and went up on the third floor, and was trying to just collect myself before I had a conversation with him and he came to me.

Q. Okay. And that's what I'm trying to say here.

A. Okay.

Q. I'm glad that you're saying that because I think they lowered the boom on you and all of a sudden you're in a predicament now that your husband is in the house, you have other kids in the house, and now there's this disclosure that they're molested again, ah, for the second time, and he's admitting that it happened. What is his reactions? What is his demeanor at that point?

A. Um, he's very quiet, very withdrawn, and not saying much. He's you know, he's not saying much at all.

Q. He comes back up to you on the third floor because –

A. Yeah.

Q. Now I'm assuming; correct me if I'm wrong, you didn't want to stay with him that night because of this disclosure?

A. No. I didn't want to – No. I needed time to myself, obviously, yes.

Q. Right.

A. I wasn't sure what was going on. My mind was going a thousand different directions.

Q. Okay.

A. I had two other kids in the house. I had two kids that had left, gone out of the home –

Q. Right.

A. - - with, you know, like you said, giving me all this information. I needed to kind of filter through things.

Q. All right. And when you went back into the house after they left off the front porch, where – where was Jim?

A. I would say probably in the kitchen or on the second floor or –

Q. And is that the first time you had a conversation about this disclosure?

A. I don't – I don't remember. I'm not trying to be obnoxious. I just – I don't remember the events after the boys left, other than I had to take care of the children, and the boys saying to me, "Whatever you decide, Mom, we'll disp – we'll support your decision. Whether you stay with him or you don't, we'll support your decision."

Q. "The boys" meaning?

A. Jeffrey and Erik.

Q. "Jeffrey and Erik"

A. Right. "Whatever you decide, Mom, we'll"

Q. Right.

A. - - "support your decision," is what they said to me.

Q. Right.

A. And we left it at that. We knew there had been a lot of -

Q. And of course they would because it's not you; it's Jim that did this.

A. Right. I understand that.

Q. And that's what they're saying to you. So, you go back in, and I'm assuming after this has been dropped on you - you had to have had a conversation with Jim. And that's what I'm-

A. After – It would have to have been after I had taken care of the boys because, obviously, I'm trying to take care of these little kids that are running through the house.

Q. Exactly.

A. - - like "What's going on? What's going on?" And, you know, I'm like – So, it was that evening and he came up to the third floor and he said, you know, he just was very quiet and didn't say much, and I told him that I basically could not discuss it with him that night. I was too distraught to talk about anything.

Q. Okay. And what point did he disclose any information to you?

A. He never did. He never came back and ever told me again. Other than, "What Suzie said was true." We –

Q. And when did he say that to you?

A. That was in the kitchen when he said – Before the boys and I had the conversation, when he came and he said "Whatever Suzie told you was true." That was when they first came to the house.

Q. So, when you first came to the house, you walked into the kitchen and – and Jeff, Erik and Kelly, and Jim –

A. And Jim were all in the kitchen together.

Q. - - were all in the kitchen together?

A. Right.

Q. And he immediately says to you –

A. No. No. No. No. First the boys say, "We need to talk to you. We want to talk to ▄▄▄▄ and ▄▄▄▄. " That's – That's – That happened first.

Q. Alright.

A. That's the first sequence of events.

Q. And what do they say that they need to talk to -

And around they go again....

Q. isn't the purpose of that meeting to disclose this in front of Jim and confront him?

A. I – I – I thought it was to tell me. To make it – To tell me. I wasn't sure. I mean obviously it was because they wanted me to know what was going on but I – didn't look at it as that being confrontational with Jim. I thought they were there to let me know because they were worried about their younger brothers. That's how I took it. That was my take on it.

Q. And to make you aware of it?

A. And to make me aware that what they had said back in 1988, and which was denied, had, you know, was then they were saying it was true.

Q. Okay.

INVESTIGATOR HART: When did Jim tell you that he was in fear of the boys and that's why he told you?

A. That – That evening when he came to the third floor.

INVESTIGATOR HART: And how'd he - How'd he say – How'd that come about? Did he just jump right out and say it, or –

A. Yes. No. He just came right upstairs.

INVESTIGATOR HART: did you ask him or –

A. Oh no. No. No. He came upstairs and he said, "I just need you to know that the reason that I admitted to anything was because I was in fear of being beaten to a pulp." That's what he said to me.

Q. Okay. And –

INVESTIGATOR HART: What was your response?

A. I didn't have much. I didn't think that was very rational. I just said, "I don't want to talk about this right now. I need some time to ingest to what they have said to me."

INVESTIGATOR HART: And he has never admitted to this, um, from that point on to you?

A. To me? No.

Q. Or to anybody else that you know of?

A. Not to anybody else that I know of, no. Not to me. And I haven't been with him in any other – with any other people that he's talked about it with.

Q. Okay. And this conversation never came back up again? It was dropped and even when you got your thoughts and got your things together the next day, nothing was ever brought up again to Jim?

A. We didn't talk about it again, no.

Q. And the only time that you ever brought it up again is when you called a lawyer for a statute of limitations?

A. I wanted to find out why – Then next day, I wanted to know why the boys had waited that amount of years, first, to come and accuse him of that. And I wondered if it was they were – wanted to bring it before the statute ran out or after the statute ran out. I was curious to know why the number of years had taken place.

Q. Who, um, I mean is that something that you thought of on your own or was it something you talked to Jim about or –

A. No. I never talked to Jim about it. My – My – ah uncle was a lawyer so I knew – I knew.

Q. So, you disclosed this to your uncle?

A. No. No. My uncle was in Wilmington. I called Attorney Reid in Dover, who was my lawyer. I wanted to know –

Q. Alright. But where did you get the idea of statute of limitations? I mean I – From my 20 years of experience, people don't typically think of statute of limitations when their kids disclose that they've been molested.

A. I don't know. I can't – You know? I didn't talk to Jim about it but I can't honestly tell you why I – I called because I was curious the number – the number of years that had gone by being just so many years why it was so many years.

Q. Okay. I guess I'm going to ask you a question.

A. Okay.

Q. Um, if you didn't believe the kids at that point, or if you did, were you concerned that there was a problem with the statute of limitations?

A. I was – I told them that if they were going to file, I thought that they needed to file within a period of time before the statute of limitations ran out. If they wanted to file – I told Jeffrey and Erik that if they wanted to file a case, that I was going to find out what the statute of limitations was, and if they were going to file, they needed to do it before it ran out.

Q. Okay. So, was that part of the conversation on the front porch?

A. No. That was afterwards. It wasn't that same night. I hadn't made the phone call yet.

There was never a conversation with Susan about statutes of limitation until she informed Kelly and I that they had run out. I put faith in her that she cared enough to inform us of the truth. As it turns out I believe she was just protecting herself and her husband, waiting for this all to go away, which it did for a while.

Q. Okay. So, the next day, or after that –

A. Or – Or sometime after that, yes.

Q. – you had a conversation with Jeffrey and Erik about the statute of limitations?

A. I don't know whether it was both of them or whether it was just Jeffrey or just Erik but I said, you know, that if they wanted to pursue this and file charges, they should find out about the statute of limitations, and I would call the lawyer and see what it was.

Q. Okay. Well, that –

A. Okay.

Q. – that –

A. See, you have to understand, I'm trying – I'm trying to think through this process –

Q. No. That's fine but that's –

A. – while you're talking to me.

Q. –that's making me understand –

A. Okay.

Q. – why you would just call someone.

A. I'm more than, you know, I'm like sort of this is so many years that so much has just like (INAUDIBLE).

Q. Yeah. And that – that makes – That helps me understand.

A. Okay.

Q. Did you talk to them about reporting this to the police after they disclosed it to you?

A. I asked them why they didn't report it. I honestly don't remember their response. I'm sorry.

Around and around and around....moving forward again...

Q. Okay. And when this came out, when the police became involved did you have conversation with Jim by phone?

A. About the police?

Q. About the police and about the charges and about what was going on?

A. Not the charges. He called me and told me that Jeffrey had called him, um, and had a conversation with him and that, um, he had gotten upset and confronted Jeffrey about being confrontational about his mother being a liar and something that –

Q. Right.

A. - - Kelly had said about perfect decorations and perfect so and so forth.

Q. Right.

A. And about ▮▮▮▮, the conversation about ▮▮▮▮ and, um, there was nothing told to me about charges or Jeffrey doing charges. I didn't know that –

Q. Anything about molestation –

A. No.

Q. – of him and Erik

A. No. No.

Q. So he didn't mention anything about that?

A. No. No. He was talking basically about the conversation he had had about Jeffrey saying – He said he confronted him about me being a liar and – um – that Kelly had made some comments about me and that he was unhappy about that. The next conversation I had with him was he said that he had been interviewed by two police detectives –

Q. Okay.

A. - - and he just said he'd been interviewed. He didn't say anything about charges being put on him or anything and he said, "I've been interviewed by two police detectives for the last two hours, um, that about the conversation that Jeffrey apparently had called me, the police were listening too. And that you probably will be interviewed next." Is what he said to me. But we never discussed charges or what was said when they were there.

Q. Well, I mean, obviously, he must have said why they were there, why the police –

A. Well, he said Jeffrey – that - Jeffrey was going to bring charges against him.

Q. Okay.

A. Okay. But we didn't discuss specific charges. He just said that the police had been up there because Jeffrey was going to press charges against him.

Q. And was there any mention of Erik?

A. No. I didn't even know Erik was involved.

Q. Okay.

A. Until, um, when he was arrested and I was told, I think, that Erik was –

Q. Okay. So, that day that he was – he was – the detectives spoke to him –

A. Right.

Q. – in Portland –

A. Right

Q. – – um, he called you and said that they'll probably be coming to talk to you?

A. Right.

Q. Did he know that or did the detectives say that or?

A. No. I don't – I don't know whether he said that or not but he told me that. He said, "They probably will be coming to interview you next." That's all he said to me.

Q. And did he say anything about what you, ah, may or may not say –

A. No.

Q. – or have to say or –

A. No.

Q. – or if you should see a lawyer –

A. No.

Q. – – or anything like that?

A. No. He knows – He knows better than to tell me what to say.

Q. Okay. Why?

A. Because I'm a very independent person and I don't listen to what he says to tell me what to say. I, you know, I don't need him to tell me, "Don't say" or "Do say"

Q. Okay.

A. No.

INVESTIGATOR HART: On the second disclosure, the one that he said afterwards that he had just agreed with them because he was scared.

A. Um hmm (affirmative response)

INVESTIGATOR HART: Did you have any fear for ▇▇▇ and ▇▇▇ after that?

A. No, I did not.

Q. None whatsoever?

A. None.

Q. Had you left them alone with him after that?

A. Yes. Um hmm (affirmative response). I also at the time that they came, the – the allegations, I was doing babysitting in my home –

INVESTIGATOR HART: The first one? The first allegation?

A. No The one in 1990 – The seven year one when they came when they were 22 and 23.

INVESTIGATOR HART: Okay. Yeah.

A. In fact, I had been watching my grandchildren for a period of time, Kelly and Jeffrey's children. Um there were three people in my home that I was watching their children, and I went to them and said there had been an allegation made against Jim and I wanted them to know that because they were in my home and Jim was living in my home still, and if they were uncomfortable about it, that I would please like them to remove their children from "their" home and they did not.

INVESTIGATOR HART: Okay.

A. And they did not. I went to three separate people. I can give you their names and you can check with them if you -

> INVESTIGATOR HART: Did you reassure them that Jim was never alone with the kids anyway?
>
> A. No
>
> INVESTIGATOR HART: That it was always you or –
>
> A. No, In fact, even with the grandchildren, he was alone at times. They lived with us for a period of time, with the two grandchildren. When they moved back from Arizona they lived with us.

Again her memory is completely off. We stayed with them for a week and a half after moving back to New Hampshire when Wolfgang was a year and a half and Kelly was pregnant with Griffin. As far as the kids being alone with Jim, unless she went out of her way to secretly make it happen...it didn't. We made damn sure of that.

The investigators once again circled back around in their questioning.

> Q. I mean he makes this vague statement after all these years, seven years, "What Suzie said is true" There must have been conversations over the years about this. I mean for him just to come out of the blue seven years later, you come home and him say, "What Suzie said is true," and understand that to mean he molested kids. I mean that must have been – There must have been something that was always stuck out in your head?
>
> A. There wasn't any more to the conversation. I still only believed it was Jeffrey at that point until we went out on the porch.
>
> Q. Right.
>
> A. - - and, um, we – did not talk about it over the years. We did not.
>
> Q. Okay. Now, as much as a strained relationship as you all had with Jeff and Erik, do you think that that might have been because of a molestation because those allegations were true and that's why they were so withdrawn and angry or –

A. I don't think so. There was – There were a lot of things that came with when – They came with a lot of different issues when the adoption took place.

Q. Did they always have them growing up –

A. Yes.

Q. – throughout?

A. Yeah. We've always had quite a few issues. They've been in counseling since they were adopted. They were both removed from the home at one point.

Q. What if – what if we were to tell you that Jim admitted to us that the molestation was true, would it shock you, would it reinforce something you had always thought, or?

A. I don't think it would shock me. I think there's always been a seed of doubt in my mind. I don't think it's a shock.

That would be as close as they would come to Susan stating that she had any knowledge of any abuse happening in her house. The only thing left was to try and understand the woman, what she thought, how she felt and what her motivations were.

The detectives had the same conversation with Susan over and over again, each time with a different result. In less than eight years my mother was able to forget the night we disclosed to her the horrors our father subjected us to as children. She was able to let the memories of begging us to *forgive her*, slip away.

An Anniversary & Brass Knuckles

(Kelly)

Det. Tarrants had gathered the statements from everyone pertaining to the case. Susan had her interview and Suzie Armstrong had been contacted and her statement was given over the phone.

We were notified that Jim and Susan had hired the services of Shaheen & Gordon, the very same law firm Jeff had approached a few years prior regarding his rights as a sexual abuse victim. A firm, to which, he disclosed information directly relating to the case against his father. On top of it there was the long list of interactions Bill Shaheen had with the Halldorson family as a Durham District Court Judge. He was the judge who helped send Jeff to the rehabilitation centers and made it possible for his parents to keep him institutionalized. He was the judge who removed Jeff from his parent's home and emancipated him at the age of 17.

As a judge he performed his duties as a judge seeing only what was presented before him: A troubled kid that went to school with his daughter, with as far as anyone could see church-going, upstanding citizens for parents. It makes sense in his ruling he hoped to *help* the troubled teen while unburdening the parents.

In my opinion he also had showed some moral character behind the bench when tearing into Jeff's mother for her locking Jeff out of the house. *What if he was cold? What if he was hungry?* He had asked.

Why would someone with seemingly strong moral focus allow his firm to represent an admitted pedophile after having discussed the allegations previously with one of the victims?

Beside myself, I knew there had to be some sort of conflict of interest. I urged Jeff to talk to Carolann about it. In addition I looked into things myself. We decided to contact the firm. We then received a letter from Shaheen himself stating, among other reasons, Jeff had not retained their counsel (because no money was exchanged) and therefore the firm believed there was no "attorney/client privilege" involved. So, despite Bill Shaheen being listed as a possible witness, were the case to go to trial, they had every intention of continuing to represent James.

We were not the only ones who took issue with Shaheen representing James Halldorson. In February of 2006, the Strafford County Attorney's office filed a motion to disqualify current counsel for the defendant.

It made the news. After getting notice from Shaheen and Gordon of their plans to continue to represent James, Jeff and I decided to write a letter to the New Hampshire Bar Association. We elicited the help of my Uncle Bob in California, a lawyer. In it we informed the NH Bar of all interactions between Jeff and Bill Shaheen as well as Bill Shaheen's response to our request to recuse himself.

It would be only a few weeks before James Halldorson's arraignment on Jeff's and my 10th Wedding Anniversary, March 6th, 2006.

When we arrived at the Strafford County Courthouse we met Erik in the parking lot and went in together. We met up with Carolann in her office then all walked to the courtroom together. Just outside the courtroom doors there are three conference rooms. We saw Sue as we walked past the first conference room, where she and Jim were meeting with the attorney from Shaheen & Gordon. We heard raised voices and witnessed angry faces. As we walked by, one of the occupants caught sight of either us or Assistant County Attorney Gentes and shut the door.

After a brief discussion in the conference room regarding what the County Attorney's office expected from the defendants camp we headed into the courtroom. Carolann sat with us. She whispered softly to us about every step, keeping us informed about all that was happening in the courtroom around us. The courtroom doors opened and in walked Jeff's mother, wearing her customary large dark sunglasses paired with a set of pursed lips. She was angry. She looked directly at us not saying or offering any kind of positive gesture.

Both Erik and Jeff were visibly shaken by her appearance in the court and clearly hurt by her coldness, though not surprised by it.

James Halldorson walked into the courtroom accompanied by his representation from Shaheen and Gordon.

We all rose as the judge took to the bench.

Please be seated.

Then out of nowhere...

Excuse me, Your Honor, but before these proceedings begin I ask to address the court.

It was Jim's attorney.

Go ahead.

Well you see Your Honor, it has come to the attention of Shaheen and Gordon that there is a conflict of interest which I am sure that you have been made aware of. Originally we thought felt as though there was no conflict but having reviewed our records we have concluded that there was more communication with one of the victims in this case than we had originally thought - therefore we have discussed it with our client and I have decided to recuse myself from representing James Halldorson.

That was it. He picked up his briefcase, turned and left the courtroom, rushing out as if he was late for some kind of urgent meeting. The judge moved on as if nothing had happened. Jim stood in front of the courtroom forced to face up to his unthinkable crimes, alone.

Well, we are here to hear you James Halldorson enter a plea to the charges against you. Are you prepared to do that? And have you contacted another firm to represent you?

Yes and yes your honor. I will be represented by the office of Lincoln Soldati.

Very well, Mr. Halldorson. The judge went on to read the charges.

What do you have to say to these charges?

Whether due to the pressure of the moment or being stranded by his legal counsel, he was disoriented. He opened his mouth but the only thing that came out was angry rambling. He made no sense, to either the judge or anyone else in the room.

There was a back and forth between the judge and James. James wanted to address the conditions of his bail among the rest of mess laid in front of him. He took issue with having to stay up in Portland and explained that he had two teen sons that he still needed to parent. He wanted to be able to stay in Durham if he so chose and have contact with Sue.

With all of his rambling and bitching he was somewhat of a show. The people in the courtroom, including our group, suppressed nervous laughter and exchanged looks of shock. The judge just wanted a guilty or not guilty plea. Jim seemed incapable of answering the question directly.

Ok sir, all I want from you at this point is a plea. We are not here for trial of this case. I don't need to know the facts. Just guilty or not guilty, that's all. Do you understand?

I – um – I just

Sir – do you understand?

And finally...

Yes.

Ok, then how do you plead? Sir? You could hear the irritation in the judge's voice.

Your Honor - I - I plead not guilty.

Sue got up and walked out. She didn't wait to speak with, or see Jim after arraignment and she made absolutely no attempt at contact with either Jeff or Erik. When she walked out of that courtroom we didn't see her again. She didn't step foot in the courtroom again, not for any subsequent hearings, not even for the sentencing.

In the end the judge went ahead and changed his bail conditions as to allow him sometime in the Dover house and contact with his biological sons and Sue. He was still barred from contact with Jeff, Erik and I and there was a limit to how close he could get to our home.

After the arraignment we met with Carolann, Asst. Eric Gentes and County Attorney and County Attorney Janice Rundles to discuss what we could expect over the next year.

Eric Gentes was the first to speak. *We believe, what is going to happen next is your father will find another lawyer then we will begin a back and forth on a plea agreement. I don't think any lawyer will attempt to take this to trial. There is too much evidence against James. He has admitted multiple times to these crimes to both witnesses and law enforcement.*

In other words any lawyer is going to advise him that it would be in his best interest to try and plead this case out. Janice entered in the discussion. *So, what we'd like to know from you all is, how do you feel about this? Is there an amount of time you'd feel is...*

Oh, I don't know. Jeff responded.

We won't take any kind of plea if you are not comfortable with it. But we can speed things up and make it easier for you all, and obviously everyone involved if we do come to a plea agreement but we'd like to know how you feel about that.

I don't care. I just want him to go away and this to be done. That was all Erik had to say on it all.

I guess I'd have to think about that. Do you have some ideas as far as time goes? I mean I don't think I'd want him in jail for less than five years.

I couldn't imagine trying to figure out an adequate punishment for someone who'd wronged me so. I, myself, being so close to the whole situation had a hard time thinking of any punishment for James that wasn't viciously primal and didn't include removal of body parts or infliction of excruciating physical pain. So, when I heard Jeff say *five years.* I thought...*what, NO WAY!*

I took a deep breath in an attempt to contain myself. I hated to see Jeff sell himself so short. All those years of pain...and all those years Jim spent free and clear? In response Jeff really thought all that was worth was five years?

I – I??

Yes, Kelly?

*I think, well – I **really** I think he shouldn't get out. Period. I - mean hasn't he been out long enough? What about –*

Yes, yes – we understand, we just need to be realistic and um – we think the reality is that he is in his 50's with a heart condition – so...

When I say, five years I mean – well – for each of us.

Oh, yes – Jeff we do think that is possible. Give it some more thought and contact us if you have any more thoughts on that - let us know – let Carolann know. We could aim for 7 to 13 years and probably get that with a plea but we'll talk more.

So, how long does the process take? Jeff asked.

Well the whole thing can take up to a year. It will depend on how back logged the court system is. We should know soon enough as to when that trial date is set. There will be some delay because his new lawyer will be allowed time to get up to speed on the case.

It wasn't long before Jim had found himself in trouble again.

On May 18, 2006, Jim was arrested for a weapons possession less than a block from our house.

In the early evening Jim was riding his bike in Dover. While doing so he ran his bike into the back of a car. Our home in Dover was directly between Susan's home and where James rode his bike into the back of the vehicle. In the report given to us by the County Attorney's office it stated that Jim was under the influence of prescription pills. His speech was slurred and slow. He was unable to complete simple tasks.

Jim appeared confused and confrontational at one point with the police officer. He was released from the hospital without injury but arrested for Possession of metallic knuckles in pursuant of RSA 159:16.

His explanation was inconsistent, first saying he had found them in his son's room and was going to throw them in the Cocheco River. Later he said that he had gotten into a fight with his wife then found them on his dresser but had no idea how they got there.

Once he was cleared medically at the hospital and all information was gathered relating to the weapons charge and his strange behavior he was released to Susan on $500.00 cash bail.

When she came to pick him up she informed the officer that earlier in the day she and Jim had been arguing over him taking the pills and that he had put her in a *headlock*. However, she was unwilling to provide a statement. Sue also informed them on April 6th Jim had tried to kill himself by attempting to overdose on the very same prescription pills.

Sue then brought him back to her home, a home where she lived with her two teen boys. Carolann called both Jeff and I the following morning to inform us as to what had transpired. She told us he was being arraigned as she spoke to us and that there were already plans to try and get his bail revoked.

On May 22nd the State filed for an expedited hearing to have Jim's bail revoked pending trial on all charges. They stated that they had concerns for the safety of the victims, the Defendant, and the general public. At the very least they wanted new conditions added to his bail.

THE STATE OF NEW HAMPSHIRE

STRAFFORD, SS.   SUPERIOR COURT

THE STATE OF NEW HAMPSHIRE

V.

JAMES HALLDORSON

Bind-Over Docket Number 06-S-192 to195

STATE'S MOTION THAT THE COURT HOLD AN EXPEDITED HEARING AND REVOKE THE DEFENDANT'S BAIL, or in the alternative REVISIT THE CONDIDTIONS OF BAIL

NOW COMES the State of New Hampshire by and through the office of the Strafford County Attorney, Janice K. Rundles, and requests that this Court hold an expedited hearing, and thereafter revoke the Defendant's bail. In the alternative, the State requests that this Court revisit the issue of bail, and impose additional conditions, including electronic monitoring by Strafford County Community Corrections.

The basis of the State's Motion is set forth in the numbered paragraphs below:

I.   THE FACTS.

1. The Defendant faces three counts of aggravated *Felonious Sexual Assault,* for allegedly performing fellatio on his two sons beginning when each was under thirteen years of age. One of the victims, now an adult, lives with his family in the same neighborhood of Dover as the Defendant.

2. Jury Selection is scheduled for September 11, 2006.

3. The Defendant remains free on $25,000 cash/corporate surety.

4. On May 18, 2006, the Defendant, while riding his bicycle in the middle of Thomas Street in Dover, collided with the rear end of a motor vehicle. The Defendant was transported to Wentworth Douglas Hospital, but was later released without injury.

5. Because of the strange way the Defendant was acting, Hospital personnel called the Dover Police Department. Officer Scott Petrin responded.

6. When Officer Scott Petrin arrived, the Defendant was about to take Inderol, Buspar and Selexa, which had been prescribed to the Defendant, and are used to treat depression and anxiety.

7. Officer Petrin noticed that there were additional loose pills in the Defendant's shoe. Also in the Defendant's shoe was a set of brass knuckles. The Defendant initially told Officer Petrin that he had found the knuckles in his son's room, and had planned to throw them into the Cocheco River. Later, he stated that he had gotten into a fight with his wife, then found them on his dresser, but did not know how they had gotten there.

8. While speaking with the Defendant, Officer Petrin noted that his speech was slurred, and slow. Officer Petrin did not smell any alcohol on the Defendant's breath or person, and concluded that the Defendant was under the influence of drugs – possibly the aforementioned prescription drugs.

9. While Officer Petrin was in the room, the Defendant tried to explain the circumstances of the accident to a doctor. The Defendant appeared to be confused, and nearly got into an argument with Officer Petrin, when Officer Petrin interjected to explain that Thomas Avenue, where the accident occurred, intersected with Central Avenue.

10. The Defendant was subsequently arrested and charged with misdemeanor *Possession of Metallic Knuckles* RSA 159:16

11. During the booking process, Mr. Halldorson was unale to follow simple commands, such as where to stand for photos, or when he was asked to sit.

12. In addition, he appeared confused about where he was.

13. During the booking process, Officer Petrin noticed scratches on the Defendant's arm. When asked how they occurred, the Defendant stated that his cat had scratched him. Thereafter, *the Defendant* asked Officer Petrin if his cat had scratched his arm.

14. The Defendant was released on $500 cash bail to the custody of his wife, Susan Halldorson. Ms. Halldorson told Officer Petrin that earlier that evening she and the Defendant had argued over the Defendant taking pills, and that he had put her in a headlock. Ms. Halldorson was unwilling to provide a statement.

15. Ms. Halldorson also told Officer Petrin that on April 6, 2006, the Defendant had tied to kill himself by taking an overdose of medication.

II. THE STATE HAS SERIOUS CONCERNS REGARDING THE SAFETY OF THE VICTIMS, THE GENERAL PUBLIC, AND THE DEFENDANT

16. Given the Defendant's: (i) strange behavior on the evening of May 18, 2005, apparently attributable to the improper use of prescription drugs; (ii) possession of an illegal and dangerous weapon; (iii) that the Defendant had apparently physically assaulted his wife earlier in the evening; and (iv) the Defendant's prior attempted suicide, the State has grave concerns that he poses an immediate danger to the Victims, other members of the community, and to himself.

17. The State requests that this Court hold an expedited hearing, after which it revoke the Defendant's bail pending trial on all charges.

18. If the court is not willing to revoke the Defendant's bail, the State requests that the Court reconsider the issue of bail, including wheather the Defendant should be placed on electronic monitoring through Strafford County Community Corrections.

19. To expedite a hearing on this matter, this Offic is sending acopy of this Motion via first class mail, and facsimile to Counsel for the Defendant.

WHEREFORE, the State respectfully requests that this Honorable Court:

A. Revoke the Defendant's bail;

B. In the alternative, revisit the issue of bail and impose additional conditions.

C. Grant such further relief as may be deemed just and quitable.

May 22, 2006

Respectfully submitted

Eric A. Gentes, Assistant Strafford County Attorney

THE STATE OF NEW HAMPSHIRE

On June 2nd the Judge and the County Attorney's office reached an agreement regarding Jim's bail.

State v. James E. Halldorson

Please be advised that on 6/02/2006 Judge Fauver made the following order relative to:

Motion to Revoke Bail; Moot

> STATE'S MOTION THAT THE COURT HOLD AN EXPEDITED HEARING, AND REVOKE THE DEFENDANT'S BAIL OR IN THE ALTERNATIVE REVISIT THE CONDITIONS OF BAIL

Motion to Modify Bail; Granted

> STATE'S ASSENTED – TO MOTION TO ADD ADDITIONAL CONDITIONS OF BAIL: "GRANTED – THE BAIL ORDER IS AMENDED ACCORDINGLY"

The Judge did not revoke bail but did allow for additional conditions which included:

Defendant be monitored by the Strafford County Community Corrections Program ("SCCC");

Such monitoring to include GPS or electronic monitoring;

> Such monitoring to include a curfew, the hours of which are to be determined by SCCC.
>
> Defendant not to consume any alcohol.
>
> Defendant not to ingest any controlled drugs, with the exception of prescribed drugs, to be taken only in the quantity and manner prescribed.

Jeff was content with the agreement. Me? Not so much. I didn't understand why his bail was not revoked. He was caught under the influence with a weapon, less than a block from our home. Not to mention the possibility that he was also being physically abusive to Sue. I was afraid that we wouldn't make it to trial without a major blow up from him.

I also started to have some concern that there might be some retaliation from the younger of the two biological sons, Sam or Will. Jim had said he found the brass knuckles in his son's room. It just got my mind turning. There was no real reason for the concern just an underlying feeling. I never had any concerns about Sam but Will...I don't know....I just worried about Will more. I worried about him hurting himself as much as anything. The whole situation had to be terrible for him. At least Sam was out of the house while at school. Will was still living with Sue (& at times Jim) full-time and in his senior year of high school. In the end neither one gave us any trouble whatsoever.

The trial was set for two weeks in September. The State had motioned for the cases (Jeff's assaults & Erik's assaults) to be combined and the judge agreed. The jury selection for the State of New Hampshire v. James Halldorson was to begin on September 11, 2006 and the trial was to start the following week, tentatively, on September 18, 2006. We were expected to be present during the entire trial.

Once again the waiting began. Jeff was extremely anxious. We knew the County Attorney's Office and Soldati had begun going back and forth on a plea agreement. The state would extend an offer and Soldati would refuse and offer up another. Considering all the evidence they had, the State didn't do much in the way of concession and remained fairly firm on their offers. We had no idea what to expect and just continued playing the waiting game.

By: Jeff & Kelly Halldorson

Plea Agreement

(Jeff)

In the late summer of 2006 we were notified that Jim's lawyer had negotiated a plea agreement. The trial was changed to a hearing. The plea agreement consisted of two options, first option being thirteen to twenty years uncontested or second, a capped plea of twenty to forty years. With the capped plea the option was left open for his lawyer to attempt to negotiate with the judge for a lesser amount of time but the max would be twenty to forty years.

With a guilty plea James would be taken into custody until sentencing. It was hard to comprehend. Jim was actually going to go to jail. It was surreal.

On September 11, 2006 we walked again through the metal detector and were ushered up to the courtroom by Carolann. When I entered my first instinct was to look around for Susan. Erik and Kelly seemed to be doing the same. The courtroom was empty except for a young man in his mid-twenties. He was holding a small pad of paper in which he was scribbling away. Kelly pointed to him and whispered.

I think that guy is a reporter. You may or may not want to talk to him...

Susan was nowhere to be found. She would not be in attendance this time. It appeared that Jim was going to be alone. We sat down and Carolann whispered to us in the seating area of the courtroom while we waited for the judge.

This won't take too long. He's just going to go in front of the judge and plead guilty. Then the bailiff will take him into custody and he will be transferred to the Strafford County jail where he will remain until his sentencing hearing.

How long will that be? Before the sentencing? Kelly asked.

It can take anywhere from 45 to 60 days. It all depends on how cooperative he is and how long the pre-sentencing investigation (PSI) takes.

The PSI will help the judge when it comes time to impose sentence. It is the main tool he will use. Jim, and most likely you two, will have to talk to Jim's assigned probation officer. Jim will have to go through a physical and talk with a lot of people to make sure that he is capable and competent enough to be sentenced. The PSI is a very important tool - as are – as are the letters that you can write to the judge. Writing a letter gives you an opportunity to be heard and say whatever you want regarding the impact that Jim and his crimes have had on you. You can also read those letters at the sentencing or I can read the letter for you if you wish, at the sentencing.

Jim walked into the courtroom. He was accompanied by his new lawyer, a man roughly the same age. They walked together whispering as they went along the aisle. He did not look scared. He was calm, as though this was all a very normal part of everyday life.

I found it disconcerting. I thought for a moment, maybe they had a trick up their sleeves. Maybe they knew some secret way to get out of this whole mess.

All rise.

We sat once again, powerless to what was going to happen.

I understand that we are here today because you want to change you plea.

Uh – yes - Your Honor...

His lawyer gestured him to stand.

Yes - Your Honor - that is correct. Jim was clear and direct.

I am assuming that the State and the Defense Counsel have come to some form of agreement. Is that correct Mr. Gentes?

Yes - Your Honor that would be correct. We will be seeking a sentencing hearing following the completion of the PSI.

All right, then to be clear Mr. Halldorson, are you fully aware of the charges that you are pleading to?

Yes - Your Honor.

And I am sure that your counsel has made you fully aware of the plea agreement?

Yes- Your Honor.

I just want to be sure that there are no questions left before you plea.

Yes Your Honor.

Ok then, James Halldorson in the case of the State of New Hampshire verses James Halldorson, you have been charged with 32 counts of Aggravated Felonious Sexual Assault on a person under the age of 13. These are all class A felonies. How do you plead?

Guilty, Your Honor.

James Halldorson in the case of the State of New Hampshire verses James Halldorson, you have been charged with 7 counts of Agitated Felonious Sexual Assault on a person under the age of 16. These are all class A felonies. How do you plead?

Guilty.

And finally, James Halldorson in the case of the State of New Hampshire verses James Halldorson, you have been charged with 1 count of Felonious Sexual Assault on a person under the age of 13. This is a class B felony. How do you plead?

Guilty, Your Honor.

Let the record state that James Halldorson has willingly and under no duress plead guilty to all charges brought forth by the State. At this time I would ask the bailiff please take Mr. Halldorson into custody where he will remain until sentencing for the above mentioned crimes. Thank you, this court will inform all necessary parties of the sentencing date.

The bailiff walked forward and without any expression of emotion Jim held out his hands to be handcuffed and walked through the door with the bailiff.

Ok well that went well. I was somewhat afraid of what Jim would be like after the last time we were here. Carolann was doing her best to keep the whole thing light and to the point. *You guys have done a great thing here. I know that this will all work out for the best. You're doing the right thing.*

We all said our goodbyes and went on our way to try and make this day seem just like all the rest.

It wasn't until three days later that Jim finely showed some sort of reaction to the fact that he just pled guilty to sexually assaulting two children.

On September 14, 2006 only three days into what was going to be a long incarceration for James Halldorson, he attempted suicide. At 5:30 in the morning Jim was brought to the hospital in Dover. There he received 15 sutures for a self inflicted laceration on his arm. Jim had used the stem of his eyeglasses to try and cut his wrist.

While in the hospital he asked the attending officer if he could contact Susan but the request was refused. He also wanted to know how he could get to see that Judge again. The officer told him that those were questions for his lawyer. Jim stated that he was not "overly pleased" with his lawyer and he wanted to revisit the plea. He thought his counsel had done a poor job representing him.

Jim was returned to the Strafford County Jail and we did not hear anything from or about him again until we receive the date for his sentencing - November 28, 2006

Sentencing
(Jeff & Kelly)

The sentencing was early in the morning. Ann (Kelly's mom), Heather (Erik's girlfriend), and Dave (Jeff's friend) all attended for emotional support.

It was the same Courtroom, yet different. A sense of finality and a touch of relief replaced the anxiousness of past visits to the Courtroom and seemed to echo loudly throughout the room. We were prepped. We knew what the expectations were. Carolann explained the process. One questioned remained. Would Susan show?

We looked around. She was nowhere to be found. She had stood by Jim for so long but allowed him to face this final hour, alone. And alone he was as he entered the Courtroom. His complexion pale, he appeared sickly dressed in a prison jumpsuit with little black slippers. He was cuffed and he shuffled his shackled feet as he was led down the aisle of the court by his lawyer.

It was hard to see him there like that. It would be hard to see anyone like that. His physical appearance was pathetic. His face remained expressionless and eyes glossed over. The jail doctors had given him his meds, no doubt.

Eric Gentes walked in, stacks of papers in one arm and a briefcase in the other. He stopped to talk with us, resting his briefcase on the bench next to us. We exchanged words and handshakes then he moved up to the front of the Courtroom, taking a minute to organize both his paperwork and thoughts at the Prosecution's table.

All rise, Honorable Judge Fauver will now bring this court into session.

We all stood as the bailiff opened the door for the judge.

Please be seated.

We watched and listened as the three of them, the Judge, Jim's lawyer and Eric Gentes spoke in their legalese. They discussed the number of charges and how many counts of what. They went over the cap plea verses the fixed plea. We watched and waited.

It was not a trial but a sentencing hearing, something you might see on an episode of Law and Order or another program like that. Except all the slow parts weren't edited out like on TV.

My understanding of the cap plea is... twenty to forty years. That would be the highest I would go, is that correct?

Yes, that is correct Your Honor.

Jim chose the cap plea. With the cap plea the County Attorney recommended twenty to forty but Jim's lawyer was allowed to argue for less. The County Attorney's recommendation was just that, a recommendation the Judge wasn't bound by it. As opposed to the fixed plea where there would have been no negotiating. Soldati must have felt he had a chance at a lesser sentence.

Ok, Mr. Gentes why don't you go ahead and give me your recommendation, I expect the victims are here and if they chose to speak or anyone else chooses to speak then I would be happy to hear them.

Yes, Your Honor, just before we begin - I just want to note that through the presentation - I will be referring to the defendant, as their father. The victims understandably have mixed feelings about recognizing that relationship but I feel it's important that we recognize that these actions took place in that family relationship if you will.

I understand that.

Jeff and Erik had made it clear they no longer considered James and Susan their parents. They didn't want to be their children anymore, wanted or not. Kelly's mother sat on the bench beside us. Where was Susan? Why wasn't she there? James had hurt her too. He had lied and torn her family apart. Yet, she wasn't there. Neither were the two younger boys, both of whom were adults at the time of sentencing.

Eric Gentes began his recommendation.

> *Your honor addressing each Doc Number 06-S192 which is Aggravated Felonious Sexual Assault against a victim with the initials E.H., a person under thirteen years of age and all of the AFSAS, Your Honor, involve the same act, that is the defendant committing the act of fellatio on the victims, the State is recommending seven and a half to fifteen years committed imposed...*
>
> *Your Honor, on Doc Number 06-S193 AFSA on a person under thirteen years of age, the victim in this case having the initials J.H., the State is recommending seven and a half to fifteen years of staying committed...*
>
> *Your Honor, on Document Number 06-S194, AFSA on a person between the ages of thirteen to sixteen years of age, but a member of the same household as the defendant, again the victim with the initials J.H. and I'll make a brief or a minor change, Your Honor, to the forms the State is recommending five to ten years imposed and that is consecutive to the other two sentences...*
>
> *On Doc Number 06-S195 that is Felonious Sexual Assault, that is sexual contact with a person under thirteen years of age, the victim with the initials J.H. and that involves the act of the defendant rubbing his genitalia on the victim's body, the State is recommending three and a half to seven years and that would be concurrent with all other sentences...*

> *If you are keeping score, that 7.5 years for the acts that they could prove against E.H. and 13.5 for the acts that they could prove against J.H.*

If Erik had submitted to the invasive grilling of Caralann's forensic grilling that they could have brought even more against Jim. We were just going to have to settle for forty felonies, I think that would suffice. He did plead guilty.

> *Your Honor, the defendant has plead guilty to forty counts of sexual assault against the children in this case, so the sentences the Court impose here today must account for forty separate occasions when the defendant committed what I think we all agree is one of the most horrific crimes imaginable and that is the assault on a child. They must account for a time for forty instances when the defendant manipulated and abused his position as a parent to target his own children.*
>
> *The sentences must account for a period of six years for one victim and three and a half years for another victim, when each night they had to go to bed and not feel safe and secure, which every child is entitled to, but wonder if that night they were going to be raped yet again by their father and if that were to happen, if things were to get even stranger, even weirder and all of this is relative when you live in this situation, Your Honor, if the defendant might do something different, like in one case, like the victims face rubbed his genitalia on his body. The sentences must account for the pain and harm caused on the victims by the defendant which has lasted far longer than the six years and the three and a half years, respectively.*
>
> *We know from reading the PSI, that J.H. still suffers from nightmares, he still suffers from flashbacks, and although his brother has elected not to participate in the PSI project or in the PSI, both bothers fully cooperated with the investigation. Your honor, both brothers had to start to tell their story again and again to police officers on video tape, to the DA in this matter, to the County Attorney, to myself and anybody who participated in that process, can tell you that both brothers are suffering from a great deal of anguish, a great deal of pain, in this matter.*

Although both brothers are extremely intelligent, extremely articulate, have the support of each other, have the support of loved ones, both brothers, we certainly hope and believe are on their way to recovery and healing, that is a process that is going to take their entire life, so in that sense, both brothers have been given life sentencing in this matter, and the sentences that the Court will impose here today must take into the account, that the victims came into the defendant's family with nobody but themselves, after suffering horrific abuse at the hands of their biological father, after being chosen to come into the defendant's family by the defendant and his wife and now almost thirty years later, both victims are estranged from that family, have really nobody but themselves and the families that they themselves have created, that they have formed, through no fault of their own.

Now Your Honor, the defendant is going to ask for far less than the state is asking in this matter and one of the things the defendant is likely to argue is that he is accepting responsibility for his actions, that he is admitting to his guilt but Your Honor, any admissions in this matter are decades to late and have been grudging at best. When he was fourteen years old when most fourteen year olds are worrying about pimples and if they are cool in school, J.H. was able to summon up enough courage to tell a neighbor, a teenage boy, like yourself, what was happening and then go on the tell this boy's mother, and there in after, because of pressure from J.H.'s family and because of love that he felt for his family, especially his mother, who was pregnant at the time, J.H. recanted and said "I made this all up."

At that time the defendant could have stepped forward and said "You know what I did was horrible, I may not be able to give an explanation for it, but I'm not going to victimize my son again for telling the truth," but instead the defendant denied the allegations, or at best remained silent brandishing his own son a liar, and disturbingly enough the abuse did not immediately end at that time, it continued for a period of time, either for a period of months or about a year and when it did end J.H. found himself, essentially spending the next two years incarcerated in various facilities that were intended to treat young people with drug addictions, incarcerated into these facilities despite the fact that he was not even using drugs at the time, that any problems he might have been suffering were certainly not coming from himself and in these facilities he did disclose, he said "I may not be using drugs," even no one believed him, but "look this is happening this is happening to me, you're right maybe I do have things to deal with" and we know that at least on one occasion there was a meeting between the councilors and J.H.'s family, his parents, and again that would have been the time for the defendant to step forward and say, "Enough, I'm not going to call my son a liar, I'm not going to victimize him again" but he did not.

The defendant had another opportunity about ten years ago to come fully clean. At that time, J.H. was asked by his mother to help install bunk beds into one of the bedrooms of his two younger brothers. The nine year old brother, suddenly out of the blue, started having difficulty sleeping at night and J.H. began to be concerned and began to fear that what had happened to him and his older brother was now happening to his younger brother, so again this young man summoned up enough courage, he contacted E.H. who also at that time decided it was time to step forward and there was a meeting between these two brothers, the defendant and their mother, and at that meeting, the defendant did admit to what had occurred, but according to a written statement by the mother given to the police in this matter, after the boys had left the defendant told her, "Look I only admitted to this because I didn't want to get beat up."

Once again explicitly, if not implicitly, brandishing these victims, once more, liars, victimizing them yet again, and even, Your Honor, during the investigation of this the matter the defendant's admissions have been at times half hearted, have been reluctant, during a one party phone conservation, during a phone conservation between J.H. and the defendant that was recorded without the defendant's knowledge, the defendant admitted to J.H. specifically what occurred, the specific conduct at issue and admitted that it could have happened hundreds of times.

Yet, just a few days later, when confronted by detectives Bilodeau and Terrance of the Durham Police Department, the defendant, at first, tried to dodge the issue and said "I was blackout drunk at that time, I'm not really quite sure what happened" and then sort of admitted well it could have happened and then finally admitted to the act but gave a number of twenty times, and most disturbing, Your Honor, is when one of the detectives asked the defendant "Did you ever do this to your two younger sons"? The defendant's reply was "Oh, no, I would never do that to my real sons", thus implying that because these two boys were adopted, because these two boys were brought into that home by choice, it was somehow less of a crime, that it was not sick to do this to them.

Your Honor, and I don't want to spend my whole time addressing what I think are the defense arrays, but I do want to address something which was raised during PSI, that this PSI says that the defendant has a clean criminal history and that was the basis of one of the recommendation, again, Your Honor, I know that the defendant has plead guilty to forty separate counts of sexually assaulting a child, assaults that occurred over a period of six years, assaults that occurred on two separate victims, I think it would be hard to say that anyone has a longer criminal history than that, now it is true that the defendant has not be sentenced before on these charges, and is certainly that is something that the Court should take into consideration, but he should not be rewarded just because he has not been caught up until now.

The final thing I want to note, Your Honor, is if this Court accepts the state's recommendation that is twenty to forty years, it will be sentencing the defendant to a total of one half to one year in jail for each instance of sexually assaulting a child.

The States recommendation, Your Honor, is taking all these circumstances into consideration, and the State's opinion is very, very restrained. Your Honor, if the Court does not accept the State's recommendations, I want to implore the Court to recognize that at the time these instances were committed they were Class A felonies. They were punishable by seven and a half to fifteen years in prison. If the Court does not accept the State's recommendation which the State feels is fully appropriate, I strongly, strongly urge the Court at least, at least to impose a sentence of seven and one half to fifteen years imposed consecutive for each victim in this matter. There are two young men that stand before you and anything less would be a true miscarriage of justice. Your Honor, it is my understanding that, at least one of the victims and several loved ones would like to address the Court in this matter. I would turn this matter over to the victim's assistant at this point and she can assist them in the process.

Eric Gentes had done his part, and had done it well. Then we'd be allowed to address the court. James' lawyer didn't seem to like the idea but agreed in the end...

Just to be clear it is my understanding that the victims have a right to address the Court. I'm not sure who he means by these other people, if they want to call witnesses to the stand, then they can - do that in a sentencing hearing, but my understanding is the victim has the right to address the Court.

Let's start with the victims. Come up sir if you want and go over to the microphone if you will, sir? Step over there, sir, if you would? Okay, before we start, if you would just give me your name, sir.

My name is Jeff Halldorson, Jeffrey Watson Halldorson. I have a question for you, Your Honor, would you mind if I turn the podium to face the defendant while I read my letter?

You certainly may.

Thank you.

It was important to face the man that had brought us all here today. There had to be no mistake that this was the end of his victimization of the people that stood before him.

It's been a long time coming to this point; you'll have to forgive me. It may take some time.

Certainly, take your time. Would you like some water? The compassion in Judge Fauver's voice was evident.

I'm going to read the letter I wrote first, because I think that bears most of how it goes, the only problem with having to write a letter is that it's thought out, it's contrived. You have the opportunity to sit there and capture your feelings. It's not your initial feelings, you have the ability to distort the facts for your benefit, but it's the best we can do.

Your Honor, it's unfortunate that I'm writing this letter, it's unfortunate that you're reading this letter, this whole letter should never have been written in the first place. As things have it, here I am writing it. Now you can read it. I started this letter many times in my head, all with new beginnings that were meant to make an impact which made myself sound strong, witty or portrayed the hurt I feel, but they all sound fake as does this one.

This letter is supposed to tell you how James Halldorson's actions against me impacted my life, how it hurt me, and what the outcome has been. I apologize if I do not do that, sir. I have spent my whole life trying to get past it. I am not sure that I know how I actually feel. Forgive me.

Take your time.

I spent a long time building this callous that you don't know which feelings I have made up, or which ones I have used to mask the true ones. James, I'm reading this for you, because I feel that I need to, not because you deserve it.

I tell you this, though, if anyone did those things to someone I truly loved, that there would be no question in my mind what I would do. The ironic part is that's exactly what happened. You may have hurt me. I can live with that, but he hurt my brother, too. He hurt him deep. Deeper than you or I could ever imagine. That I cannot live with, that is unacceptable for my brother to go, for my brother to sleep through one night sober and free from fear where thoughts from James is worth James feeling our fear, drunk and the pain that he has caused his family for the rest of his natural life, knowing that he has done this, not running from the lies, but to know that it was he who has done this.

He's in that cell because I did not let him lie anymore. I tried to let him be, I tried to live free from the past, but by doing that I was holding Erik, Erik's and my future hostage by that I let him, by letting him go, I was keeping us back, to see him have everything we wanted, a house, a family, a life, and he would piss it all away, like it meant nothing.

By: Jeff & Kelly Halldorson

I have spent my life running from, hiding and fighting my feelings about what James did to me. He took, he took something, you took something that could never be replaced. They chose us, they picked us, you picked us, you, handpicked us. We were adopted into his, we were adopted into his sick life to fulfill him. The actions of his molestation don't hurt quite as bad as that.

Erik and I needed love, we needed hope, we did not need to be raped in our sleep by a man that chose to be our father. You chose that more than anything. These people that can go out and have kids, they can breed like mice, but you went out, went through the actions and picked us, selectively.

I want nothing more than to forgive him for what he has done, I have tried. I've decided that I will never forgive you. You do not deserve it. The thing that hurts most is I know, I know now that all of this, through all this court and lawyer mess, I know now without a doubt in my mind that she knew, too.

Susan Halldorson knew the man that we called dad was slipping into our room at night and ruining our innocence. There's no proof better than having her tell me that if I feel the need to press charges to let her know so, that she may get her finances in order. No, no one will ever change my mind, nor need try. If we got up to go to the bathroom, she knew. If the dog moved from room to room, she would get up. But if James got out of one bed and into another, she slept through it? I've been able to see these things now.

Did they tell you what happened the first time I told someone? They put me in a drug rehab. There were no drugs in my system. I passed every test, Your Honor, every one, marijuana, there was nothing. They kept me there anyway, two years of my childhood, not only was my childhood stolen in bed, it was stolen right out from under my feet.

You have already heard some of the other stuff. We confronted him. We cried; we talked of change. He was going to get help.

When we asked about ▮▮▮▮ and ▮▮▮▮? James quote was, I would never do that to own my child. You know what Susan did? Nothing. Not a damn thing. Nothing. Where is she now ? Nowhere.

At home in a big house. At work. Moving on without you, moving on without us, because she knows she's just as guilty as you, and you know it, too.

I need to move forward. I only hope that ▆▆▆▆▆▆▆ *and* ▆▆▆▆ *will forgive me if I've hurt them, but this is not my fault. I did the right thing. Erik did the right thing.*

James Halldorson, you are an evil man. Susan is as much to blame as you and should be here where she belongs and has been all the time right by your side, but she's not. He has earned his place in jail. Erik and I are not alone, he has hurt many, many people in the wake of his self indulgence and destruction. Susan's mother was right. She was. You've already read this letter so you know what it says. I'll make sure to give it to you. There's something bad about this man she said. I don't know why she told me that, but she told us that when we were young.

It is unfortunate that there are things he will miss, like graduations, grandchildren being born, weddings, freedom. It is not for him that I feel it is unfortunate, but for us, these are things that we really could have used a father for.

James Halldorson has taught me one thing in life, that is how not to be a father.

I guess I will pick up from there with the family I have. You see I am lucky, I married into a family with enough love that they were to spare some for me, not some to mind and go, but enough to last a life time.

Uncle Andy taught me to appreciate the finer things in life, you could have done that.

Uncle Bob taught me that no matter what have fun, you could have done that.

Uncle Joe taught me that no matter how hard you work you can always do better; you could have taught me that.

Grampy taught me it's okay to cry; you didn't teach me that.

And Bob, my father-in-law, he's taught me that there are good men out there. You didn't teach me that.

You've seen the evidence, you've heard the tapes. The rest is up to you, Your Honor. I am now free from the fear that I feel at night. I know he's was locked up, for at least now, and my children are safe from him anyway.

So this is to conclude, the impact in my life, so the impact in my life, there are hard times, overwhelming, and yes it hurts, it hurts a lot. The outcome, well, that's more difficult.

Erik is alive and doing better. I turned out okay. So I guess we're going to have to wait and see. I am Jeff Halldorson, I am not your son. You never wanted me to be. There's only one thing that I care about now, and that is that my brother and I can move on with our lives without you.

Thank you.

Those would prove to be the last words spoken from son to father.

Thank you. The Judge was well practiced in disguising his thoughts. He sat stoic behind his bench. Compassion showed only when he spoke.

Your Honor, Kelly Halldorson, the wife of Jeff Halldorson would like to address the Court.

Your Honor, I would ask that she not take the stand. Soldati did his best to stop it.

Why? The Judge questioned?

Well, I think that this is in a sentencing hearing, other than the input from the victims, which is specifically authorized by statute. The defendant has a right to cross examine any evidence or witnesses the State produces.

I'm not going to require her to take the stand. I'm going to let her speak from the podium. This is not an inquisition; this is an opportunity for the victims and those who are frankly directly affected by any criminal conduct to speak and to assist the Court in imposing an appropriate sentence.

Soldati was put firmly, in his place.

Fine.

Kelly went to the podium.

I'm sorry. This is going to be a little hard.

Can you move the microphone a little bit closer to the podium? I know she's going to speak low.

I'm going to try really hard.

Take your time.

Your name is what?

Yes, my name is Kelly Halldorson. I'm Jeff's wife. I have a letter. I'll just read the letter I wrote.

Kelly's voice quivered as she read the letter she'd written to the judge. Unable at times to hold back the tears, as she spoke all in the Courtroom could see beyond any doubt that the pain James had inflicted went beyond Jeff and Erik. He had wounded those two so deeply the pain reverberated to all close to them as well.

> *My name is Kelly. I am victim Jeff Halldorson's wife. We've been together thirteen years and married ten of those. We have three amazing children ranging in age from nine to twelve to which Jeff is a commendable parent. Jeff is a strong, kind and caring man. He is a man with whom I feel truly blessed to be loved by. The children and I call him our Superman because often times he seems so strong and invincible. However, just like the fabled comic book hero, Jeff has his own kryptonite. For him, it's his past, his childhood and his father.*

By: Jeff & Kelly Halldorson

This is a man who was tossed around, Jeff, from family member to family member shortly after his birth until ultimately he was given up with his brother to the State. They were then moved from foster home to foster home until promised a new life by James and his wife.

Mr. and Mrs. Halldorson chose them, promised to care for them and love them. Instead the boys were made James's sick playthings. As children, these boys never knew a safe home. Never. Because James's despicable acts and his mother's blind eye these two boys were stripped of what little innocence they had left after leaving the care of their birth parents and multiple foster homes.

They were further let down when the molestation came out when the boys were teens. Jeff had disclosed the abuse to a neighbor. He felt pressured to recant and was sent away to a drug rehab. A drug rehab so strict, it was legally forced to close eventually.

Although Jeff's drug tests came back clean, he was forced to remain there for three months, three times longer than the typical thirty day stay. Jeff was then moved around a lot, including stays at a reform school, another hospital, a group home among other placements.

Overwhelmed with emotion Kelly found it difficult to carry on but did so regardless her remaining words for the court, spoken through tears.

I'm sorry

While at one of these placements, a hospital, Jeff disclosed the abuse again. The hospital brought in his mother and father to discuss. They ended up leaving Jeff in the hospital and never brought the accusations to the police. It was all brushed under the carpet and these boys were failed yet again and James was left to live his life without consequences.

My husband is a strong man but what person could endure this type of upbringing and come out unscathed. I probably know more than anyone, other than his brother, have seen his pain, I've seen his pain when I've driven him more than once late at night to an emergency room for a panic attack. I've seen his pain and he has been to different counselors on and off over the years and he has needed help of anti-anxiety and anti-depressant medications. I've seen his night time pacing, his insomnia. I've seen his concern and heartbreak for his brother, his worry over how his brother is coping.

I've seen his pain affect our intimacy, our alone time, our private time as husband and wife, and lastly, I've seen his tears. I do believe Jeff is a strong man and I think it's the only reason he's been able to live life despite all his pain and suffering. He for the most part tries to keep his pain in his past and see the good in life and family he has now. His past, I know will continue to creep up on him and his brother as well. I just hope that both he and his brother will be able to sleep just a little more soundly knowing the man who committed these vile acts against them will be locked away from them and other children for hopefully a very long time, because I know I will.

James Halldorson committed crimes twenty years ago through no fault of Jeff and his brother. He has not been held accountable until now, for all these years while Jeff and his brother have been struggling to make their relationships work, build families and move beyond their pain, James has been free, he's been free to raise two biological children, buy a summer home, spend weeks during the summer there. He's seen two biological children graduate from high school. He's gone to concerts, he's eaten out, ran in road races, he's lived, he's enjoyed life all the while his victims have been struggling to cope with all the pain and humiliation this man's caused them. I, for one, hope he doesn't get even one more second to enjoy life outside a cell. I would like to see him forced to spend all the time reflecting on his crimes behind bars.

Thank you.

Kelly returned to her seat by Jeff's side.

Your honor, it's my understanding that the second victim in this matter would like to address the Court.

Erik walked up to the podium. He didn't hesitate or even wait for instructions...

By: Jeff & Kelly Halldorson

The simple fact of the matter is that you don't think you did anything wrong.

If you could just tell me your name, sir?

Erik Halldorson. There was a short pause and he went one, staring Jim down as he spoke. You could hear rage building in his tone.

You don't think you did anything wrong. You still don't think you did anything wrong and I know it, and I know it. You don't think you did anything wrong and I know it and all the people talking about oh how bad it is.

Erik's outburst had everyone's hair on end. His face contorted in a twist of anger and disgust. He gripped the podium with white knuckle force as he towered over the thing. He was on fire.

You don't think you did anything wrong and it's twisted and it's here and it's in you and it's in your sick thought, and it's going to bend you like bent me and my brother, you don't think you did anything wrong - All these people in the room are never going to convince you and I'm going to fucking convince you right now, you did something wrong and you are a good man and I love you but you did something wrong….Are we clear?

The fire in Erik's eyes subsided as he returned to his seat. What he had accomplished was yet to be determined.

Your Honor, at this point the state has nothing more to offer.

Our case had been brought to the court. We all had done everything that we could do. There was nothing left but to hear what the defense had to say. Then the weight would be on the court to determine what was to come of the admitted sex offender.

Your Honor, I have submitted sentencing forms to the Court - and in essence - what I have done is adopted, although the numbers come out different, and I'll explain why. I've adopted the recommendation of the

PSI. The difference is that in the PSI - I'm not sure that the officer was aware that the sentences have to reflect the sentence at the time of the offense and so instead of ten to twenty, I've recommended seven and a half to fifteen, which is the maximum penalty for these offenses, not the ten to twenty which would be the sentence if the offense were committed now.

Along with the Statute of Limitation changes to the laws regarding child sexual assault in New Hampshire the punishments had changed as well. When the offenses had taken place the consequence had been less severe.

Seven and a half to fifteen years is the sentence for one count of Aggravated Felonious Sexual Assault.

Aggravated Felonious Sexual Assault (New Hampshire RSA 632-A:2) is defined as sexual penetration, however slight, into any opening (vagina, mouth, or anus) against a person's will (without consent) or when the victim is physically helpless to resist. It is considered to be a felony punishable by up to 10 to 20 years in the state prison for one count. A person is also guilty of Aggravated Felonious Sexual Assault without penetration when he or she touches the genitalia of a person under the age of 13 for the purpose of sexual gratification or arousal.

I am recommending seven and one half to fifteen staying committed in a State Prison on the indictment 06S-192 and - then concurrent consecutive if imposed, but concurrent with each other, consecutive to 192 seven and one half to fifteen suspended on 193, seven and one half to fifteen suspended on 194 and three and one half to seven, on 194 all maximum sentences but suspended but consecutive if imposed. I've also asked for a twenty year window of imposition.

We both wondered...what the fuck did that mean? It sounded like, bottom line he wanted James to do seven and a half to fifteen total by having the multiple penalties run concurrent.

I will address the rationale for the sentence which I think actually is reflected in the PSI. If I could have a moment - I believe that my client does wish to address the Court.

The Judge motioned in agreement. He stood in front of the Judge Jim looked so very alone. He had no one by his side. Nobody sat behind him in support. No sister. No wife. No sons. Still hand-cuffed he stood at the Defense table with folded hands.

Your Honor, for years I do admit that I have lived in denial, deceit and a world of- um - dishonesty. I admit those things. You did hear that Erik and Jeffrey were adopted by my wife and myself.

His words were clear and he spoke as though he was reading lines from a well-rehearsed script.

I did not select them to be objects of my – (sigh & pause) - predilections. Truly and honestly thought that we could bring those kids, those boys with love into a home and give them the things they didn't have when they came to us because they were bounced around...

...Unfortunately, I succumbed to something deep inside me that I can't explain to the State why I did it. I was wrong. I admit that I'm wrong and I'm sorry. I know from what the victims have said this morning; they don't think I feel that I am wrong? I know I'm wrong...

...I did accept responsibility the time that it was reported to the authorities in Brookside Hospital. We were told that the State was going to investigate, that it was mandatory for the counselor to report it to the State. It was documented and the State never investigated it and I can't explain that for that reason...

He turned to us, with his hands bound and eyes pleading.

...I want to sincerely apologize to the victims, Erik, Jeffrey and Kelly.

Then he looked at Judge Fauver. His look was not received well. Fauver responded with...*Don't look at me!*

I-I want to sincerely apologize to the victims: Jeffrey, Kelly and Erik. I sincerely apologize. I know I was wrong. I did take you under my wings, as your father. I know you don't accept that now, but there was a true love there. Despite what you say Jeffrey you must know with your heart that your mother never knew this went on. I was deceitful, I was dishonest and I was in denial. We know that I suffered from alcoholism and as a result of that disease one becomes a very sneaky person. Your mother never knew about it because I was sneaky.

Jeff and Erik were unable to hold back. They heckled Jim.

Where is she now? Jeff questioned.

She did not come today...she did...

You're protecting your cash. You're protecting your cash, Jim. Erik interrupted.

*Your Honor, if he could...*Soldati spoke up.

Anything else you want to say to them?

That's about it.

Anything else you want to say to them, now's your chance.

No, Your Honor.

I did admit my guilt, when Jeffrey asked me to speak to ▨▨▨▨ and ▨▨▨▨ last year; I did that in all honesty. When the police came to my office, I gave them my statement in all honesty. I couldn't tell the officer? I didn't. I cooperated.

Erik heckled again. *They have porn in the jailhouse Jim.*

By: Jeff & Kelly Halldorson

Your Honor, I'm very ashamed for my actions. When my children did confront us several years ago at the meeting with my family, my wife, Jeffrey did ask me to seek help. The very next day, I did travel to Massachusetts spoke to a counselor. I have been through intensive individual psychotherapy for that period of approximately fifteen years. I've been through two drug and alcohol rehab programs. I stand committed to participate in the twelve step program which I've done and in that program one of the first steps in being through AA is recognizing denial and that's what I just admitted to Erik and Jeffrey. I was in denial and I was sneaky...

...During the past years I have, my wife and I have raised two other brothers of Jeffrey's and Erik's. They have been successful graduated from high school, I did see them graduate. I saw Erik graduate from high school, I saw Erik graduate from Jump School. I've tried my best to be a father. I cannot explain why these actions took place but, Your Honor; they were over twenty years ago. It doesn't excuse them, it doesn't excuse them whatsoever...

...I would like to say that I have gotten my life together through alcohol and drug counseling and I would look forward to participating in sexual abuse, sexual rehabilitation so that these things never occur again, but I have lived a productive career, have raised the children at the house and I did work in a hospital where I was a volunteer and contributory admission of that hospital. I was wrong. I am guilty and I must now pay the consequences...

...I would ask that you have mercy on me so that I may participate in a sex offenders program and contribute to society as best as I can and as quickly as possible. I do understand that long term is justified and I accept that. As I stand before you, that one day I will stand before God, as a merciful and righteous God, and I will face him at that time. I am sorry for my victims, truly sincerely sorry. I hope in their heart someday they can forgive me, but they are strong, Kelly's right, they are strong. Thank you, Your Honor.

He sat down as his lawyer stood and prepared for his final address to the court.

Your Honor, first of all I think it's important to recognize that this case is about events that happened over twenty year ago. That there's no indication, whatsoever, that there's no evidence, whatsoever, and I'm somewhat disturbed by some of the innuendo of some of the individuals, but there's no evidence, whatsoever, that my client has done anything over the last twenty years, but lived a productive lawful life...

Really? No evidence, whatsoever, that James has done anything over the last twenty years, but lived a productive, lawful life??? No evidence? We wondered whether Mr. Soldati had been informed of James car accidents, DUI, or even the brass knuckle parole violation.

...He is not seeking, Your Honor, to be exonerated. He is not seeking to minimize his conduct, his conduct lasted for a period of time in his life, and it was a period of time when he was a severe alcoholic, virtually every day. One of the difficulties that he had in terms of his interactions with the police is that his alcoholism in fact did interfere with his memory. He doesn't know a lot of the details of what went on. He doesn't remember, nor did he catalog every instance. You know when Mr. Gentes says "Well you know it was twenty when it was ten". You know one of the effects of alcohol particularly when you have blackouts is that it affects your memory. I'm not saying that as mitigation of the offense, Your Honor, but it does suggest that when people are pressing the defendant to admit to things part of the difficulty he'd have was not being able to remember the whole time period, quite frankly. But what he has done here, Your Honor, is he has accepted the responsibility...

...He has entered pleas to these four indictments recognizing that there's no way for him to possibly articulate the details of each of the counts but he's accepted the guilt for these crimes, Your Honor. He didn't have to do that. We could have tried these cases. He could have

tried these cases. He has accepted it, and I think that there has to be some recognition that there is a benefit, that there is a benefit to the State, there is a benefit to victims when an individual accepts responsibility for their crime and enters a plea of guilty that is not particularly, in these types of offenses, that's not an easy thing to do in part and I think that Mr. Halldorson somewhat referenced that...

...It's not an easy thing even from the psychological stand point, because denial runs very deep in these types of conduct. He has accepted that responsibility he has not tried to minimize it, he's accepted everything that the State has alleged here, even necessarily without knowing the details or remembering the details where he may be able to fill in something that might satisfy Mr. Gentes questions or concerns. He's accepted this responsibility...

...He has, he did end this conduct. This conduct did not continue beyond a particular point in time. I don't think he knows anymore why it ended then he does why it began, but there's no evidence that it ever continued beyond sometime nearly twenty years ago, and for the past twenty years he's lived a productive life. He's cared for and supported his family; he's been a constructive member of the community...

...I don't say that that should mitigate the offenses here in any sense that he should simply be able to escape any consequence, but in fact he did not continue his conduct. It did end. Now whether it's because he got control of his alcoholism to the degree that alcohol played a role in lowering inhibitions or allowing whatever else was causing him to act out these, I don't know and I'm not really qualified to answer that but the two seem to coincide. He ended his alcoholism, he got treatment for that and these events stopped. Again, I'm not saying that the alcoholism caused these. Many people are alcoholics who don't engage in this type of behavior but it did end and he has accepted responsibility. There's not a lot more that he can do than stand up before you, Your Honor, and say I am guilty of what I am charged with and I accept the fact that at fifty eight years old I am going to remain in the New Hampshire State Prison for a long period of time and that's really where we are at...

...Nobody here is suggesting that the defendant should be sentenced to the House of Correction or that he be given a minor sentence to the State Prison. We are looking at a maximum sentence in State Prison that we are asking the Court to impose. What the State is asking you to impose is really beyond that and the State wants to basically ask this Court to sentence on the basis of vengeance on the basis of long held family issues that frankly we are not going to resolve by any of this...

That was just plain wrong. Each individual act of Aggravated Felonious Sexual Assault carried with it seven and a half to fifteen years (at the time the offences were committed), a **minimum** of seven and a half years for ONE act of Aggravated Felonious Sexual Assault. How much time for 39 separate acts? The math puts the minimum at nearly 300 years and a maximum at close to 600. Obviously things don't go exactly like that when multiple accounts of a specific crime are committed but Soldati didn't even acknowledge there were two victims in his calculation. He was suggesting his client get seven and a half to fifteen years for a single count of Aggravated Felonious Sexual Assault.

Vengeance? Really?

...But I don't think the role of the Court is to play to the vengeance of family members even those who have been hurt by a defendant. Look at the reasons for sentencing, now we look at, at least the traditional reasons. We talk about punishment and that really is the only issue here is that the defendant needs to be punished and he's going to be punished, but there's also the issue of deterrence which I don't think plays much of a role here...

...Clearly the defendant has not continued to engage in, the sentence here is being deferred for conduct he's not been engaging in for the last twenty years so that's not a major factor. The Court does not have to sentence him for a long period of time because of concern he's likely to re-offend...

There was no way to know whether or not Jeff and Erik were his only victims. There was just no way to know and suggesting that because no more victims came forward as proof he never abused anyone else was absurd.

There's very little if any, there's zero reason to believe that's he's going to re-offend and particularly now where he has accepted responsibility he has obviously expressed the shame and embarrassment that he has caused. He's obviously recognized the pain and suffering that he's caused to his family members which contributes to his own view of his own embarrassment and regrets, remorse for this. You know from the PSI that a probation officer identified or felt that the defendant was truly remorseful. This isn't an act...

...So again, I don't think deterrence is much of a factor. I don't frankly think general deterrence is much of a factor either because people who are engaged in this kind of activity, it doesn't seem to make any difference. It's not the kind of thing where you have some sort of cause and effect, oh gee, I'm not going to do this because if I'm caught I'm going to get something more at play, here. So, I don't that's a critical aspect either...

...And then there's the issue of rehabilitation. I think that does play a role here and I think actually the rehabilitation and the punishment is somewhat hand in hand here. I think it's important that the defendant here spend a substantial period of time incarcerated and that, that in and of itself is part of the rehabilitative process. I think that they actually go hand in hand, at least in this particular case...

...I also think that the defendant should and will benefit from sex offender treatment. He obviously upon his release will be a sex offender for life. He will have to report for the remainder of his life.

Again, he's now fifty eight years old. If he is sentenced to ten years he'll be nearly seventy by the time he would be eligible for parole...

...He's not a young man. You're not sentencing a young man, who we don't even know if a sentence of that length, whether or not he'll survive it. He may well die in prison with that sentence that we are suggesting, but at least it offers some possibility that he will again be able to be a productive member of society.

Absolutely, James was not a young man but what about all the years he was and was still free to live his life. Not to mention all the talk about his sobriety. Any AA member would gaff at an individual calling themselves a recovered alcoholic while at the same time popping pills.

I understand, indeed have seen throughout my career, the emotional content that expressed by the victims here, their anger is certainly evident and justified. I'm not suggesting that there's anything about their feelings that aren't justified and they have a right to those feelings, but I don't believe that the role of the Court is to substitute anger that victims experience and make that the decision or the factor that controls sentencing...

...I think if you look at the probation report and you consider what the probation officer recommended this is somebody who's neutral, not the State, where the State has other issues. It's a neutral and detached recommendation from someone who has experienced the whole spectrum of it...

We never were allowed to see the PSI. We have no idea what this parole officer that Soldati mentions suggested.

...Mr. Gentes goes through and talks about how he wants to parts in each offense and what it means for each victim and or towards the offense for each victim, I'm not sure we gain anything by that analysis. I can look at hundreds if not thousands of cases in this Court where far more egregious behavior occurred over far more lengthy period of time, and the defendants received far less than the State is

By: Jeff & Kelly Halldorson

recommending. I don't know that we benefit by any of that. We are here to sentence this individual, James Halldorson, a sentence of seven and a half to fifteen for a person with his background who has no criminal record, frankly is an enormous and incredible sentence. That's a lot of time for somebody who has never been incarcerated, never dealt with law enforcement...

...The recriminations that the State and to a lesser degree that the victims wish to go through, well over the years he didn't own up to this, didn't come forward, I'm not sure that that should really play a role here, Your Honor...

...He has from the time that he was arrested or before he was arrested, when he was interviewed by the police, he took responsibility, he acknowledged to the extent that he could in terms of what he could remember. He didn't deny anything, he didn't try to minimize anything at all and he has accepted responsibility. I think that needs to have some recognition...

It was a just a bunch of crap. Anyone that has read police interview could see that right up to the end he was still blaming the victims for being hard children. Not to mention the man did originally plead NOT GUILTY. Sure, some could argue, that is how things are done... but really? Is that truly taking responsibility?

...Now what the sentence that I've proposed does not only does it give him a substantial period of incarceration but it also holds over his head the prospect of returning for a period of twenty years until he's nearly eighty years old. It will hang over his head to possibly return but I don't really think that in realty that's likely, I mean there's certainly no evidence to suggest that he remains a threat to anyone...

...So I would ask the Court to follow the recommendation of the sentencing forms I've submitted to the Court which I think is appropriate as I think the Probation Department's recommendation has properly set forth the issues in this case... Thank you.

Anything else you have?

No, Your Honor.

Mr. Gentes?

Real briefly - I want to address the issue of if or what benefit the defendant should receive for pleading guilty. Certainly I recognize he is entitled to a benefit, but I do note that the State would be totally and completely legally entitled to ask for a sentence imposed on each count. The case law is clear on that. The State and I think it is fair to point out that the State is asking for six to twelve months for each act. We are talking about acts here and the minimum, Your Honor, that the State is asking that the defendant be sentenced for each victim seven and one half to fifteen, bare minimum. I think that anything less would be a grave injustice. We are not seeking vengeance, Your Honor, we are seeking justice and that is what the State's recommendation reflects.

Judge Fauver questions both counsel. *Since this is a procedural matter, how did we extend the sentence review possibilities at the time of the entering of the pleas?*

Soldati responds. *I think, Your Honor, because initially I thought we were waiving sentence review, but I think that if given that we went with a cap plea that sentence review remains a possibility, I guess for both of us.*

What Soldati was attempting here was to allow for sentence review. That meant that basically if they didn't like whatever the judge imposed as a sentence they could appeal it. They could request a review and/or a reduction in time.

Eric Gentes wasn't going to allow it. *Your Honor, that was very clear. It's on the record, the Court can return to the record if need be, both parties acknowledged the sentence review as being waived. The defendant has waived sentence review.*

You could hear annoyance in Soldati's voice when he responded.

That's fine, I wasn't sure. If we were negotiating that would clearly be the case. I wasn't sure with the cap plea, whether or not if that was the case, so that's why I originally checked the box you'll note on three of the acknowledgements or three of the recommendations I checked it.

Right, I don't have a specific waiver of sentence review now.

Soldati was attempting to explain why he hadn't provided the Waiver of Sentence Review as he had negotiated. *I - I didn't think we had addressed it, and I thought it would have depended on whether or not it was fully negotiated.*

Your Honor, I do recall – it was - there was a bit of a call off between the Court and Attorney Soldati where at first, Attorney Soldati was unsure and was reluctant to acknowledge that a sentence review was being waived but when the Court pointed out that this was a negotiated plea even on a cap plea that it did involve the waiver of sentence review by its own terms.

Maybe I'll look at the record. The Judge was tiring of it.

I just don't remember, Your Honor, I'm not saying he's wrong and it's not a I don't think we intend to pursue sentence review but I you know that the State would have on the cap plea given that I have some feelings about the State being able to do it anyway but none the less I think that they may so I think that clearly if we had negotiated he would a sentence review for either party would not be, I'm not clear on the cap plea.

The judge needed to settle this sentence review issue before he imposed sentence, so he decided the best thing to do was take a recess and review the records.

What I want to do is, I want to take a short recess before I pull sentence in this case and I'm going to check the record of the plea and make sure that we find out what the understanding was with respect to sentence review. I want to make sure that's clear.

That's fine.

Yea, that's fine.

I want to take a short recess and I will come back and review the record as to sentence review. I just want to make sure that's clear and not an issue.

I understand.

I agree.

We all waited and wondered what was next. Carolann assured us everything was going well. It could, of course, go either way but she felt things were leaning in our favor.

We all rose as the Judge re-entered the court room.

I listened to the tape of the sentencing of the plea rather- ah - and you first said well if we negotiate a plea we will waive sentence review, but if it's a cap plea we may not, and then I asked you another question about that and you said okay - yes we will waive sentence review.

Fair enough.

Here's the form that goes to the State and the Defense.

I apologize.

No, that's alright. I understand. I understand. It's a sort of strange way of doing it and I understand that.

Eric Gentes spoke. *Your Honor, just to avoid the confusion for the sake – ah - I would ask -I would draw that the State's recommendations that were previously recorded on that reflects that and I've made the correction to the Defense, counsel, Your Honor. Thank you very much.*

The papers were signed and put in record. Corrections made. We sat quietly while they shuffled around papers and whispered to one another. Then the judge spoke...

Alright, in all events sentence review is waived.

He had to have that waived sentence review in his hand before he would give his sentence.

Stand up, sir.

...Ah - I have been doing this a long time, sometimes longer than I should. You know in every one of these pleas of cases like this when the sentencing cases like this, it is difficult and one that most judges or all judges give a lot of thought to because you know that we've got the craft of sentencing you here which deals with rehabilitation, returns, punishment, and have to emphasize - have to balance and take into consideration all of the factors...

...Each one of these things is difficult but some are more difficult than others. And what I find so mysterious about this case and the sentencing of this case is that the crimes that were committed really have very little if any explanation. I read these pre-sentence reports in many cases and the defendants have had awful lives, they come in having been sexually assaulted as children themselves, come from broken families, come from families that are abusive in so many ways and you can look at it and you can say it doesn't excuse why somebody does something but it explains why somebody does something. What's different about this case is there is nothing in this pre sentence report to suggest that your childhood was an awful childhood or was so traumatic that your behavior which resulted in commissioning these offenses an explanation. That's what makes this difficult...

...Second of all, it was a period of your life for about four years maybe longer that this occurred and after that point undisputed, you lived in many ways an exemplary life. You had a responsible job. You provided financially for your family and there's no other conduct which is

reported which would suggest that this was a pattern of behavior which was part of your ongoing life...

...So those are two things that make this very difficult...

...I heard the two victims in these cases speak and your attorney is correct that this is not a situation where the Court sentence is based on vengeance to repair to punish for the sake of punishing, but I can't disregard in any sentence the harm that your criminal acts have caused. I have to consider that. The harm that has been caused to these victims is harm which they will live with for the rest of their lives. This is a repeated series of acts which went on and on and on and they've got to live with that and I heard from both of them and the first one who spoke was articulate in explaining how he and his life has been affected. His wife spoke about how her husband's life had been affected. The second young man who spoke obviously has been damaged. These kids have both been damaged irreparably and I can't disregard the harm in imposing sentence even though I am not going to impose sentence for the purpose of vengeance...

...To your credit you have spared these children. These young people, these young adults or these adults rather the pain of going through a trial. You've spared them the process of standing up here and telling the jury about all the things that happened, but you know I think that that the fact that you did that and the fact that you have lived an exemplary life since that time, have been factored into the cap plea...

...Let me tell you that if you had not lived an exemplary life and this had been recent and if you had put these children, these people through a trial we'd be looking at the rest of your life. We'd be looking at forty years or fifty years...

...I know that State hasn't said it but I expect that in calculating what the cap will be they've already factored in these pieces because if had been otherwise we'd be looking at a lot more time and I've done that.

Your counsel will indicate, will confirm that I have done just that and every Judge in this Court has done just that...

...My sentence is going to be going before you, twenty to forty, it is going to be broken down as follows: On 06S-192 you be sentenced to the New Hampshire State Prison for not more than fifteen years, no less than seven and one half years and that the minimum sentence of disciplinary period equal one hundred fifty days for year the minimum and the term of the sentence to be prorated for any part of the year staying committed. This is pretrial confinement credit of seventy eight days; other conditions are to participate, meaningfully, in treatment programs directed by the correctional authorities. You have waived sentence review in writing comply alter sentence.

We had heard the words of the Judge. James was given the maximum negotiated by the State. Yet, we only felt victorious for an instant. We had hoped for a strong sentence. We hoped that a strong sentence would somehow make all the pain instantly disappear. Hoped it would wipe the slate clean for all of us. Give us a new start. It didn't.

Almost immediately, the guilt began corroding away at our beautiful little family.

Inside the Prison & Beyond
(Jeff)

Seventeen years...

The doors closed behind us as we entered the prison. I knew I could leave at any point. This was only temporary, I told myself. Even though I chose to be there, being locked in the New Hampshire State Prison for Men with my cute little wife did not feel like such a great idea once we walked through the door.

I had wanted to see the inside of the place since my father was sentenced three months before. I needed to see for myself where he would be spending the next twenty to forty years of his life and at times was overcome with curiosity.

By: Jeff & Kelly Halldorson

Jim was 58 when he was taken into custody. He would be 78 years old before he would be eligible for parole. The thought of that made me detest being inside the walls of the prison even more. My lungs filled with the stale air as I walked along side my wife. The air was heavy with the loneliness and regret. There was no happiness to be found within these walls and I realized, if only for a moment, nothing positive would come from my visit.

Do you have any weapons on you, contraband or illegal substances?

Hum... no

A nod from our guide and we moved forward through the prison. Kelly and I walked among prisoners with only a small timid priest as a guard.

This is the minimum-security end of the prison...

It resembled a recycled high school cafeteria. There we met Phil, a massive man standing close to six foot four with a bulky frame. His hand was so large it engulfed mine as he shook my hand. He was to accompany us throughout our tour, which brought me some relief.

The prison was primarily what I had expected; bars and concrete, men of all shapes and sizes, some mean looking and others timid all in solid color pajamas restrained by bars and concrete. We started in the quarantine area and worked our way through the prison as every inmate enters on their arrival.

At every stop I tried to think of Jim. *How would he be handling this? Would he be mentally strong enough?* He had lived a very comfortable life. Now instead of a bed made up cozy and clean every day by Susan, it would be a cold cot and three square. Would he be able to handle it?

Jim was just one of the over 1,300 prisoners. All of them there for a different reason, some for sexual crimes, like Jim, others for theft, drugs, fraud or murder. My thoughts drifted to the rumors everyone hears about how child molesters are singled out by other inmates, threatened and beaten up. Would he survive? Did it matter? He had put himself there. No. I had put him there. His choices, his actions, his crimes had made it possible but I had put him there. I had been the one that made certain he would spend most of the remainder of his life behind those bars. Me. There were others who had helped make it happen - Kelly, Gentes, Tarrants, Erik - all of them, but I felt as though I was solely responsible. I allowed myself to bear the responsibility for both the victory and the burden.

After the quarantine area we were walked up some dark stairs, so much of the place was reminiscent of a dungeon, in Hell itself. At the top of the stairs was a long hallway. It was barred on one side and a guard stood on the opposite side of the bars. Along one side of the hallway were at least a dozen cells. We were not allowed into the hallway and could not see completely into the cell. If they came to the front of their cells, especially the cells closest to the hallway entrance, they could see us.

These cells are for the segment of the populations that have concerns for their own safety.

Are you saying some prisoners asked to be in this area?

Yes, many of these prisoners have requested added protection. We also generally house sexual offenders in here. Or as I said other inmates who have concerns for their safety – maybe they are being targeted or it's a gang-related thing.

Gang related? Are – is - um - there really a lot of gang related activity here in New Hampshire?

No, but there is some. Nashua has been a hotspot. Your father is in a wing very similar to this, in a different area of the prison.

Are they single cells?

No, most of them have a cellmate.

Some of the prisoners hooted or yelled at Kelly, others craned their necks and would lean up against the bars in an effort to get a look at what all the excitement was about. She slid behind me.

I think we can move on now.

Next stop was the yard. We walked out onto a metal staircase landing. We stopped while our guide gave us an overview of where everything was and what the rest of our itinerary would be. This part of the tour is where we saw the most prisoners. They were being ushered to and from work and recreation. They all stared at us curiously. Most of them gawked at Kelly. I was repulsed by the thought of any one of them having a visual of my wife they could later use for their own fantasies. Why had I brought her here? To have these men look at her in this way?

With all the inmates walking around I began to wonder where Jim was.

Is there any chance of seeing my father? Will he be walking to lunch or something?

Oh, no. When a victim comes to visit the prison we make special arrangements so that does not happen.

Part of me was disappointed. I hadn't realized how much I wanted to see him until that moment. I wanted to know how he was holding up.

How do you do that? Are they put in solitary?

No, they are just confined to their wing for the day. And we will not visit that area of the prison. So, it's all pretty easy to manage that way.

He would know we were there. He would know it was me. It was always me.

We walked on through the yard to the shop. Inmates were allowed to work for money if they were at a certain level. They were paid a small amount. Part of their income often would then be used for any restitution ordered by the court or they could spend it for extra toiletries and such in the inmate store.

In the shop area, inmates made everything from license plates to kitchen cabinets which were sold to New Hampshire businesses. Other jobs were available to inmates including laundry and kitchen help. These were all ways of keeping the inmates busy and giving them some purpose. Some jobs were much more sought after than others, for example, the high level wood working. To be allowed a job such as that required a high level of obedience to and respect for the prison.

So much of the prison reminded me of the various institutions I had been in as a teen. The same concept of population management ran through all of them. Keep them busy, rewards, punishments, levels, etc. If anything, I thought, he's getting a taste of what he forced upon me.

Next we were taken back across the yard. It was the lowest security area of the prison. It appeared to be three massive, rundown motel buildings. There were three floors lined with about twenty doors to a floor. There were men hanging outside on the walkway areas talking. Doors were open and inmates could be seen walking in and out of the rooms.

Each room sleeps up to six inmates.

What about security? Kelly asked.

They are checked on at a set time where they have to get up out of bed and come to the door throughout the night.

He explained most of the inmates in this area were in prison for drug related offenses. Most hadn't committed a violent offense. The rooms were really like small apartments. There was a common area in each room and then two or three bunk rooms where the inmates slept adjacent to that common area. There were no cameras inside the faux apartments. There were large front windows with curtains. Once the doors were shut and the curtains drawn there was no way to see what went on inside. During the day the prisoners were allowed to walk freely throughout the cheesy motel-type complex, while others chose to go to work in the workshops.

That's it?

Well we check on them.

But anything can happen in-between those checks.

We do what we can, but there are a lot of men and things can and do happen. But we do have a system and for the most part it works. Most of the men here just want to do their time and go home. We do what we can to see them through.

From there we went on to the more secure areas of the prison. The first area closely resembled a wing at a hospital. It had three or four hallways of rooms with kiosk in the center. We were told there were a number of these units and they were for those inmates that required a higher level of security. In the halls were televisions and exercise equipment. Inmates walked in and out of the rooms while a few sat and watched TV or read. Some looked like they were in heated discussions with the staff.

Then we hit the last area in which they housed inmates, the most secure area of the prison. Cells were single occupant and monitored 24 hours a day. The entire walls of the cells were made of a thick plexi-glass. We were not told what crimes any of these inmates had committed nor did they tell us what they might have done inside the prison to wind up in that wing. All we were told was that the men in that unit were the most dangerous in the entire prison. They looked like nothing more than animals caged and on display in a fancy zoo.

I felt ashamed and vindicated all at the same time, torn. Jim deserved to be here. He got what was coming to him. I would say that about any man who did what he did. Why was it then that I was feeling sorry for him? I couldn't see the middle. I was either praising myself for having faced up to and locked away a predator or I was condemning myself (and Kelly) for having institutionalized my father, a man I once loved. A man at times I still loved.

Though surrounded 24 hours a day with men, fellow inmates and prison staffers, Jim was alone in a fort filled with dark men and depression. His warm house, nice clothes, big TV and prescription drugs were out of reach. So too were the bodies of little boys.

Kelly and I often discussed the possibility of Jim's predilection (as James himself had labeled it during sentencing) having been satisfied by others. He traveled a lot. And those travels took him all over the globe. He had access to many children over the years. There was no way to really know the true depth of Jim's actions.

I was less likely to indulge such thoughts being far more comfortable believing Erik and I were his only prey. Kelly was more practical about it and guilt ridden for what she could have done and felt she should have done sooner. She feared for the other children he had access to over the years. There is no evidence that Jim did anything to anyone else but... I do wonder. I wonder a lot.

The weather outside hadn't changed as we exited the prison. It was dark and dreary. The visit hadn't helped in the way that I'd hoped. I walked out of there more confused and detached than when I entered.

I wondered again if Jim was going to make it. I wondered if I was going to make it. I had become more withdrawn and internally destructive than ever before. My perception of life and right from wrong was warped.

Kelly and I returned to our home, to our children and our life. At first I was at least grateful for my freedom. I slept that night in my bed and under my roof. There was no barbed wire nor were there men with guns forcing me to stay.

In the days, weeks and months that followed Kelly found me fixating on Discovery Channel documentaries on prisons, prisoners and life behind bars. The impact on me of Jim's incarceration was not going away anytime soon. I still went to work. I continued to visit and talk to Julia, in part to protect our secret. Then I would come home and argue and bicker, many nights spending the evening in front of the TV barely acknowledging Kelly's existence.

Erik did better, at least, for a while. He said he was sleeping better and he was happier.

The story should have been over. There was a beginning, middle and end. Jim had been brought to justice, Erik had made it out okay and I still had my family. I was still a father and a husband. The funny thing was, or the not-so-funny thing, was that it didn't feel over. The pain was still there. We had dragged our past out and hung it for the world to see. We had set things right… some things that is. However, secrets are only temporary. The skeletons that I had stashed away still poked their heads out from time to time. It was obvious that the more negative I was the more they wanted to come out into the light. The more they haunted me.

Yes, I had my family. I was a father and a husband but was I a very good one? I had cheated on my wife, physically assaulted her, and emotionally ravaged her. Yet she stood by my side none-the-less. I started to realize, I was a terrible husband. If I was a terrible husband what kind of father was I? Not much better, I concluded. I yelled at them, neglected them, worked too much and made excuses for not being around. Guilt seeped into every one of our lives. It may have been guilt that I carried and me that caused it but it was all of us who suffered.

It was only a matter of time before I ran into my mother at the local food market.

I can't believe you said those things about me!

Well...hello?

How could you say that stuff, about me being a liar and knowing about your father doing those things? About me only looking out for myself?

Well...I was taken aback. Was she serious?

You could have come to me. You didn't. I thought that we were close...

You didn't even show up at the sentencing...

How could I after what you told the police?!

She had no problem making a scene. I stood in front of the checkout lines while Susan tore me a new one. There was no love in her. She was a complete stranger to me now.

I just walked right around her and headed off to grab what I had come for. No goodbye or see you later, nothing. I saw no need to finish the conversation.

My chance meeting with her only fueled my depression and angst. I thought that with the end of Jim would be the end of my pain. I was sorely wrong. After everything I still didn't have a mother to love me. It hurt. I often wondered how might life, had been different if she had stood up for me all those years ago or if she had at least stood *by* me later. I thought of all the things I should have said to her, in that store. *I should have set her straight*, I thought. Where was my backbone when it came to her? Why had I let her walk on, over and around me for so long?

I looked in the mirror and couldn't handle what I saw. Could anyone with any semblance of a conscience? I had to defend myself, to myself. I was miserable. I started looking for reasons why I was so miserable. Instead of looking inward I looked outward. Then everything seemed to come to a head. I felt I was never meant to be a father or a husband. I started to gripe about Kelly to others, incredibly, even to Julia.

I started feeling like Kelly was the cause of my problems. Our money problems were getting progressively worse. Kelly was a stay-at-home mother and hadn't been working the last two years. We homeschooled the kids and I thought if she just put them in public school and got a job all my problems would disappear. I wanted a ready excuse and answer all in one.

When I did try and talk with her about my frustrations, we would only butt heads and I would blow up. I had a narrow range of emotions which consisted of anger, guilt, frustration and happy. All but the occasional high came out as anger, with all guns aimed at the one that loved me the most.

I could be brutal at times too. Anger was easy; I knew how to stomach anger. It was the rage that followed it which caused Kelly the most concern and resulted in me lashing out, even more fiercely, from guilt.

In an effort of self-preservation, Kelly started to try and live a life that inspired her and the kids. She got involved in politics and more deeply into the homeschooling groups and our eldest son's hockey. Kelly became less focused on being my wife and put her energy into being a mother and an individual. She wasn't going to allow my past or my destructive behaviors to drag her or the kids down any longer. I took it hard. I felt abandoned. When opportunities to join Kelly and the kids were presented I chose not to go with them on their adventures. I longed to be with them, yet I couldn't be around them without feeling unworthy. I blamed them for that. It was a catch-22; I was a walking contradiction.

In the summer of 2007 I started smoking again and spending more time with Julia. I would visit her at her condo for coffee and cigarette breaks when Kelly and the kids believed I was working or I would stop by on my way home. I bitched to Julia about Kelly's involvement in politics and how I wanted to put the kids into public school and Kelly to get a job.

I missed my younger brothers. I hadn't seen them and it didn't appear they had any interest in talking to me, which again made me question my decision to bring charges. I had to tell myself that Jim hurt children and for that he was monster. Jim got what was coming to him I did the right thing. *I did the right thing.*

Kelly spent more time involved in her and the kids' activities and I become more and more detached. I was, or often felt like I was always to blame for everything. As the year went on things grew worse. I experienced random violent raging outbursts where I would verbally and even physically threaten Kelly. On one occasion I grit my teeth and threatened her, *I'll knock your fucking teeth out!* Another time I squeezed my hands around her throat and held her down on the bed.

The kids did not witness this. They slept through the outbursts, incredibly, or were not home. They did, however see plenty of bickering and yelling but thankfully were spared the nastiest of it. Yet I didn't fool myself and I believe they knew exactly what kind of man I was. Although Kelly was able to keep a lid on things most of the time she was growing increasingly afraid of my escalating anger and less interested in walking on eggshells.

In the spring of 2008 Kelly became so fearful of me she called Erik and asked for his help. She asked me to go stay with him until I was able to figure things out. I went and spent the night with Erik and then went to Kelly's aunt to confess what I had done. I didn't want Kelly to have to lie anymore. I didn't want her to have to pretend I was this perfect Superman. Although I confessed my aggressive behavior, I conveniently left out the cheating.

Kelly had put her hopes so high that things would get better for us upon Jim being put away, just like I had. We were both figuring out that wasn't going to happen. When I wasn't fighting with Kelly I was professing my love to her. I even got another tattoo representing our first drive across country. I truly wanted things to be ok. I just couldn't keep myself together long enough to see that happen. At times I would badmouth and condemn her behind her back. I wanted to support her projects and even encouraged her to run for political office. I bought her a computer as a surprise gift of support. I wanted her to take the leap and run. Almost as soon as she filed the paperwork and began her campaign, less than a month later, I resented her for doing it. I resented her for finding some happiness and fulfillment that didn't involve me. The irony being, I chose not to be involved.

Kelly had to constantly feel my mood out to see how she was going to have to deal with me on a particular day or a particular moment. I was a constant contradiction. I felt torn all the time. I loved her. I couldn't stand her. I hated myself. I wanted to be a good person yet I reveled in being a bad one. Guilt consumed me, it fed me.

It all came to a head in July of 2008, less than two months after I bought Kelly the surprise computer and three months after I had gotten the tattoo representing our history together. My first serious girlfriend from high school, Sherri, contacted me online asking how I was and what my phone number was. I showed Kelly the message and said I wanted nothing to do with her. Kelly, however, left the decision up to me, even encouraged me to message her back but suggested she was a little uncomfortable with the idea of me talking to her on the phone.

I left it alone for about a week, approved the friend request she had sent on the social networking site and found myself looking through her pictures. I was intrigued. I messaged her back a short note and included my phone number.

Sherri called me three times that first day and we talked for over an hour. We opened a line of communication that was not only completely wrong and unhealthy but entirely based on lies and deceptions to each other and our families. Sherri filled me in on her life, her kids and her marriages. I told her I worked hard and needed a break. Even though she was married herself, she joked about taking me to her father's house in Myrtle Beach. She asked if we could get drinks together. I declined, telling her *I don't think Kelly would like that*.

I didn't tell Kelly about the conversations with Sherri, in part, out of guilt and in part because I didn't know if I wanted to talk to her again and thought if I told Kelly about the conversation I wouldn't be able to. I had already crossed a line.

Over the next few days I talked with Sherri more and more. She called me multiple times a day and texted me relentlessly. She told me about her first failed marriage and that she was planning on getting a divorce from her current husband. She told me they had grown apart that everyone grows apart and that marriage shouldn't be hard. Things should be fun. She dropped not so subtle hints that she was interested in a relationship with me and had no problems keeping it from my wife. She even changed the song on her social networking page to *All Summer Long* by Kid Rock, a song reminiscing about a teen romance.

Less than a week into the phone conversations with Sherri, Kelly and the kids were invited sailing with a homeschooling family a few hours away and overnight trip. I was invited but chose not to go using work once again as my excuse. I used the opportunity to drive up to Concord and meet with Sherri at a bar after work. Nothing happened physically between us that night other than hugs between old friends but our talks got more intense and sexual. I started to call her more.

Ten days after that first phone call from Sherri, I left my family and pursued a relationship with her. Kelly had made dinner. The kids were calm, it was quiet. There was no fight. I was sulking by the computer and Kelly asked what was bothering me and I just told her, *I'm leaving you.* Dumbfounded, she cried and asked me to at least stay the night. I stayed with her then left in the morning without, so much as, a word to the kids. I walked out; leaving Kelly to explain to them I wasn't coming home. To Kelly and the kids this was all completely out of the blue. They had come to expect my instability and volatility but never dreamed I'd walk out. I had always told Kelly and the kids I would never leave them. I had made that mistake, once, when Wolfgang was a baby and never intended to repeat it.

When I walked out on Kelly, I started building an enormous web of lies. Only days after I left I called her parents, friends, aunt, and grandfather to tell them that I had left her and that it was entirely her fault, not once mentioning I was already seeing another woman. Kelly was inundated with friends and family pressuring her to fix all she had done wrong. They told her I was burnt out from working so much and she needed to get job. The kids needed to go to public school and she needed to drop out of the State Senate race. I presented myself as the martyr, the hardworking husband who was neglected, overworked and unappreciated and Kelly as the ungrateful money grubbing and demanding wife.

A week after I left, Kelly got our cell phone bill and discovered I had been talking to Sherri. I claimed I wasn't talking to her anymore which the phone records verified because a few days earlier I had bought a separate pay-as-you-go phone (that Kelly wouldn't be able to track) to talk to Sherri on. I told Kelly and the kids I was staying at Erik's but spent the weekends with Sherri at the home of another old high school friend partying, a few miles from our family home. I leaned heavily on Sherri for support. She told me I was doing the right thing and that life shouldn't be hard. *People grow apart and it's no big deal. Kelly will be fine. She'll find someone, you need to be happy.* I ate it up, once again, embracing any excuse to revel in destructiveness, in my own destructiveness.

A few weeks into the affair Sherri filed for divorce from her husband and started light-heartedly pressuring me to move in with her. *We both need to find somewhere to live. We can be roommates.* When I objected she said it was no big thing she and her daughter could share a room. The same fifteen year old daughter she brought with her one night to the friend's house we partied and slept together at. She did this after I had already told her I had no desire to meet her kids. Her daughter then became a regular fixture at the parties. Sherri asked to meet my kids many times. I refused. I felt the pressure but tried to blow it off.

I didn't think there was any way I could go back to Kelly after what I'd done. I had gone too far. I didn't want to be alone and Sherri was a lot of fun to be with. All she wanted to do was drink and that is exactly what I did. Together we did our best to drink my problems away.

The financial burden of it all was taking its toll. I told Sherri I couldn't afford to text her all day long with the phone I'd bought I was charged ten cents for every text. She bought me a phone on her plan so she could continue to text me. And she did all day long, every day. *Where are you? What's up? Are you going to hang out this weekend?*

Sometimes I would have the Sherri phone off and she would text me on my other phone asking where it was. She wanted to talk all the time. At the time it felt good, like she was really interested in me. But looking back it was likely much more about keeping track of me. She did know where I was, nearly every minute of the time I spent away from Kelly. And when Kelly became suspect of my relationship with Sherri she "friended" her on the social networking site and Sherri accepted. So not only did she know everything I was doing she knew most everything Kelly was doing too.

It was at least clear to me that Sherri wanted much more from me than I was willing or had any desire to give but I played along to some extent. Sherri would ask when I was planning on filing for divorce or at least separation and I'd tell her I didn't know what was happening or make some excuse about money being a factor. She would ask to meet my children and I would say *that isn't happening anytime soon.* If she talked about taking me to Myrtle Beach, I'd say *someday maybe.* I always left things open with her.

The truth was I don't think that I ever had any real intention of leaving Kelly. There were times I thought I did but I could never bring myself to fill out the paperwork.

And a big part of me was terrified of Kelly finding out as I continued to spend at least two or three nights a week with Kelly. I couldn't let her go. I even told Sherri early on, *I can't stop kissing her - Every time I see her - I can't *not* kiss her.* It got harder and harder for me to be away from Kelly. I would try and shut her out most days I didn't even answer the majority of Kelly's calls or would just shut off my phone completely. When I did take calls from Kelly I spent the time screaming insults and threats at her or lying to her about my whereabouts whilst drilling her about her activities. Then I when I saw Kelly, in person, I had to be with her. I would spend the nights with her then hate myself in the morning for it and by the following afternoon I would start taking that anger out on Kelly with the threats and nasty phone calls.

Finally, for the first time in our lives together, Kelly completely crumbled. The roller coaster ride I forced her onto was too much for her. She believed all the lies I was feeding her and everyone else. She believed she was the cause of it all. She believed I was the righteous one, that she had hurt me. Worst of all, she doubted what kind of a mother she was. I had convinced her family that homeschooling was bad for the kids. Everything I was using as distractions for my own wrongdoings became her undoing. I overestimated her strength. I wonder if there was a part of me that was testing her. Kelly ended up spending four nights in New Hampshire Hospital, a psychiatric facility.

This should have awakened me to the pain I was causing. It should have had me coming to my wife's aid as she had come to mine so many times. Instead Kelly's crisis fueled my recklessness. I saw her as weak and undeserving and saw Sherri as an escape and Julia as an ear. While Kelly was in the hospital I sent the kids to stay with her parents and called to talk but didn't visit them. I stayed at our house in Dover, alone. Kelly picked the kids up when she got out of the hospital. Meanwhile, despite tiring of Sherri, I put a deposit down on a trailer rental in another town closer to her home and work, further stretching my family's finances.

Thankfully, when Kelly emerged from New Hampshire hospital she had awakened. She had renewed confidence and began taking a different approach when talking to me. She did a lot of listening. She apologized, for breaking down. She listened with compassion to what was happening with me. She seemed to understand more which parts were truly her doing and which ones were not. She stopped taking responsibility for all of our failures as a couple.

She started working part-time mornings at a relative's machine shop and she began, again, building back her independence while being clear with me that what she truly wanted was to work things out between us. Kelly wasn't always strong but she managed overall pretty well. She tried to focus on our friendship. *I want us to be friends again. I want you to like me again.* It did not take long from there on to start seeing her again for who she was and I started panicking for what I had done to tear her down but I continued to separate myself from her and the kids.

Then one afternoon she called while I was at work to ask me about an email I had sent her. After spending the previous night with her I told her in the email we could never be together again. She called to confront me about the email. I felt put out and she had caught me in a bad mood. I lost it on her and completely unrelated to the conversation called her a *money grubbing cunt*. She hung up the phone and text me, *You win. I hate you.*

That was it. That was the turning point.

I couldn't imagine a world where she hated me, really hated me. We'd had arguments before over the years where she'd said that to me, out of anger, but never had it felt so real. I panicked. I tried calling her repeatedly and begged her for forgiveness. She responded calmly but sternly. She apologized for her words but told me she had reached her limit and I was free to pursue a divorce and she would not contest.

I had already begun to slowly end my relationship with Sherri. I wanted it to die a slow natural death. I had become concerned she might do something and Kelly might find out. My time with Julia was now spent bitching about Sherri. It had become clear to me Sherri was lying to me as much as I was lying to her. I grew tired of her drinking and advice. It was obvious, she was wrong. Things were not *going to be alright*. The romantic picture Sherri kept trying to paint seemed more and more ridiculous by the day.

Julia ironically became a cheerleader for Kelly and a sounding board for me. A few days after the, *I hate you* text from Kelly I was at a party with Sherri but spent the time texting Kelly on the porch. Eventually I just got up and left without even telling Sherri or anyone else I was leaving. Sherri sent me angry texts. *You are an asshole! Where did you go? We are supposed to be your friends here.* With those texts I became even more concerned about Sherri and her stability.

A few days after Wolfgang and Griffin's birthdays, near the end of October Kelly showed up on the jobsite we were working at together. Riddled with guilt I lashed out at her demanding she leave and told her about the phone Sherri had bought for me. I was on an emotional rollercoaster. I wanted to force an end to it all. But I didn't. Later that evening at my trailer I promised Kelly I was done talking to Sherri. I even made a show of it by pretending to throw the phone in a pond. What I really threw in the pond was the phone pay as you go phone I had bought while keeping the phone Sherri had bought safe and hidden.

Through my entire crisis I was unable to remain long from Kelly and her bedroom. I needed her body. I craved her all the time, even when I was angry which just fueled my self-loathing and guilt. I ran Kelly through the ringer both physically and mentally. Sherri and I had unprotected sex and as a result of my carelessness Kelly wound up in the hospital.

Kelly had a feeling something was wrong a couple of weeks after getting out of New Hampshire hospital but tried to go on with life. She didn't want to appear weak in my eyes again. Two nights before Halloween, just a week after I had pretended to throw the phone in the pond. Kelly developed a sudden high fever. I already had plans to spend the night with her so I was at the house. During the night her temperature spiked above 104 then broke after she took a fever reducer. She woke in the morning and felt better so she went on with the day which included working in the morning.

That evening was Begger's Night in Dover and Kelly had plans to take the boys trick or treating. Zoe was spending the night at a friend's house. By lunchtime Kelly spiked another high fever. She went to the doctor's office but they told her to go directly to the hospital. They suspected appendicitis.

She didn't go to the hospital. She went home instead, took some Advil and called me to come take the boys trick or treating. When I arrived she was bundled up on the couch and she was burning up but was refused to go to the hospital. She kept trying to make deals with me *I'll go if my temp hits 101.* Then that became *I'll go if my temp hits 102* and so on.

The boys finally convinced her to get checked out. I drove her to the hospital got her registered and then went back to the house to take the boys out trick-or-treating.

When I returned to the hospital the doctor informed us Kelly wasn't going to be going anywhere for a few days. It wasn't appendicitis. Kelly had an infection that had spread to her kidney and it required IV antibiotics and fluids. This time I didn't send the kids to her parents. I cancelled my plans for the weekend, which included seeing Sherri and working. I stayed at the house in Dover with the kids.

The magnitude of all my actions was sinking in. I continued to talk to Sherri as well as Julia while telling Kelly and the kids we were going to be a family again. The day Kelly got out of the hospital I spent the night with her at the house but in the morning I headed off to the trailer I had rented to work on the property instead of joining her and the kids for Wolfgang's hockey game. While I was working outside an unexpected visitor pulled up. It was Sherri. I didn't want her there. It was finally becoming crystal clear to me that I could no longer do this. I smoked a cigarette with her, told her I was working on my relationship with Kelly and asked her to leave.

I ran from what I had become and what I was. The next few days I barely spoke with Sherri, only texting her briefly each day. Then the following Friday evening Kelly brought Wolfgang to his weekly homeschool teen, roller skate gathering. When Kelly went to pick him up she found Sherri roller skating with her daughter and the friends I had been partying with. I had no idea Sherri was going to be there or I would have suggested Kelly take Wolfgang elsewhere. There is no way to tell for sure Sherri's intentions in choosing to go to that specific roller skating rink, over an hour from her house, on a Friday night. Maybe it was coincidence, maybe it wasn't. What is clear though, is she knew my son did this on a regular basis and she neglected to mention to me that she had plans to go.

After seeing a group of people pointing at her and Wolfgang and putting that together with the pictures she'd seen online Kelly figured out who they were and called me, livid and crying. At this point I had told her about the phone and that I had seen Sherri a couple of times but was still denying any kind of sexual relationship with her. Three days later I mailed the phone back to Sherri and severed my relationship with her. She continued to make attempts to contact me through friends and I was told she even drove by my trailer with a friend on at least one occasion. I ended my relationship with Julia shortly after, calling her the day before Thanksgiving telling her I needed to get my family back on track.

In many ways I was grateful to let all of it go. I had had enough with the game that I had created. Yet, I still wasn't honest with Kelly about the extent of my betrayal. It would take nearly a year for it all to come out and the majority she would find out through her own detective work, including searching phone bills, questioning me, talking to Sherri's husband and putting the pieces together.

On returning to my family, I was finally willing to look at what I was and where I wanted to go as a person. I began to, within my ability, to make amends for the pain I caused. I met with and apologized to Sherri's husband. I came clean with friends and family with regards to my leaving Kelly. I got more involved with the kid's homeschooling life. I stopped using needing to work as an excuse to avoid Kelly and the children.

I will not profess to be an expert on what it means to be a survivor of sexual assault. Although I have survived for so long I have hardly mastered it. I don't know if I ever will. That right there, that piece in itself is worth all the knowledge in the world. There may not be an end and learning to accept that it may be a piece of what has made me but it need not be one that defines me.

Being a survivor, regardless if it was physical, sexual or emotional abuse and knowing that there is no way to go back and change what happened allowed me to move forward with this piece of my life.

What matters now is that I know there is a life I want to live. Whether Jim dies in prison or Susan finds a man to love her and dies happy, whether my two kid brothers find peace or never speak to me again... what matters is that I have now taken back my life. I have given it completely to the children and the woman I love and will no longer let the past be an excuse for today or tomorrow.

It remains a struggle. I continue to be confronted by the consequences of my own actions. In September of 2009 near the end of the writing of this book, Kelly found out about my affair with Julia through a text from Sherri. I had been able to keep the secret for four years. I had convinced myself it was dead and buried but with all skeletons, they don't sleep. They always resurface. We had been close to healing our relationship from the damage my affair with Sherri had inflicted; now we were forced backwards. It was all too much for me. I exploded and crumbled at the same time. I truly reached my rock bottom. Kelly and the children asked me to admit myself for psychiatric care. I did and I spent nearly a week in Concord Hospital's psychiatric ward.

As a result of my treatment in the hospital it came to light that I have Borderline Personality Disorder. A reminder that what happened will always be a part of me. I am choosing to not allow it to define me. I'm working daily to be a better husband and father. There are days when failure is the only word I can find to describe that day. Thankfully there always seems to be a new day and opportunity to follow.

Together with Kelly I am facing my past as well as my choices despite painful reminders which continually crop up unexpectedly. Days after I was released from Concord Hospital I was driving in Concord with my eldest son, Wolfgang. Sherri spotted me while she driving. She rolled down her window and started shouting my name. I heard something, looked in my rearview mirror and realized it was her. I immediately rolled up my own window and tried to ignore her. She followed us, through a couple of streets. I pulled over and got out. I stood ten feet or so away from her vehicle and yelled to her *never contact me again! Never follow me! Our relationship was all a huge mistake, I love my wife!* All things which should, already, have been clear to her, for nearly a year at that point.

Once again the rippling effects of my actions resulted in pain to my family. My 14 year old son had to witness that exchange.

I have so much damage to repair from my destructiveness. I hurt my family. I am overwhelmed at times but determined to take responsibility for the wrongs I have made. I accept that I may falter. There are days when I hate who I am and I want to cut the ties to the pain I have caused and run. There are days when it causes me physical pain to see my reflection and know that there are people that I have hurt. There are days when hate is all there is to explain what I feel about myself, my past and my indiscretions. I live now for the days in between; to see those painful days drift further and further from me.

I have often been asked if I forgive Jim for what he did to us. My answer is this:

Every day I wake up hoping that Kelly can forgive me for the things that I have done to her. I don't look to a God in the sky to absolve me of my sins. I look for Kelly's forgiveness with my actions and my words. I hope that she and my children can find me worthy of that.

Jim has never shown any remorse for the pain he has inflicted on others. He finds forgiveness in a God that he has chosen. He has only asked for forgiveness in the face of a judge with the fear of a penalty. It is hard to look back at my childhood and not feel sorry for myself. I went through four parents and ended up with none.

Here I am at 36 looking back and looking forward. What do I have to say for myself? I did the right thing putting Jim in prison and not giving up; letting everyone know what he did and what he was. With the help of my loving wife and a well-knit support group we put him behind bars.

I do not know if Jim's sexual predilections started and ended with Erik and me. Now that he is behind bars we at least know he will not have the chance to fall back on his old ways.

I believe it is important, for many reasons, that victims seek justice. It should not be our fate to go through life with our abusers haunting us.

People asked "Why now?"

Is it so different now than when it happened? Does it matter? He still did these things to children and just because it was years ago, it doesn't mean that it should be forgotten.

For those who have been sexually assaulted or physically abused, it doesn't just go away. There isn't a point where you can say *Ok that's it, I am never thinking of this again.* The effects Susan and Jim have had upon me will echo throughout my entire life, whether I want them to or not.

There is no *right* time. Though, Kelly would argue the sooner the better, as close to the assault/s as possible. If it falls into the statutes of limitation and a victim wants to search for justice then that is their right, as it was my right. I was lucky in a lot of ways. It was easy to prove what Jim did. He and Susan were so willing to prove me wrong, that they only proved me right. I had a wife to hold me up in the hard times and the legal system worked in my favor.

Kelly and I took a chance. From the moment I walked into that police station Kelly and I put everything on the line, our names, our reputation and our sanity. We came out with a victory and we came out with heartache.

I may never overcome the past. Being willing to accept it for what it is and where I have come from has been far more valuable than trying to conquer it. It cannot be conquered. The past is just that. Accepting it for what it is was the first step, for me towards, living a better life. So many suits in leather chairs with $100 an hour fees have told me in great detail how I need to let the past go or put it behind me. That's a nice thought, but highly unrealistic. Our experiences and actions of yesterday make us who we are today. Everything I have seen, done or felt has in some way contributed to who I am.

I could try, woefully, to put it behind me or move on. I have chosen instead to allow it to rest beside me. I accept what was done to me as a child and allow the pain to come when it does. To hide from it feeds resentment and in my experience causes me to act destructively to myself and my relationships. The pain is going to be there. I understand and accept that and I am empowered by that and resolve to deal with it, appropriately, when it comes.

I am not to blame for the abuse I endured. Jim's actions are that of his own. We as a society feel guilt for what has been done to us as individuals, that in some way we are dirty because of perversions done to us as innocents. The only blame that I would accept is for my inaction as an adult, *if* anything happened to my two younger brothers or any other child.

As a survivor of Jim's sexual assault it was my responsibility to other possible victims to inform the world of what he was, despite my early failed attempts. It was a long battle and it did in the end come out. I could have fought harder sooner. So, could have everyone involved Kelly, Erik, my neighbors, Susan, Brookside hospital...everyone.

It is our duty, to ourselves, our loved ones, and humanity to find the strength within us, trust those around us and to stand together against the fear that holds us back from protecting the next possible victim.

If we as victims no longer lie down and allow those who have inflicted these crimes against the weak and small, stand together and fight back we will overwhelmingly triumph. For far too long the demons of the night have been allowed to inflict pain and fear. I can tell you from personal experience that it is not worth living with secrets, such as these. No matter how scary it is to reveal them. We also must not allow others to fall victim to the hands of those who have victimized us. Their wrong doings cannot - must not - be allowed to drive us into a secrecy that will free them to take advantage of others.

Was all the pain worth the result? I don't know.

It is safe to say that Erik and I have both ended up damaged from what that family did to us. We will forever have them invading our shadows, wanted or not.

That is our sentence, to be broken shadows of what we could have been. It is hard not to think about that. What could I have been if I had been adopted into a loving family which didn't have a sexual predator for the head of the house? Would I be a better father, better partner in life? Would right from wrong more defined? Would Kelly have had a husband who carried her more than he used her for a crutch?

I do not wish to go through life blaming my actions on the past and what has been done to me. By doing that I give it power. It retains a control over my thought process that I in turn allow to be displayed by my actions. This is not a power I wish to give it. If I do choose to accept responsibility for my actions then I am free to accept the past for what it was, past. However, in doing so I am now also responsible for accepting the consequences for those actions. This is my choice; I do not care to blame Jim or Susan for that matter, for the wrongs that I have committed.

I have a hole where my mother's love should be. It will never be filled and I will take it to my grave. I know that that love missing from my life has affected me in negative ways. Once again though, allowing it to have those affects had given it power. Realizing it was important to choose to walk away from it has proven to be very difficult at times.

I often ask myself, were my problems caused by not having a mother who loved me? Was it because my father hurt me as a child? Or because I was just born to be a failure?

If I step back and look at things from an outsider's perspective, I know that my past, the way that I was raised, and all that was laid on me as a child carried over to my adult life, contributing to my Borderline diagnosis. I do not blame my actions on the past but realize my past has molded me and the way I think, act and interact with others, especially with those closest to me. It would be foolish not to take my life's experiences into consideration when I analyze the actions I've taken and the decisions that I've made.

It has had some negative impact as can be expected. One major impact it has had on me is my unrealistic way of dealing with separation. For instance when Kelly left Arizona after our son was born, the lack of her physical presence made it hard for me to maintain our emotional bond. This has carried out for us on many occasions. When in Kelly's presence, I felt a strong need and desire for her. However when I was away from her, I often developed a negative detachment and turned on her with venomous anger and rage or neediness and jealousness.

It is interesting to note that my separation detachment carried out to other relationships as well. As unfortunate as this was with regards to my friends and Erik, it worked in my favor with Julia (and Sherri). Turning my attention from her and focusing it on my wife and family, where it belonged, left me forgetful of why I even had encounters with Julia. The more time that separated Julia and I without any form of contact, or the need for me to hide my secret, the less I felt for or about her. It was easy for me to walk away with little to no words between us.

The only person that I have not been able to detach from in this was would have to be Susan... though even now she slips further from me every day.

After the sentencing of Jim, losing my younger brothers and Susan, I had enough knowledge as an adult to distinguish right from wrong. Yes, I had an unfortunate childhood. Yes, I was treated badly as a teenager and I did have a right to be mad. I didn't, however, have any right to transfer my pain to the lives of others.

I have heard so many times that those who have been abused end up abusing others. I always understood that to mean the same type of abuse. If a victim was sexually abused, they would go on to sexually abuse others, if the abuse had been physical, they would become physical abusers and so on. Therefore, I felt, the saying didn't apply to me. I had never sexually abused anyone. So, I had beaten the odds, right? Wrong. I had dragged the ones who loved me through the ringer, and hurt Kelly in so many ways that counting them would only make me sick.

It took leaving and breaking up my family, causing mass destruction to the foundation of my marriage, and hurting my children for me to confront my actions openly and truly see the depth of how Jim's abuse shaped my soul, my mind and my capacity for deep interpersonal relationships.

Hopefully with enough time and effort, love and attention for Kelly and the kids, as well as a greater focus and commitment to mindfulness practice I will be able to live a life I can be proud of.

So, again I ask myself. Was it worth it? I don't know.

But, what I do know is...

Jim is where he belongs. I believe that if we victims stand strong, don't run and let our skeletons be heard...maybe in the future there won't be as many of them.

My next step is finding a way to forgive, myself.

Addendum

The following pages contain the Statutes regarding child sexual assault for all fifty states, at the time of writing. The laws may or may not have changed since the publication of this book. And the information provided is for reference purposes and is not meant to constitute any type of legal advice.

Alabama

Civil Statute of Limitations

- <u>2 year SOL for Suits Based on Sexual Abuse</u> : Actions for most injuries may be brought within 2 years. There is no general statutory exception for sex-related actions. Ala. Code § 6-2-38(l).

- <u>Delayed Tolling for Minors</u> : 19 years old + 2 years: Ala. Code § 6-2-8.

- <u>No Discovery Rule</u> : The Alabama Supreme Court has declined to allow an action based on sexual abuse when suppressed memories of the event surface after the statute of limitations had run out. *See Travis v. Ziter*, 681 So. 2d 1348 (Ala. 1996).

Criminal Statute of Limitations

- No SOL for Sexual Offenses Against Victims Less Than 16 Years Old : Ala. Code § 15-3-5(4). For older victims, most sexual offenses are classified as felonies, which generally have a 3 year statute of limitations. Ala. Code § 15-3-2; see §§ 13A-6-60 through -70. A small number of sexual offenses are misdemeanors, which have a 1 year SOL.

Alaska

Civil Statute of Limitations

- No SOL for Suits Based on Serious Sexual Offenses, 3 Years for Lesser Offenses : Actions for felony sexual abuse of a minor, felony sexual assault, or unlawful exploitation of a minor may be brought at any time. Alaska Stat. § 09.10.065. Suits based on misdemeanor sexual abuse of a minor, misdemeanor assault, incest, and felony indecent exposure must be brought within 3 years. *Id.*

- Delayed Tolling for Minors : 18 years old + 2 years. Actions for misdemeanor abuse of a minor that accrue when the person entitled to bring such action is under 18 years old may be brought within 2 years after that person attains full age. Alaska Stat. § 09.10.140(a). Noting that § 09.10.140(a) limits this extension such that "the period within which the action may be brought is not extended in any case longer than two years after the [victim reaches the age of majority]." This language actually reduces some windows for bringing suit compared to their window without this statute: a victim of misdemeanor sexual abuse who is age 17 years and one day (and is not entitled to the discovery extension) has only two years after his 18th birthdays to file an action (for a total of some time less than three years), whereas victims below that age have the full three years allotted by § 09.10.065.

- Discovery/"Should have discovered" Rule: 3 year extension : There is a 3 year SOL for actions based upon misdemeanor sexual abuse of a minor from after "the plaintiff discovered or through reasonable diligence should have discovered that the act caused the injury or condition." Alaska Stat. § 09.10.140(b).

- Retroactivity: to Effective Date (October 1, 2001) : The effect of Alaska Stat. § 09.10.065 (eliminating the SOL actions based on serious sexual offenses) was limited to claims that were not time-barred on October 1, 2001. 2001 Alaska Sess. Laws 86 § 4; *Catholic Bishop of N. Alaska v. John Does 1-6*, 141 P.3d 719, 725 (Alaska 2006). The state legislature may, however, retroactively revive time-barred actions by a clear and explicit showing of intent to do so. *Id.*

Criminal Statute of Limitations

- **No SOL for Sexual Offenses Against Minors** : Sexual offenses perpetrated against children under age 18 as well as sexual offenses involving children (e.g. prostitution) have no statute of limitations. Alaska Stat. § 12.10.010(a).

Arizona

Civil Statute of Limitations

- **2 year SOL for Suits Based on Sexual Abuse** : Actions for most injuries may be brought within 2 years. There is no general statutory exception for sex-related actions. Arizona Rev. Stat. § 12-542.

- **Delayed Tolling for Minors** : 18 years old + 2 years: Arizona Rev. Stat. § 12-502.

- **Discovery Rule** : "[A] cause of action does not accrue until the plaintiff knows or with reasonable diligence should know the facts underlying the cause." *See Doe v. Roe*, 191 Ariz. 313 (1998).

Criminal Statute of Limitations

- **No SOL for Sexual Conduct with or Molestation of Minor Victims Less than 15 Years Old** : Arizona Rev. Stat. §§ 13-107(A), -1405, -1410. A charge of sexual conduct with a minor between 15 and 18 years old generally may be brought within 7 years, Arizona Rev. Stat. § 13-107(B)(1), although there is no statute of limitations if the perpetrator is the minor's parent, step-parent, adoptive parent, legal guardian, foster parent, or the minor's teacher or clergyman or priest. § 13-1405. Sexual abuse of a minor under 18 also has a 7 year statute of limitations. §§ 13-107(B)(1), -1404. Misdemeanor sex offenses have a 1 year SOL. § 13-107(B)(2).

- **Discovery Rule** : Tolling periods for criminal charges only begin after the actual discovery of the offense by the proper authorities or the discovery "that should have occurred with the exercise of reasonable diligence..." Arizona Rev. Stat. § 13-107(B).

Arkansas

Civil Statute of Limitations

- **Delayed Tolling for Minors** : 21 years old + 3 years. While there is no explicit SOL for actions based on child sex acts, any action that accrues when the person entitled to bring such action is under 21 years old may be brought within 3 years after that person attains full age. Ark. Code Ann. § 16-56-116.

- Discovery Rule : There is a 3 year SOL for actions based upon sexual abuse of a minor from "the time of discovery of the sexual abuse." Ark. Code Ann. § 16-56-130. "'Time of discovery' means when the injured party discovers the effect of the injury or condition attributable to the childhood sexual abuse." Id.

- Retroactivity to Effective Date Only : The above statute of limitations was retroactive to the effective date only (August 13, 1993). 1993 Ark. ALS 370. Arkansas is a "vested right" jurisdiction and does not allow the legislature to expand a statute of limitations that would revive a cause of action already barred. See Branch v. Carter, 933 S.W.2d 806 (Ark. 1996).

Criminal Statute of Limitations

- SOL is 6 Years for Serious Sexual Crimes Against Minors, 3 or 1 Year(s) for Others : The statute of limitations is 6 years for serious sexual felonies, including first degree sexual assault and rape. Ark. Code Ann. § 5-1-109(b)(1)(A). Rape is defined to include intercourse or deviate sexual activity with a victim less than 14 years old and incest with a victim less than 18. Ark. Code Ann. § 5-14-103. First degree sexual assault entails sexual intercourse or deviate sexual activity by certain government employees engaged in family services, by certain professionals "in a position of trust and authority over the victim" who uses that trust to engage in sexual intercourse or deviate sexual activity, or by someone employed by the victim's school district; and the victim is less than 18 years old. Ark. Code Ann. § 5-14-124.

    3 years for other sexual felonies, and 1 year for sexual misdemeanors. § 5-1-109(b)(2)-(3).

- Delayed Tolling for Minors : 18 years old + 6, 3, or 1 year(s). If the victim of a sexual crime is a minor, the SOL does not run until he or she reaches 18. § 5-1-109(h).

California

Civil Statute of Limitations

- Special Childhood Sexual Abuse SOL : 18 years old + 8 years. Ca. Civ. Proc. Code § 340.1(a).

- Limited Discovery Rule : 3 years. Actions against a person for committing childhood sexual abuse may be brought "within 3 years of the date the plaintiff discovers or reasonably should have discovered that psychological injury or illness occurring after the age of majority was caused by the sexual abuse . . . ." Id. Actions for liability against a person who owed the victim a duty of care and actions against a third party whose intentional act was the legal cause of the sexual abuse are barred on the victim reaches age 26, unless that person failed to take reasonable steps to prevent future unlawful sexual conduct by an employee or representative that it knew or had reason to know had engaged in such conduct. *Id.* § 340.1(b).

- 1 Year Window : From January 1, 2003. *Id.* § 340.1(c)

Criminal Statute of Limitations

- Delayed SOL for Most Sex Crimes Against Victims Less than 16 : Until victim is 28 years old. Ca. Penal Code § 801.1 allows prosecutions for a number of felony sex crimes committed against victims younger than 18 to be brought any time before the victim's 28th birthday. Felony sex crimes are sodomy, oral copulation, and sexual penetration of victims less than 16, §§ 286, 288a, 288.7, and performing lewd or lascivious acts against a child under the age of 14, § 288.

- Reporting Window: 1 year : After the above SOL has expired, prosecutions for a sexual crime committed against a victim younger than 18 may be brought within 1 year of the date a report is filed with a state law enforcement agency. Ca. Penal Code § 803(f). In this case, the allegations must be corroborated by admissible, independent evidence other than the victim's own testimony. *Id.*

Colorado

Civil Statute of Limitations

- Delayed Tolling for Sexual Offenses Against Minors : 18 years old + 6 years. Colo. Rev. Stat. § 13-80-103.7. This extension does not apply to claims brought against a person other than the perpetrator of the sexual offense. *See Sandoval v. Archdiocese of Denver*, 8 P.3d 598 (Colo. App. 2000).

- Discovery Rule: 6 years : State courts have read a discovery rule into the above statute, stating that a suppressed memory is a "disability" that triggers the 6 year SOL only after the memory surfaces. *Id.* at 600.

Criminal Statute of Limitations

- No SOL for Felony Sexual Offenses Against a Child (Age Varies) : Colo. Rev. Stat. § 16-5-401(1). Most sexual offenses are felonies if committed against a child less than 15 years old, including various types of sexual assaults, §§ 18-3-402, -405, -405.3, as well as unlawful sexual contact, § 18-3-404, internet luring of a child, § 18-3-306(3), and internet sexual exploitation of a child, § 18-3-405.4. Crimes related to child trafficking and prostitution are generally felonies if the victim is less than 18 years old. E.g. §§ 18-3-402 through -406. Aggravated incest, for which the victim must be under 21 years old if a child of the actor or less than 10 years old for other relations, is also a felonious sexual offense. § 18-6-302.

- No Discovery Rule : Sexual offenses are not included in the statutory list of offenses having a run-at-discovery SOL. *See* Colo. Rev. Stat. § 16-5-401(4.5).

Connecticut

Civil Statute of Limitations

- 30 Year Delayed SOL for Victims under Age 18 : Conn. Gen. Stat. § 52-577d.

    In actions for personal injury based on events for which the actor was convicted of first degree sexual assault, there is no statute of limitations. § 577e.

- No Discovery Rule : *See, e.g., Rosado v. Bridgeport Roman Catholic Diocese Corp.*, 1997 Conn. Super. LEXIS 2496 (Conn. Super. Ct. Sept. 15 1997).

- Retroactive : The 30 year delayed statute of limitations, enacted in 2002, has recently been applied retroactively by the state's highest court. *See Doe v. Norwich Roman Catholic Diocesan Corp.*, 279 Conn. 207 (2006).

Criminal Statute of Limitations

- No SOL for Class A Felony Sexual Offenses; 5 year SOL for Most Others : *See* Conn. Gen. Stat. § 54-193(a). Class A felony sexual offenses include first degree and aggravated sexual assault if the victim is less than 16 years old, §§ 53a-70, -70a, and employment of a minor in an obscene performance, § 53a-196a. All felonious sexual offenses are or may be punished with imprisonment in excess of one year, e.g. § 53a-71 (sexual assault in the second degree), § 53a-191 (incest), and therefore carry 5 year statutes of limitations. § 54-193(b). Other sexual offenses (i.e. misdemeanor) must be prosecuted within 1 year of the offense. *Id.*

- Delayed SOL for Sexual Abuse of Minors: 30 Years : Prosecutions for sexual abuse of minors may be pursued within 30 years of the date the victim attains the age of majority (18), or within 5 years of the date the crime is reported to any police officer, whichever is earlier. Conn. Gen. Stat. § 54-193a.

Delaware

Civil Statute of Limitations

- No SOL for Suits Based Upon Sexual Abuse of a Minor : Del. Code Ann. 10, § 8143. Such suits may be based on any sexual act that constitutes a criminal offense. *Id.*

- 2 Year Window : Open from July 1, 2007. *Id.*

Criminal Statute of Limitations

- No SOL for Sexual Offenses Except Sexual Harassment and Indecent Exposure : *See* Del. Code Ann. 11, § 205(e). But, prosecutions may not "be based upon the memory of the victim that has been recovered through psychotherapy unless there is some evidence of the corpus delicti independent of such repressed memory." *Id.*

District of Columbia (D.C.)

Civil Statute of Limitations

- Delayed SOL for Minors : 18 years old + 3 Years. There is no specific SOL for suits based on sexual acts, *see* D.C. Code § 12-301, but the period does not begin tolling until the victim reaches age 18. *Id.*, § 12-302.

- Discovery Rule : "[T]he statute of limitations begins to run when a plaintiff either has actual knowledge of a cause of action or is charged with knowledge of that cause of action." *Cevenini v. Archbishop of Washington*, 707 A.2d 768 (D.C. 1998).

Criminal Statute of Limitations

- 15 Year SOL for Child Sexual Abuse, 10 Years for Most Other Child Sex Offenses : First and second degree child sexual abuse may be prosecuted within 15 years of the offense is committed. D.C. Code § 23-113(a)(2). Other forms of sexual abuse, using or promoting a minor in a sexual performance, and incest have 10 year statutes of limitations. § 23-113(a)(3). Other felonies must be brought within 6 years and misdemeanors within 3 years. §§ 23-113(a)(4)-(5).

- Delayed Tolling for Minors : 21 years old plus 15 or 10 Years depending on the act. D.C. Code § 23-113(d).

Florida

Civil Statute of Limitations

- Delayed SOL for Actions Based on Sexual Abuse or Incest Against Minors : 18 years old plus 7 Years. Fla. Stat. § 95.11(7).

- Discovery Rule : 4 Years from the date a victim knew or should have known that the injury and abuse were causally connected. *Id.* The recovery of repressed memories of abuse also qualifies as such as "discovery." *Hearndon v. Graham*, 767 So. 2d 1179 (Fla. 2000).

Criminal Statute of Limitations

- No SOL for Serious Sexual Crimes and Some Felonies Committed Against Minors; 4 or 3 Years for Other Felonies; 2 for Most Misdemeanors : Capital and life felonies may be prosecuted at any time, as may any first degree felonious sexual battery committed against a victim less than 18 years old. Fla. Stat. §§ 775.15(1), (14). Sexual battery against a victim less than 12 years old is a capital felony, §§ 794.011(2)(a), (8)(c), while first degree sexual batteries include those committed by a person in familial or custodial authority, § 794.011(8)(b), and those committed with force or violence, § 794.011(4). Other first degree felonies, which have an SOL of 4 years, § 775.15, include aggravated child abuse, § 827.03. Felonies that may be prosecuted for 3 years include incest, § 826.04, child abuse that does not cause great bodily harm, § 827.03(1), and non-violent sexual battery, § 794.011(5). Luring a child under 12 for an unlawful purpose is a first degree misdemeanor, § 787.025, and may be prosecuted for 2 years, § 775.15.

Georgia

Civil Statute of Limitations

- Delayed SOL for Most Sexual Offenses Against Minor Victims : 18 years old + 5 Years. The SOL for childhood sexual abuse is 5 years once the victim reaches age of majority (18). Ga. Code Ann. § 9-3-33.1 "Childhood sexual abuse" is broadly defined to include acts related to rape, molestation, enticing a child, incest, sexual battery, and other sexual acts. *Id.*

- Discovery Rule Unlikely : Georgia's highest court has held that the common law discovery rule only applies to injuries that "develop only over an extended period of time." *Corp. of Mercer Univ. v. Nat'l Gypsum Co.*, 258 Ga. 365, 366 (1988). While the state Supreme Court has not directly ruled on whether injury resulting from sexual abuse is such an injury, the Court of Appeals for the 11th Circuit, applying Georgia law, has held that it is not. *M.H.D. v. Westminster Schs.*, 172 F.3d 797, 804 (11th Cir. 1999).

- No Retroactivity : Statute only applies from effective date, July 1, 1992. Ga. Code Ann. § 9-3-33.1 (Ga. L. 1992, p.2473 § 2, not codified by the Assembly, provided for prospective application only.)

Criminal Statute of Limitations

- 7 Year SOL for Most Sexual Offenses Against Victims Under Age 18 : Prosecutions for crimes punishable by life imprisonment or by death, and felonies committed against victims under age 18 may be brought within 7 years. § 17-3-1(b)-(c). Misdemeanors must be prosecuted within 2 years. § 17-3-1(d).

- Delayed SOL for Most Sexual Offenses Against Victims Under Age 16 : Prosecutions for cruelty to children, rape and statutory rape, sodomy, child molestation, enticing a child for indecent purposes, and incest of a victim less than 16 years old do not begin to run until the victim reaches that age or reports the crime, whichever is earlier. § 17-3-2.1.

- No SOL for Sexual Crimes If Identity of Accused is Based on DNA Evidence : § 17-3-1(c.1).

- Limited Discovery Rule : No SOL period runs while the person who committed the crime is unknown or the crime itself it unknown. § 17-3-2.

Hawaii

Civil Statute of Limitations

- Delayed SOL for Suits Involving Minor Victims : 18 years old + 2 Years. The general SOL for personal injury actions is 2 years, Haw. Rev. Stat. § 657-1(4), but tolling is delayed until the victim reaches 18, § 657-13.

- Discovery Rule : The discovery rule is such that the SOL begins to run when the victim knows or should have known that their injury and the abuse was causally related. *See Dunlea v. Dappen*, 924 P.2d 196 (Haw. 1996).

Criminal Statute of Limitations

- 6 Year SOL for Serious (Class A) Sexual Felonies, 3 Years for Others : Haw. Rev. Stat. § 701-108(2)(b), (d). Sexual offenses that are Class A felonies include first degree sexual assault (most victims under age 16 and sexual act committed by strong compulsion), § 707-730, continuous sexual assault of a minor under 14 (offender resides in the same house as the minor or has recurring access, and engaged in three or more sexual acts while the minor is under 14), § 707-733, and first degree promotion of child abuse (including production or participation in the preparation of child pornography), § 707-750. Most other sexual offenses are non-Class-A felonies, e.g., incest, § 707-741, second and third degree sexual assault, §§ 707-731, -732, second and third degree promotion of child abuse, §§ 707-751, -752, first and second degree electronic enticement of a child, §§ 707-756, -757.

- Delayed SOL for Felony Offenses Against Victims Under Age 18 : The SOL is tolled until the minor victim reaches the age of 18. § 701-108(6)(c).

Idaho

Civil Statute of Limitations

- Delayed SOL for Child Abuse Suits : 18 Years Old + 5 Years. Idaho Code § 6-1704.

- Discovery Rule : The SOL begins to run when the victim discovers or should have discovered the injury and its causal relationship to the abuse. *Id.*

- No Retroactivity : The statute explicitly applies prospectively. § 6-1705 (effective July 1, 1989).

Criminal Statute of Limitations

- No SOL for Most Sexual Offenses Against Victims Under Age 16 : Idaho has no statute of limitations for prosecuting sexual abuse of a child, or lewd conduct with a minor, under age 16, § 19-401, or for rape of a victim under age 18. *Id.* Felonies carry 5 year SOLs. § 19-402. *Accord, e.g.*, § 18-6602 (incest), § 18-1507 (sexual exploitation of a child), § 18-1508a (sexual battery of a minor) § 18-1509a (enticing a child over the internet) with § 18-111 (defining felonies).

Illinois

Civil Statute of Limitations

- Delayed SOL for Childhood Sexual Abuse Suits : 18 Years Old + 10 Years. 735 I.L.C.S. § 5/13-202.2(b)-(d).

- Discovery Rule : Suits for childhood sexual abuse may also be brought within 5 years of the date the victim discovers or reasonably should have discovered the act of abuse and the injury caused. § 13-202.2(b).

Criminal Statute of Limitations

- Delayed SOL for Most Sexual Offenses Against Minor Victims : 18 Years Old + 20 Years. 720 I.L.C.S. 5/3-6(j). Such offenses include criminal sexual assault, aggravated criminal sexual assault, predatory criminal sexual assault of a child, or aggravated criminal sexual abuse. *Id.*

Indiana

Civil Statute of Limitations

- Delayed SOL for Personal Injury Suits : 18 Years Old + 2 Years. The general SOL for personal injury actions is 2 years, Ind. Code § 34-11-2-4, although the statute is tolled until the victim turns 18, §§ 1-1-4-5 (defining a minor as being "under a disability"), 34-11-6-1 (tolling SOL while victim is "under a disability").

Criminal Statute of Limitations

- 5 Year SOL for Most Sexual Felonies Against Minor Victims, and Barred After the Victim Reaches 31 Years Old : Most sexual crimes against minor victims are classified as Class B, C, or D felonies, and must be prosecuted within 5 years. Ind. Code § 35-41-4-2(a)(1), although some are classified as Class A felonies—which have no SOL, § 35-41-4-2(d)—if committed by using or threatening to use deadly force or result in serious bodily injury. *See, e.g.*, § 35-42-4-1(b) (rape), § 35-42-4-3(b) (child molestation), § 35-42-4-5(a)(3) (vicarious sexual gratification).

- Age Limit: 31 Years Old : Prosecutions for the following child sex crimes may not be brought once the victim reaches age 31: child molestation, vicarious sexual gratification, child solicitation, child seduction, and incest. Ind. Code § 35-41-4-2.

Iowa

Civil Statute of Limitations

- 5 Year SOL for Sexual Abuse or Exploitation By A Counselor, Therapist, or School Employee; 2 Year General SOL for Personal Injury Suits : IOWA CODE § 614.1 (2008).

- Discovery Rule for Actions Based on Child Sexual Abuse : For actions based on child sexual abuse, a claim may be brought within 4 years of the discovery of the date of a causal relationship between the injury and the sexual abuse. § 614.8A.

- Delayed Tolling for Minors : 18 years of age plus 1 year. § 614.8(2).

Criminal Statute of Limitations

- 10 Year SOL for Sexual Abuse, Incest, and Sexual Exploitation by a Counselor, Therapist, or School Employee Committed Against a Minor; 3 Years for Most Other Sexual Offenses : First, second, and third degree sexual abuse, incest , and sexual exploitation by a counselor, therapist, or school employee may be prosecuted within 10 years of the offense if committed against a minor victim. IOWA CODE §§ 802.2,

802.2A (2008). Felonies and aggravated or serious misdemeanors may be prosecuted within 3 years of the offense. *Id.* § 802.3.

Kansas

Civil Statute of Limitations

- Later of Delayed SOL (18 + 3 Years) or Discovery Rule (3 Years) : Actions based on child sexual abuse may be brought until the later of three years from the victim's 18th birthday or three years from the date the victim "discovers or reasonably should have discovered that the injury or illness was caused by childhood sexual abuse . . ." KAN. STAT. ANN. § 60-523(a) (2008). The statute clarifies that "[d]iscovery that the injury or illness was caused by childhood sexual abuse shall not be deemed to have occurred solely by virtue of the person's awareness, knowledge or memory of the acts of abuse." *Id.* § 60-523(c).

- Retroactivity : Allows any action commenced "on or after July 1, 1992, including any action which would be barred by application of the period of limitation applicable" prior to the effective date. *Id.* § 60-523(d).

Criminal Statute of Limitations

- 5 Year General SOL : KAN. STAT. ANN. § 21-3106(4) (2008).

- Delayed Tolling/Discovery/Repressed Memory Rule May Toll SOL Until Victim Turns 28 Years Old : The SOL is tolled if two or more of the following conditions are supported by substantial competent evidence: (i) the victim was a child under 15 years of age at the time of the crime; (ii) the victim was of such age or intelligence that the victim was unable to determine that the acts constituted a crime; (iii) the victim was prevented by a parent or other legal authority from making known to law enforcement authorities the fact of the crime whether or not the parent or other legal authority is the accused; and (iv) there is substantially competent expert testimony indicating the victim psychologically repressed such witness' memory of the fact of the crime, and in the expert's professional opinion the recall of such memory is accurate and free of undue manipulation, and substantial corroborating evidence can be produced in support of the allegations contained in the complaint . . . . *Id.* § 21-3106(5)(f). However, no prosecution delayed by this statute may be brought after the victim's 28th birthday. *Id.*

Kentucky

Civil Statute of Limitations

- Latest of 5 Year SOL, Delayed Tolling (18 + 5 Years), and Discovery Rule (5 Years) for Actions Based on Child Sexual Assault or Abuse : KY. REV. STAT. ANN. § 413.249(2)

(2008). Discovery here means knowledge of the act. *Id.*

Criminal Statute of Limitations

- No SOL for Felonies; 5 Year SOLs for Other Sexual Misdemeanors Against Minors : KY. REV. STAT. ANN. § 500.050 (2008). Felonies include all forms of rape, *id.* §§ 510.040-.060, most forms of sodomy, *id.* §§ 510.070-.090, sexual abuse in the first degree, *id.* § 510.110, unlawful use of electronic means to include a minor to engage in sexual or other prohibited activities, *id.* § 510.155, and incest, *id.* § 530.020.

Louisiana

Civil Statute of Limitations

- Delayed SOL for Sexual Abuse of a Minor : 18 years of age plus 10 Years. LA. REV. STAT. ANN. § 9:2800.9 (2008).

- Discovery Rule : Louisiana courts have appeared to apply a year one discovery rule where "some cause of action in not known or reasonably known by the plaintiff, even though his ignorance is not induced by the defendant." *Wimberly v. Gatch*, 635 So.2d 206, 211 (La. 1994) (quoting *Rajnowski v. St. Patrick's Hospital*, 564 So.2d 671 (La. 1990).

Criminal Statute of Limitations

- Delayed SOL for Most Sexual Offenses Against Minors (18 + 30 Years); No SOL for Particularly Serious Offenses : There is no time limitation for prosecutions of crimes for that are punishable by death or life imprisonment, including aggravated rape and forcible rape, LA. REV. STAT. §§ 14:42-42.1 (2008). LA. CODE CRIM. PROC. art. 571 (2008). Prosecution for the following crimes, when committed against a minor, may be begun within 30 years from the time the victim reaches age 18: sexual battery, LA. REV. STAT. ANN. § 14:43.1 (2008), second degree sexual battery, *id.* § 14:43.2, oral sexual battery, *id.* § 14:43.3, felony carnal knowledge of a juvenile, *id.* § 14:80, indecent behavior with juveniles, *id.* § 14:81, molestation of a juvenile, *id.* § 14:81.2, crime against nature, *id.* § 14:89, aggravated crime against nature, *id.* § 14:89.1, incest, *id.* § 14:78, or aggravated incest, *id.* § 14:78.1. LA. CODE CRIM. PROC. art. 571.1 (2008).

Maine

Civil Statute of Limitations

- No SOL for Actions Based on Sexual Acts Against Minors : ME. REV. STAT. ANN. tit. 14, § 752-C (2008).

- Retroactivity Unlikely : The federal District Court for the District of Maine has ruled that "[a]lthough later amendments to Section 752-C allow persons who were victims of sexual abuse as minors to pursue their claims at any time, the Legislature clearly did not intend for this expanded statute of limitations to revive claims that were already "barred by the previous statute of limitations in force" prior to the amendments. See Me. P.L. 1991, Ch. 551, § 2; Me. P.L.1999, Ch. 639, § 2." *Guptill v. Martin*, 288 F.R.D. 62 (D. Me. 2005).

Criminal Statute of Limitations

- No SOL for Most Sexual Offenses Against Victims Under Age 16 : "[I]f the victim had not attained the age of 16 years at the time of the crime, a prosecution for: incest; unlawful sexual contact; sexual abuse of a minor; rape or gross sexual assault, formerly denominated as gross sexual misconduct, may be commenced at any time." ME. REV. STAT. ANN. tit. 17-A § 8 (2008).

Maryland

Civil Statute of Limitations

- Delayed SOL for Actions Based on Child Sexual Abuse (18 + 7 Years); Delayed SOL for Most Other Personal Injury Actions (18 + 3 Years) : Child sexual abuse actions may be brought within 7 years of the date the victim turns 18 years old. MD. CODE ANN., CTS. & JUD. PROC. § 5-117 (2008). Most other claims based on injury caused by sexual acts on a minor that do not constitute sexual abuse fall under the general SOL, which is 3 years, *see id*. § 5-101, although this period will be tolled until the victim turns 18. *Id*. § 5-201.

- Discovery Rule Possible But Unlikely : While the Maryland Court of Special Appeals has declined to extend the common law discovery rule to child sexual abuse actions, see, e.g., *Doe v. Archdiocese of Washington*, 689 A.2d 634 (Md. Ct. Spec. App. 1997), those decisions predate the expansion of the SOL for such actions in 2003 (see above) and generally relied, at least in part, on the fact that the Legislature had created no SOL exception for child sexual abuse actions. *See id*.

- No Retroactivity : Effective date, October 1, 2003. 2003 Md. Laws 360, sec 2.

Criminal Statute of Limitations

- No SOL for Felony Offenses; 1 Year SOL for Misdemeanors : Maryland has no time limitation for prosecutions of felonies. *See Clark v. State*, 744 A.2d 113, n.8 (Md.

2001). Most sexual offenses are classified as felonies. MD. CODE ANN., CRIM. LAW §§ 3-301 to -324 (2008). Misdemeanors may be prosecuted within 1 year. MD. CODE ANN., CTS. & JUD. PROC. § 5-106 (2008).

Massachusetts

Civil Statute of Limitations

- Later of Delayed Tolling for Minor Victims (18 + 3 Years) and Discovery Rule (3 Years) for Assault and Battery Actions Based on Sexual Abuse of a Minor : MASS. GEN. LAWS ch. 260, § 4c (2008). "Sexual abuse" is defined broadly to include many forms of sexual actions. *See id.*

Criminal Statute of Limitations

- No SOL for Most Sexual Offenses Committed Against Minor Victims : However, independent evidence is required if prosecution is brought more than 27 years from the date of the offense. MASS. GEN. LAWS ch. 277, § 63 (2008).

Michigan

Civil Statute of Limitations

- 2 Year Personal Injury SOL; No Specific SOL for Suits Based Upon Sexual Abuse of a Minor : MICH. COMP. LAWS § 600.5805(2), the general Personal Injury statute, allows 2 year SOL for action charging assault, battery, or false imprisonment.

- Delayed Tolling for Minors : If victim was under the age of 18 or insane, claimant has 1 year after the disability is removed (through death or otherwise) to bring a claim if the SOL has otherwise run. MICH. COMP. LAWS § 600.5851

- No Discovery Rule : No discovery rule for memory claims or claims that victims did not realize a causal connection between the sexual abuse and their injuries. *See, e.g. Lemmerman v. Fealk*, 201 Mich. App. 544, 507 N.W. 2d 226 (1993).

Criminal Statute of Limitations

- SOL Depending on the Nature of the Offense : No SOL for criminal sexual conduct in the first degree. MICH. COMP. LAWS § 764.24(1). For criminal sexual conduct in the second to fourth degree, and assault with intent to commit criminal sexual conduct, must file within 10 years after the offense is committed or victim's twenty-first birthday, whichever is later. MICH. COMP. LAWS § 764.24(2)(a). All other indictments may be found and filed within 6 years after the offense is committed. MICH. COMP. LAWS § 764.24(5).

- DNA Exception : If evidence of the violation is obtained and that evidence contains DNA that is determined to be from an unidentified individual, an indictment against that individual for the violation may be found and filed at any time after the offense is committed. However, after the individual is identified, the indictment may be found and filed within 10 years after the individual is identified or by the alleged victim's twenty-first birthday, whichever is later. MICH. COMP. LAWS § 764.24(2)(b).

Minnesota

Civil Statute of Limitations

- Delayed Tolling for Sexual Offenses Against Minors : 18 years of age plus 6 years. MINN. STAT. § 541.073 (2008).

- Discovery Rule : Minnesota's discovery statute specifies that an action: (a) must be commenced within six years the victim knew or had reason to know that the injury was caused by the sexual abuse, (b) the victim need not establish which act in a continuous series of sexual abuse acts caused the injury, and (c) the knowledge of a parent or guardian may not be imputed to a minor. MINN. STAT. § 541.073(a-c). The Minnesota Supreme Court held that the six-year period provided in the delayed discovery statute began to run when victim reached majority, *D.M.S. v. Barber*, 645 N.W.2d 383 (Minn. 2002). The Supreme Court applied the state's discovery rule to sexual abuse cases, but rejected a "realization" definition of discovery. *Blackowiak v. Kemp*, 546 N.W.2d 1 (Minn. 1996).

Criminal Statute of Limitations

- SOL Depending on the Nature of the Offense : If a minor when the acts occurred, the victim must bring a claim "within nine years after the commission of the offense or, if the victim failed to report the offense within this limitation period, within three years after the offense was reported to law enforcement authorities." MINN. STAT. § 628.26(e) (2008). 3 years for all other offences. § 628.26(k).

- Other Grounds for Tolling : However, if victim is coerced/prevented from reporting the three year limit is ignored. *State v. Danielski*, 374 N.W.2d 322 (Minn.App. 1985). In such situations, the incest victim must tell someone who actually brings information to proper authorities before statute runs. *State v. French*, 392 N.W.2d 596 (Minn.App. 1986).

- DNA Exception : There is no SOL for criminal sexual conduct in first to third degrees if DNA evidence was preserved. § 628.26(f).

Mississippi

Civil Statute of Limitations

- 3 Year Personal Injury SOL; No Specific SOL for Suits Based Upon Sexual Abuse of a Minor : The general personal injury statute allows 3 years within which to bring an action. MISS. CODE ANN. § 15-1-49 (2008). In actions for which no other period of limitation is prescribed and which involve latent injury or disease, the cause of action does not accrue until the plaintiff has discovered, or by reasonable diligence should have discovered, the injury. (However, see *Doe v. Roman Catholic Diocese of Jackson* below.).

- Delayed Tolling for Minors : The SOL is tolled until the victim reaches the age of majority (18 years of age). MISS. CODE ANN. § 15-1-59.

- Discovery Rule in Child Sex Abuse Cases Unlikely : Discovery rule did not apply to toll limitations period in alleged sexual abuse victim's case as there was no latent injury; acts of abuse alleged were physical acts of which person would be generally aware when events occurs. *Doe v. Roman Catholic Diocese of Jackson*, 947 So.2d 983, (Miss.App. 2006).

Criminal Statute of Limitations

- Generally No SOL for Sexual Battery of a Minor : No limitation if the victim is age 14-16 while abuser is 3+ years older, victim is under 14 while abuser is 2+ years older, or victim is under 18 while abuser is in position of authority or trust. MISS.CODE ANN. § 99-1-5 (2008). No limitation for touching or handling of children for lustful purposes. § 97-5-23. For other purposes, within 2 years of the offense. § 99-1-5.

Missouri

Civil Statute of Limitations

- Later of Delayed Tolling for Minors (21 Years of Age plus 10 Years) or Discovery (3 Years After Discovery) : A victim must commence an action within ten years of attaining the age of 21 or within three years of the date when a victim discovers or reasonably should have discovered that an injury was caused by the abuse, whichever occurs latest. MO REV. STAT. § 537.046 (2009).

- Retroactivity : The statute specifies that it "shall apply to any action commenced on or after August 28, 2004, including any action which would have been barred by the application of the statute of limitation applicable prior to that date. § 537.046.

Criminal Statute of Limitations

- Delayed Tolling for Minors; 20 Year SOL for Most Offenses; No Limitations for the Most Serious of Offenses : Actions must be commenced within twenty years after the victim reaches the age of eighteen unless the prosecutions are for forcible rape, attempted forcible rape, forcible sodomy, kidnapping, or attempted forcible sodomy in which case such prosecutions may be commenced at any time. § 556.037.

- Discovery Rule : The tort claim does not begin to run until both the injury and the damage is ascertained by the victim. See Powel v. Chaminade College Preparatory, Inc., 197 S.W.3d 576 (Mo. 2006).

Montana

Civil Statute of Limitations

- Three (3) Year SOL from Time of the Abuse or Until Discovery of the Injury : An action must be brought within 3 years of the act constituting abuse or within three years after a victim discovers that they have sustained an injury caused by the abuse. MONT. CODE ANN. § 27-2-216 (2007).

- Delayed Tolling for Minors : The statute is tolled for the period of disability (minority). § 27-2-401.

- Discovery Rule : In Werre v. David, 913 P.2d 625 (Mont. 1996), the Montana Supreme court ruled that the SOL does not being to run until the victims discovers the connection between the injury and his/her childhood sexual abuse. In addition, the Court ruled that the statute applies to acts against the perpetrator as well as to acts of negligence by non-perpetrator third parties.

- Retroactivity : The Montana legislature specifically provided that the statute be given retroactive effect: "[This act] applies to all causes of action commenced on or after October 1, 1989, regardless of when the cause of action arose. Section 5, Ch. 158, L. 1989. This action of the legislature was upheld in Cosgriffe v. Cosgriffe, 864 P2d 776, (Mont. 1993).

Criminal Statute of Limitations

- SOL Depending on the Nature of the Offense; Delayed Tolling for Minors : For felony offenses including sexual assault, sexual intercourse without consent, or incest (defined by Mont. Code Ann. §§ 45-5-502, 45-5-503, and 45-5-507(4), respectively), an action may be commenced within 10 years of the time the victim reaches the age of 18 if the victim was less than 18 at the time the offense occurred. A misdemeanor may be commenced within 5 years after the victim reaches 18 years of age if the offense was committed when the victim was less than 18; otherwise 1 year. Mont. Code Ann. § 45-1-205(1)(b) (2007). For offenses including those defined by Mont. Code Ann. §§ 45-5-504, 45-5-505 (deviate sexual conduct), 45-5-507(1), (2), (3), or (6) (incest), 45-5-625 (Sex abuse of children for pornographic purposes, etc.), or 45-5-627 (ritual abuse of minor) may be commenced within 5 years after the victim reaches 18 years of age if the victim was less than 18 years of age at the time that the offense occurred. Mont. Code Ann. § 45-1-205(1)(c).

- DNA Exception : "If a suspect is conclusively identified by DNA testing after a time period prescribed in subsection (1)(b) or (1)(c) has expired, a prosecution may be commenced within 1 year after the suspect is conclusively identified by DNA testing." § 45-1-205(9).

Nebraska

Civil Statute of Limitations

- Four Year Personal Injury SOL; No SOL Specific to Child Sexual Abuse : A personal injury action must be brought within four years from the time when the cause of action accrues. NEB. REV. STAT. § 25-207 (2008).

- Delayed Tolling for Minors : The SOL is tolled if the victim "at the time the cause of action accrued [is] within the age of twenty years... [and] shall be entitled to bring such action within the respective times limited by this chapter after such disability is removed." § 25-213.

- Limited Discovery Rule : The Nebraska Supreme Court has held that the application of a discovery rule is determined by focusing on when the discovery of the injury occurs and not on when the injured party recognizes whose conduct is responsible for the injury. *Teater v. State of Nebraska,*, 559 N.W.2d 758 (Neb. 1997).

Criminal Statute of Limitations

- No SOL for Most Criminal Prosecutions : No SOL for sexual assault of a child in the first degree under § 28-319.01 or for sexual assault of a child in the second or third degree under § 28-320.01. Nor is there any time limitations for prosecution or punishment for sexual assault in the third degree under §28-320 when the victim is under sixteen years of age at the time of the offense. NEB. REV. STAT. § 29-110(5) (2008).

Nevada

Civil Statute of Limitations

- 10 Years from the Later of Delayed Tolling to Age of Majority or Discovery : A victim has ten years to bring an action arising from sexual abuse of a minor from the time that the victim reaches the age of 18 or discovers or reasonably should have discovered that the injury was caused by sexual abuse, whichever occurs later. NEV.REV. STAT. §11.215 (2008).

Criminal Statute of Limitations

- SOL Depending on Nature of Sexual Abuse; Delayed Tolling; Discovery : Nevada has unified the discovery rule, delayed tolling, and a bright line rule for child sexual abuse prosecutions. For felony sexual assault, the general rule is a 4 year SOL. NEV.REV. STAT. § 171.085 (2008). Other felonies are 3 years, misdemeanors are 2 years for gross misdemeanor and 1 year for simple. §§ 171.085, 171.090. For minors, an action may be brought for any offense constituting sexual abuse of a child: (1) Twenty-one years old if he discovers or reasonably should have discovered that he was a victim of the sexual abuse by the date on which he reaches that age; or (2) Twenty-eight years old if he does not discover and reasonably should not have discovered that he was a victim of the sexual abuse by the date on which he reaches 21 years of age. §171.095(1)(b). However, if a written report for a sexual assault is filed with a law enforcement officer during the limitation period, the limitation is removed. § 171.083.

New Hampshire

Civil Statute of Limitations

- Later of Delayed Tolling (18 + 12 years) and Discovery Rule (+ 3 years) for Minor Victims : Actions based on sexual assault and related offenses, N.H. Rev. Stat. § 632-A et seq, or incest, § 639.2, committed against a victim under age 18 may be brought within the later of 12 years from the victim's 18th birthday or 3 years of the time the victim "discovers, or in the exercise of reasonable diligence should have discovered, the injury and its causal relationship to the act or omission complained of." § 508:4-g.

- Retroactivity : The 12 year delayed tolling law went into effect Jan. 1, 2009. The previous version of the statute, including the enactment of the discovery rule, went into effect July 22, 2005.

Criminal Statute of Limitations

- Delayed Tolling for Minor Victims: 18 + 22 years : Sexual assault and related offenses, New Hamp. Rev. Stat. § 632-A et seq, and incest, § 639.2, committed against a victim under age 18 may be prosecuted within 22 years of the victim's 18th birthday. § 625:8.

New Jersey

Civil Statute of Limitations

- Discovery Rule : 2 Years. "In any civil action for injury or illness based on sexual abuse, the cause of action shall accrue at the time of reasonable discovery of the injury and its causal relationship to the act of sexual abuse. Any such action shall be brought within two years after reasonable discovery" N.J. Stat. Ann. § 2A:61B-1(b).

- Delayed Tolling : A court is also entitled to toll the statute on other grounds including "the plaintiff's mental state, duress by the defendant, or any other equitable grounds." N.J. Stat. Ann. § 2A:61B-1(c).

Criminal Statute of Limitations

- No SOL for sexual assaults; 5 years for other sexual crimes : Prosecutions for sexual assault and aggravated sexual assault may be commenced at any time. N.J.S.A. § 2C:1-6(a)(1). These offenses cover victims less than 13 years old, as well as victims between 13 and 18 if the abuser is either a relative, has supervisory powers over the victim, or stands *in loco parentis*. N.J.S.A. § 2C:14-2. All other sexual crimes carry 5 year SOL periods. *See* § 2C:1-6(b)(1).

- Delayed SOL and Discovery Rule for Sexual Contact and Child Endangerment : Prosecutions for criminal sexual contact, N.J.S.A. § 2C:14-3, and endangering welfare of children, § 2C:24-4, may be brought within 5 years after the victim reaches age 18, or within two years following the reasonable discovery of the offense by the victim, whichever is later. § 2C:1-6(b)(4).

New Mexico

Civil Statute of Limitations

- Later of Delayed Tolling (18 + 6 years) and Discovery Rule (+ 3 years) for Minor Victims : Actions based on childhood sexual abuse may be brought within the later of 6 years from the victim's 18th birthday or 3 years of the time the victim "knew or had reason to know of the childhood sexual abuse and that the childhood sexual abuse resulted in an injury to the person, as established by competent medical or psychological testimony." N.M. Stat. Ann. § 37-1-30. "Childhood sexual abuse" is defined, *id.*, as behavior that would constitute criminal sexual penetration of a minor, § 30-9-11, criminal sexual contact with a minor, § 30-9-13, and criminal sexual exploitation of a child, § 30-6A-1 *et seq.*

Criminal Statute of Limitations

- No Limit for Only Most Serious Child Sex Offenses, 5 or 6 years for Most Others : There is no SOL for prosecutions of first degree felonies, a 6 year SOL for 2nd degree felonies, and a 5 year SOL for third and fourth degree felonies. § 30-1-8. Criminal penetration in the first degree (committed against a child less than 13 years old) is a first degree felony, in the second degree (committed against a child 13 to 18 years old and by the use of force or coercion) is a second degree felony, and in the fourth degree (committed against a victim 13 to 16 years old by someone over 18, more than 4 years older than the victim, and not the victim's spouse; or against a victim 13 to 18 years old by someone in the victim's school who is over 18, more than 4 years older than the victim, and knows or learns that the victim is a student in that school) is a fourth degree felony. § 30-9-11. Criminal sexual contact with a child is a second degree felony, and entails sexual contact with the unclothed intimate parts of a child under 13 years old, or a child between 13 and 18 when the perpetrator is in a position of authority over the child and uses that authority to coerce the child to submit, uses force or coercion that results in injury or is aided or abetted by another person, or uses as a deadly weapon. § 30-9-13(B). Any other sexual contact (i.e. not with the child's unclothed intimate parts), under the same conditions, is a third degree felony. § 30-9-13(C). Manufacture of child pornography is a second degree felony, while most other child pornography-related crimes are third or fourth degree felonies. §§ 30-6A-3, -4(C). Hiring or profiting from child prostitution is a second degree felony, unless the child is less than 13 years old, in which case receiving a profit is a first degree felony. § 30-6A-4.

- <u>Delayed Tolling for Minor Victims</u> : Tolled until the victim is 18 years old. The statute of limitations for prosecutions of criminal sexual penetration or contact with a child does not run until the earlier of the victim reaching age 18 or the reporting of the offense to law enforcement. § 30-1-9.1.

New York

Civil Statute of Limitations

- <u>Delayed Tolling for Sexual Offenses Against Minors</u> : Five years for certain first degree sex offenses. N.Y. C.P.L.R. § 213-c. Three years for other offenses. § 214. Tolling is delayed with minors until the age of 18. § 208. The statute is also extended to 7 years from the date of the crime or 10 years from the conviction itself depending on the offense if the same defendant has been convicted of a criminal offense. § 213-b. Alternately, a civil claim may be brought within five years after the conclusion of a criminal action. § 215(8)(b).

- <u>No Discovery Rule</u> : "[T]he Statute of Limitations must run from the time of the act until the Legislature decrees otherwise." *Goldsmith v. Howmedica, Inc.*, 67 N.Y. 2d 120, 124 (1986); *See also Bassile v. Covenant House*, 594 N.Y.S. 2d 192, 193 (1993) *lv denied* 82 N.Y.2d 656.

- <u>No Retroactivity</u> : The current Statute of Limitations applies as of the effective date of the Act, June 23, 2006. 2006 N.Y. Laws ch. 3, sec. 5.

Criminal Statute of Limitations

- <u>SOL depending on the nature of the offense</u> : No SOL for first degree offenses. N.Y. Crim. Proc. Law § 30.10(2)(a). Five years for all other felony sex offenses. §

30.10(2)(b). Two years for misdemeanor sex offenses. § 30.10(2)(c).

- Delayed SOL for Sexual Abuse of Minors : Criminal SOL tolls until the 18th birthday of victim or until it is first reported to law enforcement, whichever comes first. N.Y. Crim. Proc. Law § 30.10(3)(f).

North Carolina

Civil Statute of Limitations

- Three Year Statute of Limitations for Personal Injury : Actions for personal injury must be brought within three years of the occurrence. N.C. Gen. Stat. Ann. § 1-52(5).

- Discovery Rule : For latent injuries resulting from personal injuries actions, the cause of action does not accrue until the harm to the victim becomes apparent, or ought to have reasonably become apparent. No cause of action will accrue "more than 10 years from the last act of the defendant giving rise to the cause of action." N.C. Gen. Stat. Ann. § 1-52(16). *See also Soderlund v. Kuch*, 546 S.E.2d 632, 638 (N.C. Ct. App. 2001) (primary purpose of discovery statute is to protect latent injuries).

- Delayed Tolling for Disabilities/Minors : Persons under 18 years of age claiming personal injury may bring their cause of action within three after reaching the age of majority. N.C. Gen. Stat. Ann. § 1-17(a)(1).

Criminal Statute of Limitations

- No Statute of Limitations for Any Sexual Offense Felony : Sexual offenses that are classified as a felony have no statute of limitations. Sexual intercourse and sexual offenses with minors are considered felonies. N.C. Gen. Stat. Ann. § 15-10; *State v. Hardin*, S.E.2d 74, 75 (N.C. Ct. App. 1973); N.C. Gen. Stat. Ann. §§ 14-27.7.2A, 14-27.4A, 14-27.7.

North Dakota

Civil Statute of Limitations

- Two Year Statute of Limitations for Sexual Assault and Battery Claims : A sexual abuse claim must be commenced within two years of the alleged abuse. N.D. Cent. Code § 28-01-18; *Peterson v. Huso*, 552 N.W.2d 83, 84 (N.D. 1996).

- Discovery Rule : North Dakota Courts affirmed the use of a discovery statute that allows the accrual of an action for sexual abuse to begin only when "the claimant knows, or with reasonable diligence should know, that a potential claim exists."

Peterson v. Huso, 552 N.W.2d 83, 84 (Dakota 1996); *Osland v. Osland*, 442 N.W.2d 907, 909 (N.D.1989).

- Delayed Tolling for Minors : 18 years old + One Year. Persons under 18 years of age may bring their cause of action within one year after reaching the age of majority. N.D. Cent. Code § 28-01-25.

Criminal Statute of Limitations

- Seven-Year Statute of Limitations For Prosecution of Child Sexual Abuse : The sexual abuse of minors must be prosecuted within seven years of the offense, or if the victim fails to report the abuse, within three years of the reporting. However, if the victim is under 15 years of age, the statute of limitations does not begin until the victim turns fifteen. N.D. Cent. Code §§ 29-04-03.1, 29-04-03.2

Ohio

Civil Statute of Limitations

- Twelve Year Statute of Limitations For All Childhood Sexual Abuse Claims : Any cause of action brought by a victim of childhood sexual abuse claims must be brought within 12 years of the date of accrual. Accrual begins on the 18th birthday of the victim. Ohio Rev. Code Ann. § 2305.111(C) (2009).

- Discovery Rule : In any action on or after the effective date of the statute (8/3/06) where the defendant has fraudulently concealed facts of the abuse claim, the statute of limitations will begin at the "time when the plaintiff discovers or in the exercise of due diligence should have discovered those facts." Ohio Rev. Code Ann. § 2305.111(C) (2009).

- Retroactivity To Effective Date of 8/3/06 : The new statute of limitations applies to all civil actions for claims resulting from childhood sexual abuse that occurred prior to the effective date of the act, and where a civil action for assault and battery has never been filed and the previous statute of limitations had not expired before the effective date of the statute. Act effective Aug. 3, 2006, c. 97, sec. 3, § 2305.111, 2907.01, 2006 Ohio Legis. Serv. Ann. (West).

Criminal Statute of Limitations

- Twenty-Year Statute of Limitations for Criminal Prosecution of Child Sexual Abuse : Criminal prosecutions of child sexual abusers must be commenced within 20 years of the occurrence. The statute of limitations will be tolled until the victim turns 18 or when responsible adult (not including family members) who has a legal duty to report abuse is aware of such abuse. Ohio Rev. Code Ann. §§ 2901.13(I)(1), 2151.421 (2009);

State v. Elsass, 105 Ohio App.3d 277, 663 N.E.2d 1019 (Ohio Ct. App. 1995); *State v. Turner,* 91 Ohio App.3d 153, 631 N.E.2d 1117 (Ohio Ct. App. 1993)

Oklahoma

Civil Statute of Limitations

- Two Year Statute of Limitations for Childhood Sexual Abuse Claims : Child sexual abuse victims have two years after the last incident of abuse that caused the injuries to file their claims. Okla. Stat. Ann. 12 § 95(6)(a) (2008).

- Delayed Tolling for Minors : Generally, persons under 18 years of age may bring their cause of action within two years after reaching the age of majority. Or, alternatively, if the abuser is in a state, federal or local correctional facility or jail, the victim has five years from their release to file their claim. The statute of limitations will begin to run at whichever date is later. Okla. Stat. Ann. 12 § 95(6)(b) (2008).

- Twenty Year Statute of Limitations for Claims Against Incarcerated Abusers : Victims may file claims against at any time during the incarceration of the offender for injuries caused by criminal actions, but any action against an incarcerated abuser must be commenced within twenty years of the victim turning 18. Okla. Stat. Ann. 12 § 95(6)(b), (7) (2008).

- Discovery/"Should Have Discovered" Rule: Two-Year extension : Victims alternatively have two years from the "time the victim discovered or reasonably should have discovered that the injury or condition was caused by the act or that the act caused the injury for which the claim is brought." Okla. Stat. Ann. 12 § 95(6)(b) (2008).

Criminal Statute of Limitations

- Twelve-Year Statute of Limitations for Felony Sexual Offenses; All Others Three Years : A 12-year statute of limitations exists for sexual offenses against minors that are classified as felonies after discovery of the offense. Discovery means the date that the crime against a minor was reported, or one year after the victim turns 18. For all other offenses, there is a three-year statute of limitations after the date of the offense. Okla. Stat. Ann. 22, § 152(C)(1), (H), (F) (2008).

- DNA Evidence Exception : A prosecution against these offenses may be brought any time after the offense as long as the victim reported the abuse with in 12 years after discovery, physical evidence which can provide a DNA sample was collected, and the abuser can be identified by this DNA. The prosecution must be commenced within three years from the date on which the identity of the suspect is established by DNA testing. Okla. Stat. Ann. 22, § 152(C)(2) (2008).

By: Jeff & Kelly Halldorson

Oregon

Civil Statute of Limitations

- Delayed Tolling for Sexual Offenses Against Minors : 18 years of age plus 6 years. Victims have six years from their 18th birthday to commerce their claims. Or. Rev. Stat. Ann. § 12.117(1) (2008).

- Discovery/"Should Have Discovered" Rule: Three-Year Extension : Accrual of the statute of limitations for a civil action may commence "not more than three years from the date the injured person discovers or in the exercise of reasonable care should have discovered the injury or the causal connection between the child abuse and the injury." Or. Rev. Stat. Ann. § 12.117(1) (2008).

- Retroactivity of 7/8/93 O.R.S. 12.117 Statute : The legislature has deemed that the six-year statute of limitations and the three-year discovery statute are retroactive, and apply to all causes of action that arise before, on or after the effective date of act (7/8/93), and revive any cause of action that was previously barred by the 1991 statute. Also, any claim brought before the 1993 statute that was previously barred by the 40 years of age constraint was now free to be brought up until one year after the commencement of the 1993 statute. *P.H. v. F.C.*, 873 P.2d 465, 466, 127, Or.App. 592 (Or. Ct. App. 1994); Act effected Aug. 10, 1993, c. 622, sec. 2, § 12.117, 1993 Or. Laws (West).

Criminal Statute of Limitations

- Six-Year Statute of Limitations for Felonies; Four Years of Misdemeanors : Certain felonies, including incest, sexual abuse in the first and second degree, have a six-year statute of limitations after the commission of the offense. If the victim is under 18 years of age, criminal proceedings must be brought before the victim turns 30, or within twelve years of the after the incident is reported to legal authorities, which ever occurs first. For other misdemeanors involving sexual abuse in the third degree, the prosecution must be brought within four years of the offense. Or. Rev. Stat. Ann. § 131.125(2) (2008). If the victim was under 18 years of age, "anytime before the victim attains 22 years of age or within four years after the offense is reported to a law enforcement agency." Or. Rev. Stat. Ann. § 131.125(3) (2008).

- Application of 6-Year SOL to Sexual Offenses : The Court of Appeals found that the extended six-year statute of limitations for sexual offenses, rather than the three-year limit for other felonies, applied to sexual abuse charges although amended limitations statute did not specify the offenses charged. *State v. Sharp*, 949 P.2d 1230, 1233, 151 Or.App. 122 (1997).

Pennsylvania

Civil Statute of Limitations

- Delayed Tolling for Minors; Twelve-Year Statute of Limitations for Childhood Sexual Abuse : Victims who were minors when the abuse occurred have twelve years from their 18th birthday to bring a civil action regardless of whether or not the victim brings a criminal proceeding as well. 42 Pa. Cons. Stat. Ann.§ 5533 (2008).

- No Discovery Statute for Repressed Memories : The courts will not toll the statute of limitations in childhood sexual abuse cases regardless of the victim's inability to bring suit due to repressed memories. The Court reasoned that the discovery statute is for when "the injury is not readily discernible as opposed to cases where it is the incapacity of the plaintiff which causes the delay in bringing suit." *Dalrymple v. Brown*, 701 A.2d 164, 168 (1997); *Pearce v. The Salvation Army & Crouch*, 674 A.2d 1123 (Pa. Super. Ct. 1996); *Seto v. Willits*, 638 A.2d 258 (Pa. Super. Ct. 1994).

- No Retroactivity for Previously Time-Barred Claims : The statute will not revive any claim which has been barred by a prior existing statute of limitations. Act. No. 2002-86, sec. 3, § 5533(b), 2002 Pa. Laws (West).

Criminal Statute of Limitations

- Statute of Limitations for Childhood Sexual Abuse Charges End When the Minor Victim Turns 50 : Prosecution of childhood sexual abuse charges must be commenced before the minor victim turns 50 years old. 42 Pa. Cons. Stat. Ann.§ 5552(c)(3) (2008).

- DNA Exception : If a DNA test can identify an otherwise unidentifiable perpetrator, prosecution may be commenced within the previously stated statute of limitations, or one year after the identity of the perpetrator is discovered, whichever is later. 42 Pa. Cons. Stat. Ann.§ 5552(c.1) (2008).

Rhode Island

Civil Statute of Limitations

- 7-year SOL for Suits against Perpetrators Based on Sexual Abuse : Claims based upon intentional conduct, i.e. against a perpetrator, must be brought within 7 years of the act of abuse, or 7 years from when the victim discovered or reasonably should have discovered that his/her injuries were caused by the sexual abuse. R.I. Gen. Laws § 9-1-51(a)(2008).

- **3-year SOL for Non-Perpetrators** : Claims against non-perpetrators must be brought under the general tort statute of limitations. Suits must be filed within 3 years of the acts constituting negligence. R.I. Gen. Laws § 9-1-14(b) (2008).

- **Discovery Rule** : Statutorily defined as against perpetrators (see above). Under Rhode Island law, discovery rule does not extend to claims against non-perpetrator defendants for damages arising from childhood sexual abuse and are governed by the general three-year statute of limitations for personal injuries. *See Ryan v. Roman Catholic Bishop of Providence*, 941 A.2d 174 (R.I., 2008).

Criminal Statute of Limitations

- **No Limit for Criminal Acts of Sexual Assault in the First Degree or Child Molestation in the First or Second Degree** : No limit for First degree sexual assault (§ 11-37-2), First degree child molestation sexual assault (§ 11-37-8.1), Second degree child molestation sexual assault (§ 11-37-8.3) R.I. Gen. Laws § 12-12-17(a). For any other criminal offense, within three years after commission of the offense. R.I. Gen. Laws § 12-12-17(c) (2008).

South Carolina

Civil Statute of Limitations

- **6 Years After Victim Reaches Age 21 or 3 Years From Discovery of Injury and Causal Relationship Between Abuse and Injury** : S.C. Code Ann. §15-3-555(A)(2008).

- **Discovery Rule** : A Court may suspend the SOL during the period in which a victim psychologically represses his or her memory of sexual abuse. The Supreme Court of South Carolina has stated that SOL begins to run on the date a reasonable person in the victim's circumstances was no longer repressing memories of abuse and the resurfacing memories would have put a reasonable person on sufficient notice, i.e. an objective standard. The victim may attempt to recover damages when those memories are triggered and remembered. *Moriarty v. Garden Sanctuary Church of God*, 341 S.C. 320, 534 S.E.2d 672 (S.C. 2000).

- **No Retroactivity** : Cannot be used to revive claims that expired prior to amendment effective August 31, 2001. A new statute cannot be used to revive a claim that had expired prior to its passage pursuant to the due process clause of the South Carolina constitution. *Doe v. Crooks*, 364 S.C. 349 (S.C. 2005). Prior to 2001, the limitations period was provided by §§ 15-3-530(5) and 15-3-535.

Criminal Statute of Limitations

- NO SOL for Any Criminal Prosecution in South Carolina : Sexual conduct with a minor is considered a first degree felony if offender engages in sexual battery with a victim who is under 11 or who is under 16, and offender has previously been convicted of or pled guilty to a sexual offense. It is considered a second-degree felony if offender engages in sexual battery with a victim who is at least 11 but under 14 or who is at least 14 but under 16, and offender is in a position of familial, custodial, or official authority to coerce victim to submit. However, a person may not be convicted of a second-degree felony if he is 18 or younger when he engages in consensual sexual conduct with another person who is at least 14. S.C. Code Ann. § 16-3-655 (2008). Incest is also a crime under S.C. Code Ann. § 16-15-20.

South Dakota

Civil Statute of Limitations

- 3-year SOL for Childhood Sexual Abuse : Suits must be brought within 3 years of the act or within 3 years of discovering that the injury was caused by the act (or reasonably should have discovered that the injury was caused by the act). S.D. Codified Laws § 26-10-25 (2008).

- Retroactivity : South Dakota's SOL, allowing for child sexual abuse civil cases brought within three years of date victim discovered or should have discovered that claimed injury was caused by abusive act, could be applied retroactively to cover abuse occurring prior to passage of statute. *DeLonga v. Diocese of Sioux Falls*, 329 F.Supp.2d 1092 (2004); *Stratmeyer v. Stratmeyer*, 567 N.W.2d 220 (SD 1997) (overruling *Koenig v. Lambert*, 527 N.W.2d 903 (S.D. 1995).

Criminal Statute of Limitations

- No limitation on class A, class B, or class C felonies : Including any rape where the victim is under the age of 13. S.D. Codified Laws § 23A-42-1 (2008).

- 7-year SOL for other prosecutions : S.D. Codified Laws § 23A-42-2 (2008).

- SOL Tolled Until Age 25 for Rape Victims : Victim of any offense under SDCL § 22-22-1 can bring charges at any time prior to the time the victim becomes age twenty-five or within seven years of the commission of the crime, whichever is longer. S.D. Codified Laws § 22-22-1 (2008). Furthermore, a charge brought for sexual contact with a person under 16 may be commenced at any time before the victim becomes age twenty-five or within seven years of the commission of the crime, whichever is longer. S.D. Codified Laws § 22-22-7 (2008).

Tennessee

Civil Statute of Limitations

- <u>1-year SOL For All Personal Tort Actions</u> : There is no special statute of limitations for survivors of sexual abuse. Personal tort actions must be brought within one year of the date the cause of action accrued (began to run, in most instances, when the injury was inflicted). Tenn. Code. Ann. § 28-3-104 (West 2008).

- <u>Tolling If The Person Injured Was Under 18</u> : The suit can be brought within one year of reaching 18 (i.e., the limitations period will expire the day before a victim's 18th birthday). Tenn. Code. Ann.§ 28-1-106 (West 2008).

- <u>Common Law Discovery Rule</u> : While the discovery rule is applied in common law, it is strictly applied. *Hunter v. Brown*, 955 S.W.2d 49 (Tenn. 1997) (statute of limitations begins to run when injury is discovered, or in the exercise of due care and diligence, plaintiff discovers that he or she has a right of action; limitations period is tolled only during period when plaintiff has no knowledge at all that a wrong has occurred and, as a reasonable person, was not put on inquiry.) Note that because the Plaintiff in Hunter had continuous memory of her abuse, the court stated that the case did not fairly raise the issue of repressed memory and specifically reserved decision on the applicability of the discovery rule to repressed memory "for another day."

Criminal Statute of Limitations

- <u>SOL Depending on the Nature of the Offense; 15-Year SOL for a Class A Felony; 8-Year SOL for a Class B Felony; 4-year SOL for a Class C or Class D Felony</u> : See Tenn. Code. Ann.§ 40-2-101 (West 2008). Class A felonies include aggravated rape of a child (§ 39-13-531) and rape of a child more than three (3) years of age but less than thirteen (13) years of age (§ 39-13-522). Class B felonies include aggravated rape (§ 39-13-502) and Rape (§ 39-13-503). Class C and D felonies include statutory rape by an authority figure (§ 39-13-532) Tenn. Code. Ann. § 40-2-101 (West 2008), Sexual battery by an authority figure of a child 13 yrs or older but less than 18 yrs old (§ 39-13-527), Incest (§ 39-15-302).

- <u>Tolled until age 18 or 4 years after the offense was committed if committed against a child prior to July 1, 1997</u> : and offense is Aggravated rape (§ 39-13-502), Rape (§ 39-13-503), Aggravated sexual battery (§ 39-13-504), Sexual battery (§ 39-13-505), or Incest (§ 39-15-302) unless the offense was committed prior to November 1, 1989. Tenn. Code. Ann.§ 40-2-101 (West 2008).

- <u>Tolled until age 21 if committed against a child prior to July 1, 1997</u> : and offense is Aggravated rape (§ 39-13-502), Rape (§ 39-13-503), Aggravated sexual battery (§ 39-13-504), Sexual battery (§ 39-13-505), Incest, or Rape of a child more than three but under 13 (§ 39-13-522). Tenn. Code. Ann.§ 40-2-101 (West 2008).

- SOL of 25 years after victim turns 18: for any offense committed against a child on or after June 20, 2006 : that constitutes any of the following criminal offenses: Aggravated rape (§ 39-13-502), Rape (§ 39-13-503), Aggravated sexual battery (§ 39-13-504), Sexual battery (§ 39-13-505), Rape of a child more than three (3) years of age but less than thirteen (13) years of age (§ 39-13-522), Sexual battery by an authority figure of a child 13 yrs or older but less than 18 yrs old (§ 39-13-527) or Incest (§ 39-15-302). Tenn. Code. Ann.§ 40-2-101 (West 2008).

- SOL of 25 years after victim turns 18: for any offense committed against a child on or after July 1, 2007 : that constitutes Aggravated rape of a child (where victim is 3 years of age or less) (§ 39-13-531) or Statutory rape by an authority figure (§ 39-13-532). Tenn. Code. Ann.§ 40-2-101 (West 2008).

Texas

Civil Statute of Limitations

- 5-year SOL : including sexual assault, aggravated sexual assault, or continuous sexual abuse of a young child or children. Tex. Civ. Prac. & Rem. Code Ann. § 16.0045 (Vernon 2008).

- Delayed Tolling for Minors : If the victim was a minor, the SOL does not begin to run until his/her 18th birthday. Tex. Civ. Prac. & Rem. Code Ann. § 16.001 (Vernon 2008).

- Discovery Rule : The Texas Supreme Court applies a case-by-case discovery rule. As a rule, they have held that the SOL will begin to run when a wrongful act causes some legal injury, even if the fact of injury is not discovered until later, and even if all resulting damages have not yet occurred. However, there have been cases where the SOL did not start to run until the plaintiff discovered, or through the exercise of reasonable care and diligence should have discovered, the nature of the injury. *See S.V. v. R.V.*, 933 S.W.2d 1 (Tex. 1996); *Vesecky v. Fenwick*, 880 S.W.2d 804 (Tex. App. 1994).

Criminal Statute of Limitations

- No SOL for Most Prosecutions : for sexual assault or aggravated sexual assault of a child (§§ 27.011(a)(2), 27.012(a)(1)(B)), continuous sexual abuse of a young child (§ 21.02), indecency with a child (§ 21.11)(if the offense was not barred prior to Sept. 1, 2007), or sexual assault, if during the investigation of the offense biological matter is collected and subjected to forensic DNA testing and the testing results show that the matter does not match the victim or any other person whose identity is readily ascertained. Tex. Code Crim. Proc. Ann. art. 12.01(1) (Vernon 2007).

- 10 year SOL : for sexual assault (§ 22.011) and aggravated sexual assault (§ 22.021). Tex. Code Crim. Proc. Ann. art. 12.01(2)(E) (Vernon 2007).

Utah

Civil Statute of Limitations

- Delayed Tolling For Minors: 18 years old or "Discovery" + 4 years : A person shall file a civil action for intentional or negligent sexual abuse suffered as a child within four years after the person attains the age of 18 years or, if a person discovers sexual abuse only after attaining the age of 18 years, that person may bring a civil action for such sexual abuse within four years after discovery of the sexual abuse, whichever period expires later. Utah Cod Ann. 1953 § 78B-2-308(2) (West 2008).

- Application of the Discovery Rule : Utah courts have allowed only narrow and limited application of the statutory discovery provisions. In *Olsen v. Hooley*, 865 P.2d 1345 (Utah 1993), the Utah Supreme Court held that the "exceptional circumstances" provision of the state discovery rule is applicable to a "totally repressed" memory case. The limitations period begins to run at the point the plaintiff recalls the abuse. *Colosimo v. Roman Catholic Bishop of Salt Lake City*, 865 P.2d 806, 811 (Utah 2007). See also *Burkholz v. Joyce*, 972 P.2d 1235 (Utah 1998) (refusing to apply discovery rule when Plaintiff had knowledge of the claim at age 19). In *Franklin v. Stevenson*, 1987 P.2d 22 (Utah 1999), the court reversed a jury verdict and ruled that repressed memory testimony should not have been admitted at trial because its scientific reliability was not established in the trial court.

Criminal Statute of Limitations

- SOL Depending on the Nature of the Offense : No SOL for the rape of a child, object rape of a child, sodomy on a child, sexual abuse of a child, aggravated sexual abuse of a child. Utah Code Ann. 1953 § 76-1-301 (West 2008). 8 yr SOL for forcible sexual abuse, provided that the offense was reported to a law enforcement agency within 4 yrs after commission of the offense. 4 yr SOL for all other felonies. Utah Code Ann. § 76-1-302(1)(a) (West 2008). 2 yr SOL for all misdemeanors. Utah Code Ann. § 76-1-302(1)(b) (West 2008).

- DNA Exception : For the following offenses, prosecution may be commenced at any time if the identity of the person who committed the offense is unknown but DNA evidence is collected that would identify the person at a later date (except that the provision does not apply if the SOL on an offense has run as of May 5, 2003, and no charges have been filed. U.C.A. 1953 § 76-1-302. If the statute of limitations would have run but for the provisions of Subsection (2) and identification of a perpetrator is made through DNA, a prosecution shall be commenced within one year of the discovery of the identity of the perpetrator. U.C.A. 1953 § 76-1-302(2)(b)-(3)): child abuse, §§ 76-5-109(2)(a) and (b); abuse or neglect of disabled child, §§ 76-5-110; abuse, neglect, or exploitation of a vulnerable adult, § 76-5-111; endangerment of child or elder adult, § 76-5-112.5; rape, §76-5-402; rape of a child, § 76-5-402.1; object rape, § 76-5-402.2; object rape of a child, § 76-5-402.3; forcible sodomy, § 76-5-403; sodomy on a child, § 76-5-403.1; forcible sexual abuse, § 76-5-404; aggravated sexual abuse of a child and sexual abuse of a child, § 76-5-404.1; aggravated sexual assault, § 76-5-405; sexual exploitation of a minor, § 76-5a-3. Utah Code Ann. 1953 §§ 76-1-302, 76-3-203.5 (West 2008).

Vermont

Civil Statute of Limitations

- Delayed Tolling for Sexual Offenses Against Minors : 18 years of age plus 6 years. Within 6 years of the act, Vt. Stat. Ann. Tit. 12, § 522(a), or 6 years of turning 18 and/or the removal of a disability including insanity or imprisonment (12, §551) or incapacity from damages caused by childhood sexual abuse (12, § 560).

- Discovery Rule : Within 6 years of the time of discovery. Victim need not establish which act caused the injury, if the abuse was continuing. 12, § 522(a).

Criminal Statute of Limitations

- The criminal SOL is generally 6 years except is tolled until age 24 when the victim was under the age of 16 : "Prosecutions for sexual assault, lewd and lascivious conduct and lewd or lascivious conduct with a child, alleged to have been committed against a child 16 years of age or under, shall be commenced within the earlier of the date the victim attains the age of 24 or six years from the date the offense is reported, and not after." Vt. Stat. Ann. tit. 13, § 4501(c). In cases for the same offenses where the child is under 18 but over 16, the 6 year statute of limitations applies. 13, § 4501(b). But, there is no limitation for aggravated sexual assault or kidnapping. 13, § 4501(a).

Virginia

Civil Statute of Limitations

- Delayed Tolling for Minors : Most personal injury claims have SOLs of 2 years after the cause of action accrues. Va. Code Ann. § 8.01-243 (2003); or, 2 years from removal of disability including legal incapacity and minority. § 8.01-229 (2003).

- Discovery Rule : 2 year limitation period will run from removal of disability (see above), or when the fact of the injury and its causal connection to the sexual abuse is first communicated to the person by a licensed physical, psychologist or clinical psychologist. § 8.01-249 (2003).

Criminal Statute of Limitations

- No SOL for any felony : *See* Va. Code Ann. § 19.2-8 (2003) (only non-felonious offenses subjected to time limitations to prosecution in this section).

Washington

Civil Statute of Limitations

- Delayed Tolling for Sexual Offenses Against Minors : The SOL of three years is tolled until the minor victim reaches the age of 18. Wash. Rev. Code Ann. § 4.16.340(1).

- Discovery Rule : Until victim discovered or reasonably should have discovered that the injury or condition was caused by said act. Wash. Rev. Code Ann. § 4.16.340(1)(b). Or, until victim that the act caused the injury for which the claim is brought. § 4.16.340(1)(c).

Criminal Statute of Limitations

- Most offenses are within 3 years of the CSA victim's 18th birthday or within 7 years of the offense, whichever is later. : *See* Wash. Rev. Code Ann. § 9A.04.080(1)(c). Excepting if a 1st or 2nd degree rape victim was under 14 years old at the time of the offense and it was reported to the police within one year after its commission, then action must be brought within 3 year of victim's 18th birthday or 10 years after the commission, whichever is later. Wash. Rev. Code Ann. § 9A.04.080(1)(b)(iii).

West Virginia

Civil Statute of Limitations

- Delayed Tolling for Sexual Offenses Against Minors : West Virginia has not adopted a SOL specific to child sex abuse. Nonetheless, the personal injury SOL 2 years and is tolled until the victim turns 18. W. Va. Code § 55-2-15.

- Discovery Rule : The burden is on the victim to demonstrate that he/she was prevented from knowing of the claim at the time of the injury by reason of fraudulent concealment, inability to comprehend the injury, or other extreme hardship. Mere ignorance of existence of cause of action or of identity of wrongdoer does not prevent running of statute of limitations. Nor can the discovery rule be used to extend past the 20 year statute of repose set forth in W. Va. Code § 55-2-15. *See Donley v.*

Bracken, 192 W.Va. 383 (1994).

Criminal Statute of Limitations

- No SOL for any felony; 1 year for misdemeanors : Felonies include sexual assault and sexual abuse in the first degree as defined by W. Va. Code § 61-8B-3, 4, 5, and 7. Sexual abuse by a parent, guardian, custodian, or person in a position of trust to a child is a felony. § 61-8D-5. Incest is also a felony. § 61-8-12. Sexual abuse in the second and third degree as defined by § 61-8B-8, 9 are misdemeanors.

Wisconsin

Civil Statute of Limitations

- Action Must Be Brought Before the Victim Turns 35 : *See* Wis. Stat. Ann. § 893.587. Wisconsin's Legislature has adopted a bright line rule allowing victims of several classes of abuses including those defined in §§ 948.02, 948.025, 948.06, 948.085, or 948.095 or would create a cause of action under § 895.442 to bring a claim until the age of 35.

Criminal Statute of Limitations

- SOL depending on the nature of the offense : No limitation for first degree sexual assault of a child, or engaging in repeated acts of sexual assault of the same child including class A and class B felonies. Wis. Stat. Ann. § 939.74(2)(a). For second degree sexual assault of a child, repeated class C sexual assault of the same child, incest with a child, sexual assault of a child placed in substitute care, and sexual assault of a child by a school staff person or a person who works or volunteers with children, the action must be brought before the victim turns 45. § 939.74(2)(c). Other actions must be brought within 6 years of the act if a felony and within 3 years of the act if a misdemeanor. Nonetheless, a majority of claims fall within the bright line rule embodies in § 939.74(2)(c).

Wyoming

Civil Statute of Limitations

- Delayed Tolling for Sexual Offenses Against Minors : Wyo. Stat. §1-3-105(b) provides that an action for childhood sexual abuse may be brought within the later of: 8 years after a minor's 18th birthday, or 3 years after discovery.

- Discovery Rule : Although explicitly mentioned in § 1-3-105(b)(ii), "discovery" has been defined by the Wyoming Supreme Court to be the moment the victim discovered or in the exercise of reasonable diligence should have discovered the psychic trauma regardless of when the physical trauma had occurred. *See McCreary v.*

Weast, 971 P.2d 974 (Wyo. 1999)

Criminal Statute of Limitations

- <u>No SOL for any criminal prosecution</u> : *See Boggs v. State*, 484 P.2d 711 (Wyo. 1971).

www.ingramcontent.com/pod-product-compliance
Lightning Source LLC
Chambersburg PA
CBHW022051160426
43198CB00008B/189